"Football! Navy! War!"

# "FOOTBALL! NAVY! WAR!"

## How Military "Lend-Lease" Players Saved the College Game and Helped Win World War II

Wilbur D. Jones, Jr.

*Foreword by Beano Cook*

McFarland & Company, Inc., Publishers
*Jefferson, North Carolina, and London*

LIBRARY OF CONGRESS CATALOGUING-IN-PUBLICATION DATA

Jones, Wilbur D.
 "Football! Navy! War!": how military "lend-lease" players saved the college game and helped win World War II / Wilbur D. Jones, Jr. ; foreword by Beano Cook.
        p.    cm.
 Includes bibliographical references and index.

 ISBN 978-0-7864-4219-5
 softcover : 50# alkaline paper ∞

 1. Football — United States — History — 20th century.
 2. College sports — United States — History — 20th century.
 3. Football players — United States — Biography.  4. United States. Navy — Biography.  5. Navy-yards and naval stations — United States — History — 20th century.  6. Football and war — United States.  7. World War, 1939–1945.  I. Title.
 GV959.5.U6J66   2009
 796.332'63097309044 — dc22
                                                            2009014121

British Library cataloguing data are available

©2009 Wilbur D. Jones, Jr. All rights reserved

*No part of this book may be reproduced or transmitted in any form or by any means, electronic or mechanical, including photocopying or recording, or by any information storage and retrieval system, without permission in writing from the publisher.*

On the cover: College football players pose during their Marine Corps training at Parris Island, SC, in 1942 (Franklin D. Roosevelt Library)

Manufactured in the United States of America

*McFarland & Company, Inc., Publishers*
 *Box 611, Jefferson, North Carolina 28640*
  *www.mcfarlandpub.com*

To those World War II servicemen
who played military and college football
to harden them for combat,
then lost their lives fighting for our country
on foreign battlefields, particularly those United States Marines
who died on Iwo Jima and Okinawa in 1945.

These include former Camp Lejeune coach Lieutenant Jack Chevigny (Notre Dame, coach Chicago Cardinals), who was killed in action on Iwo Jima, and twelve Marines who played in the Mosquito Bowl on Guadalcanal in December 1944, who died on Okinawa:

4th Marines: end Jim Quinn (Amherst); end David Nathan Schreiner (All-America Wisconsin); tackle Bob Bauman (Wisconsin); and tackle Hubbard Hinde (Southern Methodist);

29th Marines: end Chuck Behan (DeKalb Teachers, Detroit Lions, Camp Lejeune 1943, Navy Cross); end George Edward Murphy (Notre Dame, Lejeune 1943); tackle Ed Van Order (Cornell); tackle John Hebrank (Lehigh); center Red DeGreve (Michigan); back Tony Butkovich (Illinois, All-America Purdue); back Wayne "Rusty" Johnston (Marquette); and back Johnny Perry (Wake Forest, Duke, Navy Cross).

# *Acknowledgments*

I am exceptionally grateful to several people for pointing my research in the right direction, and helping me turn a burning idea into a manuscript. My friend and World War II navy veteran Leo Bednarzyck introduced me to Marine Corps sports historian Col. John Gunn, USMC (Ret.), an enormous reservoir of material and expert on World War II football who believed in my project. John, a retired newspaper sports editor and author of two books on Marine Corps football, allowed me full access to his vast sports library in his Gulf Breeze, Fla., home and put me in touch with several World War II players for interviews. He loaned me game programs, annual periodicals, books, and personal files.

John, even though (at this writing) your health condition has diminished your capability to pursue your occupation, I want you to know how much I appreciate receiving your advice and facilitating my task. I also thank your children, Bruce, Vikki, Becky, and Laura, for giving me permission to use your material and for donating your library to the University of North Carolina–Wilmington (UNCW).

Through John's weekly online column, three football history enthusiasts stepped forward. Jack Hilliard, a retired Greensboro, N.C., television producer and football collector, provided me with tons of material, particularly on Bainbridge Naval Training Center and Charlie "Choo Choo" Justice. His continuing interest in my success — our success — inspired me. With Gunn and Hilliard providing me a major portion of my research material and urging me on, producing the manuscript was a cinch.

Having ESPN's Beano Cook, the country's premier college football historian and commentator, write the foreword to this book is a rare professional honor and a personal coup. I had him in mind for several years as the right person to approach, but how would I do it? Through sheer coincidental good luck, his ESPN producer associate, John Lukacs, was a passenger on the Valor Tours World War II Battle of the Bulge tour I led in June 2008. Because of John's intervention, Beano's ageless analytical charm and omnipotent memory give this book a special appeal. The fact that Beano found me someone with whom he could rap about the football days of his youth probably was one reason for our resulting frequent phone conversations.

Early in my research, Mike Miklas of Charlestown, Md., dedicated to preserving the Bainbridge memory through the Bainbridge Naval Training Center Historical Association, arranged and hosted my exploratory visit to the old site. I spent the day with Mike for a tour and interviews with locals who remembered the facility, and garnered significant research material. The Cecil County (Md.) Historical Society, home to old Bainbridge, publicized my effort through historian Mike Dixon and sent me material.

Larry Clark, dean of the Cameron School of Business at UNCW, loaned me 1940s football guides of the National Collegiate Athletic Association, vitally rich sources to which I constantly referred. Jerry Parnell, a first-class reference librarian at UNCW's Randall Library, conducted valuable literature searches.

The Naval Academy sports information office facilitated an interview with the fabulous Clyde "Smackover" Scott, of Little Rock, Ark., my World War II military football hero. We had a marvelous conversation. I also enjoyed informative discussions with a number of other World War II players, including Julian Pressley, George "Sonny" Franck, and Dave Rankin.

John Thorpe, of DeBary, Fla., sent me substantial information about the Great Lakes navy team. John Witt, of Elkmont, Ala., loaned me his scrapbook of his father's participation with the Keesler (Miss.) Air Field and Hawaii Air Force teams.

I also thank two organizations in particular for granting me permission to use photographs: the National Collegiate Athletic Association and Street & Smith's/*The Sporting News* Annuals.

My wife, Carroll, my loyal and best constructive critic and soundboard, as always urged and helped me immensely. My sons Andrew, a sports journalist with Buster Sports in the North Carolina Triangle, and David, a Los Angeles marketer, frequently advised me. Sportswriter Brian Hendrickson, whose beat is the Portland Trail Blazers, and historian and author Dr. Chris Fonvielle, a UNCW professor, also played devil's advocate in reviewing and improving my work.

## Table of Contents

| | |
|---|---|
| *Acknowledgments* | vii |
| *Foreword by Beano Cook* | 1 |
| *Preface: "Saved from the Junk Pile"* | 7 |
| *Introduction: "The Most Awesome Melange"* | 13 |

1. "A Roster Out of Football's 'Who's Who'": The Bainbridge Eleven — 25
2. "Ideological Arsenal": The Impact of Football on the War Effort, Morale, and Fighting Spirit — 43
3. "Lend-Lease Football": Navy and Marine Corps College Officer Training Programs — 56
4. "A War Game in Miniature": Reacting, Adjusting, and Playing the Game — 73
5. "Shifty and Smart, Harder to Stop than Superman": Charlie Justice, Glamor Prodigy — 94
6. "All Hail to the Navy": Great Lakes, Fleet City, Pre-Flights, and Midshipmen — 107
7. "Every General Liked to Have His Own Base Football Team": Ramblers, Fighting AA's, Flyers, and Cadets — 130
8. "Rollicking, Boisterous, Macho": Flying Marines and Sea Lions — 149
9. "Around the Globe the Message Winged": The 1942–45 Seasons — 161

10. "All America Will Cheer a Champion, Whether He
    Is Black, Brown, Yellow or White": Black Players
    and Professional Football   189
11. "Not Satisfied to Listen to Short-Wave Broadcasts":
    Overseas Football, Postseason Games, and the Postwar   199
12. Clyde "Smackover" Scott and Bob Steuber: Personalities,
    Vignettes, and Anecdotes   210

*Glossary: Wartime Football Expressions, Abbreviations, and Jargon*   225
*Chapter Notes*   231
*Selected Bibliography*   241
*Index*   247

Player collegiate loyalties "came down like the Wall of Jericho," noted sportswriter Furman Bisher, who wrote postwar, "of sacrifice in return for loyalty to country by male athletes who found themselves campus nomads in the military system.... Many a football career was born on service fields ... and heaven only knows how many were left there, not to mention those left under white crosses in military cemeteries." Lieutenant Paul Brown, wartime Great Lakes (Ill.) Naval Training Center coach and future member of the professional Hall of Fame, stated: "Things like football tended to dim in importance to men who, two or three months later, might be lying dead on some beach in the South Pacific. It was something I never could reconcile myself to while coaching service football" (Bisher and Brown quoted in Bisher, "You're in the Army, Mr. Trippi," *Southern Living*, September 1984).

# Foreword
## by Beano Cook

Since the late nineteenth century, Americans have done two things better than anyone else: fight wars and play football. So it's hardly a coincidence that the relationship between the two has been one of the most enduring in this nation's history. If you don't think our proud military tradition and our national passion are joined at the hip pads, how else do you explain the roar of Air Force jets flying over your stadium? The snappy color guard standing at attention during the playing of the national anthem? The precise brassy, Sousafied sounds of marching bands?

The evidence abounds. From Operations Goalpost and Varsity in World War II to Operation Linebacker in Vietnam, the military has long demonstrated an affinity for football terminology. And try to go one fall weekend without hearing television commentators utter the words "blitz," "trenches" or "bomb." It can't be done.

A more challenging task, though, is pinpointing the exact point in history when the link between football and war became embedded in our national consciousness. It's like trying to make an open-field tackle on Jim Thorpe.

The similarities of war and football probably seemed vaguely familiar to the spectators watching the lines of Princeton and Rutgers clash in 1869, which was, after all, just four years after Appomattox. Maybe the connection was made when America's earliest gridiron stars marched off to the Spanish-American War. You may not know that the famed football stadium at West Point is named for Captain Dennis Michie, the "father of Army football," who was killed in Cuba in 1898. Or perhaps it was during the Roaring Twenties, an era when coaches, radio announcers and poetic sportswriters, many of whom had witnessed World War I firsthand, used battlefield imagery in their descriptions of games.

One thing, however, is for certain: there was never a time, and probably never will be, when war and football were more closely coupled than World War II. That's because football, in so many ways, saved America. And the war, in turn, saved football.

It's a forgotten yet fascinating era of conjoined football and military history which, thankfully, Wilbur Jones has expertly exhumed and chronicled in these pages. The association was born out of both necessity and natural design. It is perhaps appropriate to presume that had the Associated Press conducted a poll shortly after December 7, 1941, the United States would likely not have received a single a vote. Pearl Harbor had left the nation battered, humiliated and uncertain of the future. The Rose Bowl game, after all, had to be moved from Pasadena and played in a misty rain in Durham, North Carolina. There were losing battles abroad and on the homefront: the manpower drain and travel restrictions would force hundreds of colleges to drop football for anywhere from one season to the duration of the war. A game plan for the nation's survival, as well as the survival of the game, had to be devised.

Fortunately, as Stanford coach Clark Shaughnessy said, football is "a great war game"—the solution was already in place. After all, where better than college campuses to train young men to study and lead—and gridirons to teach them to fight? And what better teachers could one envision than the coaches of the era, many of whom could be considered drill instructors in their own right? "When Paul Brown sends a team on the field it's as tough mentally and physically as any commando unit." This is just one of the gems unearthed by Jones in his extensive research. And Brown is just one of the coaching legends that appears in these pages. There are cameos from Paul "Bear" Bryant and Bud Wilkinson, just to name two. There are also some unfamiliar, yet noteworthy names such as Lt. Jack Chevigny, the Knute Rockne–era Notre Dame star who coached the University of Texas in the 1930s and who was killed on Iwo Jima.

While the U.S. Army limited its personnel to intramural sports, the Navy, Marine Corps and Coast Guard ultimately placed thousands of males in more than 130 schools that had been awarded NROTC, V-5, V-7 and V-12 training programs. Put simply by Jones, "the Navy had rescued football." The result was a win-win situation. Because of their love of competition, physical prowess and single-minded pursuit of victory, athletes—football players especially—made excellent officers, soldiers, sailors and Marines. Only the helmets and uniforms changed—the attitude stayed the same.

If I had to be in a huddle or a foxhole, I would want to be surrounded by Marines. Jones writes that Marine V-12 players received two Navy Crosses, seven Silver Stars, three Bronze Stars and other assorted decorations for valor on Iwo Jima and Okinawa. As far as individual hardware goes, the Heisman Trophy and Maxwell Award pale in comparison.

A section of this book that is of particular interest to me describes the role of Admiral Thomas Hamilton, my former boss at the University of Pittsburgh, in formulating the Navy's V-5 pre-flight training program. Hamilton wore many hats during his long career — he was a player, coach and athletic director at the Naval Academy, athletic director at Pitt and commissioner of the Pacific Eight Conference, as well as executive officer on the USS *Enterprise* during the war — but he is most famous for saying, after he eschewed the opportunity to kick a tying field goal in the famous Army-Navy game in 1946, that "a tie is like kissing your sister." Hamilton was on to something. From 1941 through 1945, ties were not acceptable either.

Another win was the fact that the situation provided America with some of the best — and most bewildering — football that the game would know. As their training progressed, players were transferred between schools so often that Jones appropriately calls them "Lend-Lease players." For example, during one strange season, the University of Michigan used ten former Wisconsin Badgers to beat Wisconsin. Another player/trainee commenced his career at North Carolina, played a few games for Duke, then returned to Chapel Hill in time to suit up against the Blue Devils. So strange was the situation that Minnesota's Golden Gophers once lost to an Iowa Navy Pre-Flight team coached by none other than their own legendary pre-war mentor, Major Bernie Bierman of the USMC.

Simultaneously educational and entertaining, this book is as solid a playbook as I've read. Jones left no game program or annual unpersued, no archive unused. His meticulous research and storytelling style combine to form a potent pairing that rivals that of wartime football's most famous duo, Army's Doc Blanchard and Glenn Davis, "Mr. Inside" and "Mr. Outside." Only question remains for me: How did the WAVE cheerleaders compare to the USC Song Girls?

From tales of Heisman Trophy winners and hobbled combat veterans to 4-Fs and feared tacklers, there are plenty of stories here. There's the odyssey of Bob Steuber, perhaps the only player in history to play collegiately after playing professionally. There's the Penn coach who worked in a defense plant mornings and coached during afternoons. There are the stories behind the origins of some of the game's famous nicknames, such as Elroy "Crazy Legs" Hirsch, Clyde "Smackover" Scott, and Charlie "Choo-Choo" Justice.

As for Justice, you'll learn just how close he was to attending Duke — the University of North Carolina's archrival. Blue Devils fans, you can thank Admiral Yamamoto for that one. You'll also learn how Justice eventually came to call Chapel Hill home. All I can say is that it was one incredible package deal; the recipient of his scholarship probably had the slowest time in the 40-yard dash in the program's football history.

Although the majority of this book deals with the military's relationship to the Saturday game, there's plenty of information on the war's effect on the National Football League, including the records of such war-necessitated combination teams as the "Steagles"—the joint Pittsburgh Steelers–Philadelphia Eagles hybrid that toughed out a 5-4-1 record during the 1943 season and helped keep professional football going.

Oh, and you can't forget the names. There's Sgt. Harvard Yale Princeton, "a paratrooper player at Fort Benning." And a key member of the staff at Great Lakes Naval Training Center was named Steve Belichick—yes, the father of NFL coach Bill Belichick.

This book, with its breakdown of almost every key player's height and weight and major military training station's football history and records, is a stats junkie's dream. You'll learn about some of football's forgotten dynasties, wartime wonders such as the Bainbridge Navy Commodores, the El Toro Flying Marines, the Great Lakes Bluejackets, the Iowa Pre-Flight Seahawks, the Fleet City Bluejackets, the Norman Naval Air Station Zoomers, the North Carolina Pre-Flight Cloudbusters, the St. Mary's Pre-Flight Air Devils, the Tuskegee Army Air Field Warhawks, the Keesler Field Commandos, the Fourth Air Force Flyers, and the Randolph Field Skymasters. As a youth growing up during the war, I remember when some of these strange names appeared, fleetingly, in the AP poll. Thanks to Jones, they take the field once again.

Unlike the war, this narrative does not end with V-J Day. You'll also read of postwar showdowns including the celebrated clash between Fleet City and El Toro after which several El Toro players were reportedly shipped to China and Japan for occupation duty as punishment for losing. Talk about high stakes. There were poignant postseason honors, too, such as the "All–Purple Heart Collegiate All-America" team whose members had recovered from combat wounds to star for their college squads.

"During the war," writes Jones, "American armed forces transported freedom and football around the globe." American troops played everywhere from Algeria to Ireland. Even in Nagasaki, Japan, where the bizarre "Atom Bowl" was played amid the rubble and radiation on the site where the second atomic bomb was dropped.

Technological advancements were not limited to the battlefield. Working on gridiron laboratories, coaches helped propel the game into the modern era. While manpower shortages necessitated the suspension of the freshman-eligibility rule, some military teams with manpower surpluses used two different squads for different offensive formations, an evolutionary step toward the eventual multiple-platoon system. There were also schematic improvements that not only would change the way the game was played, but also the way it was coached and appeared to spectators. Improvements in pass protection, the use of motion and multiple offensive sets to spread defenses, as well as free substitution and fluid defensive schemes developed during World War II would all fuse into the modern incarnation we watch on television today.

But these innovations and ramifications were merely the residual effects of a more significant achievement. Indeed, as Jones writes, "American football, as perhaps no other sport, justified itself during World War II." In early September 1945, another poll, one infinitely more important than the one which was soon to be tabulated by the Associated Press, was released. And the United States sat atop the rankings. We have the sacrifices of millions of men and women — plus football — to thank for that.

Consider this book your ticket to the story of great games, greater names and perhaps the most important era the game of football will ever see. Thumb your way through the pages, shuffle down the row and take your seat. That's it right there, in the national nostalgia section, right on the fifty-yard line. As for the popcorn, well, that's your responsibility.

*Beano Cook, a well-known ESPN commentator and historian, is widely considered one of the most knowledgeable media personalities in the business. He has been around college football in various capacities for more than fifty years.*

## *Preface: "Saved from the Junk Pile"*

> *"College gridiron circles which staggered through 1943 face 1944 with conditions much improved.... In future years when anything resembling a naval station wants a football game from a top flight team, do it. For college football has been saved by the navy from the junk pile of non-essentials scrapped in these war days."*[1]

Popular Blue Network sportscaster Harry Wismer, predicting the 1944 college football landscape in the middle of World War II, lavishly credited the Department of the Navy for its role, its "inestimable value," in saving wartime football by allowing its college officer candidate trainee-students to play on the varsities.[2] The army refused its college students this opportunity.

The National Collegiate Athletic Association, the college sport's governing organization, mightily underscored Wismer's affirmation. After reviewing the previous two seasons just completed under arduous uncertainties, and of course without knowing when war would end, the NCAA enthusiastically thanked the navy for its endorsement of football to supplement the war effort.

The Department had intentions besides saving college football, important as that could be. It had a war to win at sea and on Pacific islands. It needed tough, disciplined, motivated naval surface and submarine officers and aviators, and Marine Corps lieutenants and all their crews. At the outset of the war, naval and Marine officials inaugurated vigorous physical and mental conditioning programs to train and develop teamwork, and leaders' motor skills, endurance, and fortitude. A whole new wartime force of yesterday's casual civilians had to be constructed. Football fit this need perfectly.

The title of a training manual on rigorous physical and mental strength shouted out its demonstrative motto and organizational credo: "Football! Navy! War!" Created overnight by flight training director Commander

Thomas J. Hamilton, a carrier pilot, former Naval Academy head coach, and the Football Writers Association's 1942 "Man of the Year," the rallying cry symbolized the immediate transformation of civilians into fighters. This book's title recognizes football's exceptionally effective motivational role.

Harry Wismer, the NCAA, school administrators, and the public wondered what would happen to this revered sport, college football. They must have asked questions. What would become of the game and the public's appetite and demand for it? Would it go extinct, be discarded, hibernate, be realigned or downsized? And how did all this bear on the war?

With the U.S. entry into World War II on December 7, 1941, football faced a choice of bitter harsh realities. What was the gridiron role in the massive mobilization of men, weapons, equipment, and morale, if any? At once, both by necessity and choice, conditions thrust football smack into the middle of the war effort as a vital participant. Thus the military and colleges joined forces in these tumultuous times to prepare fighting men for combat and, as a calculated by-product, prevent dismemberment of the game and sustain robust enthusiasm. The military and colleges championed and collaborated on competitive programs absolutely essential for war victory. Their zeal likely influenced the simultaneous survival of the National Football League.

It was a national emergency and the NCAA got it right. The Department of the Navy's vision, organization, and drive truly proved to be the engine of wartime football. After early and serious evaluation, emboldened by vocal leadership from the president and naval officials, the altered sport persevered as well as possible under exceptionally extenuating circumstances. Sometimes unconventionally administered, fluctuating and unpredictable, football and other sports generated the competitive regimen which also provided a huge morale boost for the home front, both civilians and military. Within two seasons, stability would return, interest explode, and the wartime experiment begin fading into memory.

## Terminology

In this book:

(1) The words "military" and "services" mean any and all of the armed forces which in World War II included the army (including the army air forces), navy, Marine Corps, and Coast Guard;
(2) The Department of the Navy included the Marine Corps (always) and the Coast Guard (during wartime);

(3) To distinguish the service academies from the rest of the army and navy, capitalized "Army" and "Navy" denote the service academies at West Point, N.Y., and Annapolis, Md.—and their football teams;
(4) "War Department" and "the army headquarters" denote the same;
(5) The words "colleges" and "schools" include universities;
(6) Team won-lost-tied records are indicated like so: 6–4–1;
(7) "Troop(s)" implies uniformed personnel of all services;
(8) "Eleven" was a contemporary synonym for a football team (from its eleven players).

See the glossary for keys to team records, players and coaches, player positions, military facilities, jargon, and other terminology.

## "Fighting a Desperate War"

"We are fighting a desperate war," navy secretary Frank Knox reminded Americans in 1943. He raved about football's importance as an essential, body-contact, physical conditioning training mechanism in helping prepare men for warfare, particularly in the Pacific. In underscoring his civilian boss, the Marine Corps commandant equated rapid reactions on a football field to the same in the jungle and on the battlefield.[3]

This book is about more than just what happened to the college sport. After setting the table, it concentrates primarily on the multitude of military-base elevens which dotted the country. The armed forces likely would have played football in some manner anyway, regardless of college actions. The reader will see that all branches formed teams, scheduled opponents from colleges and other bases, and did their best to promote football for morale and entertainment as well as conditioning. Consequently, the game at both levels intertwined and proceeded, largely mutually dependant and cooperative. In all reported instances the effort succeeded.

In praising the navy's 1942 actions, a leading magazine foresaw a debt accruing to the department at the war's conclusion. Without heavy navy and Marine Corps participation, it stated, college football would have been very informal at best, and mostly campus intramural leagues at worst. But by then the outlook called for nearly the same robust schedule of games as before the war.[4] After a ragged organizational and jurisdictional start in 1942, both college and military football regained its footing and was played out for the remainder of the wartime seasons of 1942–45 for the good of participants, fans, and the war effort.

## Sensing an Untold Story

Having forgotten this sports story of my wartime childhood growing up in Wilmington, North Carolina, I encountered it head-on while writing an obituary in 2003. When North Carolina football icon and illustrious native son Charlie "Choo Choo" Justice died in Cherryville, on October 17, the *Wilmington Star-News* asked me to write his obituary. As their military analyst, I had covered Operation Iraqi Freedom extensively and penned op-ed pieces on North Carolina World War II history.

Justice began the road to national football immortality as an Asheville high school phenomenon in the early 1940s, and achieved folk-hero enshrinement as the state's most famous football player (some might say most-famous athlete as well, with due respect for Wilmingtonian Michael Jordan). His death evoked a deluge of memories of his twice-All-America exploits for the Tar Heels, my college alma mater — he graduated in 1950; I entered in 1951 and never saw him play — but few people remembered his long-ago overshadowed World War II naval service.

My Wilmington buddies and I idolized Justice and his team. In those days Chapel Hill was a thousand miles and scarce tickets away, and radio was the medium of choice. My father preferred that I perform Saturday chores and allowed me time off only to hear the games if broadcast.

Following interviews with his wife Sarah and Carolina teammates, and further research, I submitted the obituary on deadline. But my attention simultaneously focused on something else. The name Bainbridge kept surfacing. Bainbridge, the old naval base? Certainly. Justice trained at the Bainbridge Naval Training Station in Maryland, starred on their base team in 1943-44, and later in Hawaii in 1945. Referring to his team as the "Bainbridge eleven" reflected the days of two-way players, playing both offense and defense prior to the platoon system.

The historian in me sensed a gem. I began compiling information on Bainbridge, Justice, and the story of military and college football during the war. Its enormous historical value began consuming me. Why hadn't someone previously written about all of this? Without stopping to answer that question, I dived right into the subject.

But let me backtrack. As a high school and Carolina student, I worked part-time in the *Star-News* sports department beginning in 1950. Then I envisioned myself as a career sports writer, went to college to study journalism, and imprinted novice business cards with "Grantland Rice Jones" after the era's foremost sports journalist. More than half a century later, having majored in history instead, I see this book as the result of my early dream. After I retired and moved back to Wilmington in 1997, the *Star-News* and I renewed our working relationship. My occasional op-ed and feature pieces and letters have brought me statewide journalism awards and immensely helped in my efforts to preserve North Carolina World War II history. I knew that I need not worry about the book's timing, because until now other sports and military historians have ignored my subject.

The availability of numerous popular football periodicals that continued wartime publication, game programs, military-base newspapers, and additional contemporary accounts facilitated my research. Several excellent secondary sources included: *College Football's Twenty-Five Greatest Teams; The History of American Football: Its Teams, Players, and Coaches; The Navy V-12 Program: Leadership for a Lifetime;* and John Gunn's two superb books on Marine Corps football history. A highlight of my research was visiting Bainbridge.

To fill an untapped four-year void in the history, lore, and participants of World War II military and college football—and its impact on the war effort—I wrote this book to please football fanatics, Saturday-only watchers, sports lovers, and military history enthusiasts. The appeal doubles by the fresh historical insight into the World War II procedures for assigning and training for combat mass numbers of military personnel, particularly officer candidates, and the government's mixed signals in determining the role of sports.

## The Bainbridge Eleven

The most famous wartime military eleven was the Bainbridge Naval Training Station (later Center) Commodores, both a boot camp and advanced training facility. It also showcased the period's most sensational player, the storybook teenaged halfback "Choo Choo" Justice. Bainbridge gridiron fortunes peaked with an undefeated 1944, ranking fifth in the Associated Press poll, sporting a roster of All-Americas and NFL veterans.

Bainbridge merits recognition as the archetypical successful wartime service team. Besides being extremely colorful, full of stars, and winning their first twenty-one games over three seasons, their exploits gleam with human interest and, with Justice the central figure, help shape the book's story line. The sailors' saga highlights players, coaches, big games, spirit, and well-earned national prominence. The whole scene just got to me.

Three decades after the war, the navy closed Bainbridge. Named for a naval hero of the War of 1812 and never on any map, it sprouted in 1942 in the northern Chesapeake Bay, meeting a wartime demand. Now overrun with weeds, its fenced location can be found by asking around Port Deposit, Maryland. Wild vegetation wraps badly decaying structures and covers the unrecognizable football field. Entry is by a prearranged, guided tour from dedicated locals struggling to keep its faded memory alive through a small historical society. This book reviving its glory days might help. Both the navy and football long ago foreclosed on Bainbridge.

A case can be made for spotlighting the fabulous Great Lakes (Ill.) Naval Training Center Bluejackets, but I decided not to. Their highly productive elevens posted a 33–11–3 wartime mark (they twice defeated Notre Dame, the era's crown prince of college football, and tied them once) and likely created more of a stir than any other service program. But the Great Lakes began during World War I and it is still an active facility. Bainbridge has more mystique, color, and elan. Thus I focused on Bainbridge.

# Introduction:
# "The Most Awesome Melange"

*"While football went into various degrees of retrenchment on college campuses, it broke out like the measles in some of the most unlikely places."*[1]

Years after World War II, prominent Atlanta sportswriter Furman Bisher reflected on the success of military football in those "unlikely places." He recalled that base commanders recognized not only footballs' superb combat conditioning value but also its entertainment value, a way to keep "the more fractious out of trouble." Players figured they could score points with superiors and perhaps postpone the date they would be sent overseas.[2] See what else wartime football did for the national spirit?

By the fall of 1942, with America's war nine months old, an optimistic annual football publication forecast that the sport would be more stable than the season before. The armed forces, anxious for officer material, began recruiting heavily in colleges, pushed football as a conditioner and encouraged schools to continue playing.[3] As colleges, conferences, and the National Football League reviewed their options, the country nervously preoccupied itself with far more serious matters and burgeoning wartime unknowns.

Football publications and prognosticators held reservations. Finding, retaining, and conditioning players was only one aspect of continuing the game. Scheduling, transportation, and other restrictions required factoring. The *Football Pictorial Yearbook* warned that the upcoming season would be "the most awesome melange of fact, fiction, turmoil, contradiction, recrimination, patriotism, and general uncertainty ever loosed on the American sporting public."[4] In other words: sports fans, watch out. The old game will never be the same. Could myriad uncertainties be sorted out amidst such a fluid, unsettled atmosphere, both to support the war effort and satisfy the public's wishes?

Like the prospects for victory over the nation's enemies, the football melange would be settled in due time. But temporarily, at least, the games persisted, a case of the military, colleges, and pros being obligated to play with cards they were dealt.

This book will examine how the game surmounted enormous obstacles — or skirted them — and survived, and how "the melange" sputtered, hit-or-miss, into and out of 1942, its residual effect continuing in varying degrees throughout the remaining three wartime seasons. It concentrates almost entirely on wartime military and college football, but briefly addresses the professional game in chapter 10, mainly as it applied to the national emergency. The story of how military football helped to win the war starts by identifying up front the indelible link it had with the colleges. Neither could have sustained football without the other: interdependency and an accommodating, mutually beneficial and lasting marriage of convenience was forged by strong vision, foresight, leadership, determination, and flexibility.

## The State of Football on December 7, 1941

When the United States entered the war, baseball was the king of American spectator and team sports. Football reigned supreme on college campuses, but its nascent professional version had yet to grab the fascination of the press and fans. To most Americans without the collegiate experience, football "was a pastime that thrived detached from most of the nation's urban centers," wrote Mike Vaccaro in his book about the year 1941.[5] Small towns such as Tuscaloosa, Palo Alto, Chapel Hill, and South Bend dispatched teams to meet giants from Los Angeles, Atlanta, Boston, and Chicago.

Baseball bore the scars of the Great Depression, however. President Franklin D. Roosevelt encouraged major league baseball to continue for its morale factor, which it did, although weakened in player quality during the war. Sports historian Benjamin G. Rader maintained that college football weathered the economic down times easier than professional baseball.[6] Richard O. Davies wrote that collegiate sports "naturally reflected the nation's capitalistic creed.... The economic malaise naturally affected American sports.... And the sparkling performances of athletes no longer seemed all that thrilling. The Golden Age of American sports gave way to a dour and disconsolate era that reflected the tough times of the 1930s," even cutting stars "down to size."[7] Basketball, with the excitement and attachment to the National Basketball Association and college hoops, far from being a headline sport, would wait for a postwar boom.

Rader further believed that college football's popularity grew partly by generating potent symbols. "While restoring the loyalty of a burgeoning alumni, college teams often evoked symbols that transcended the college itself." Citizens developed state pride in their university teams and became engulfed in "symbolic battles for superiority between states and regions, sometimes even ethnic groups, religions, and ideologies." The annual Army-Navy game vaulted into a national spectacle overshadowing the classic Yale-Harvard rivalry, evoking immediate endearing attachments to either side.[8]

The passive role of the National Collegiate Athletic Association during World War II barely translates into that organization's current powers and responsibilities. Colleges established the NCAA as their own governing body for intercollegiate sports in 1910 from an earlier conglomerate. Member colleges limited the NCAA's authority primarily to making rules for its various sports and supervising national tournaments. The NCAA had limited authority to enforce its principles and resorted to moral suasion. "Traditionally, colleges had accepted the basic premise that, being honorable institutions, they should police themselves." This proved inadequate. In 1941 colleges approved a new NCAA constitution providing for expulsion of members who failed to abide by association rules, but none were expelled during the war.[9]

"College football faced the forties hindered with renewed attacks by critics who assailed its very legitimacy and place in institutions of higher learning," according to historians Douglas A. Noverr and Lawrence E. Ziewacz. Once war broke out, American sports tried maintaining course and speed, a normalcy lasting only two years. Among the major college programs disbanding football, the University of Chicago cited it as "a handicap to education," noting that half of all Big Ten players were majoring in physical education. Some schools dropping football publicly said that the game was inappropriate when totalitarianism and fascism threatened freedoms, traditions, and institutions.[10]

## Team Sports to Train the Surge

Shortly after December 7, the federal government began expanding or constructing vast numbers of facilities to train the huge surge of men and women entering the armed forces. Their numbers included many professional and college football players and coaches. The president acceded to the military's requests to allow maximum sports participation in order to emphasize and exhort physical training, toughness, leadership, teamwork, and camaraderie.

From 1942 to 1945, the navy, Marine Corps, and Coast Guard placed thousands of male officer candidates in colleges for preliminary training through their NROTC, V-5, V-7 and V-12 training programs, explained in chapter 3. Many, including All-Americas and professionals, played on varsity teams and the five navy pre-flight schools located on campuses. For example, in 1943-44, 13 of 25 college All-Americas were Marine-affiliated students. Without this massive student infusion — some might say saturation — numerous colleges, especially small, private ones experiencing rapidly declining male enrollments, would have closed their doors. Roosevelt saw the V-12 as "a grand chance to save some little college" which otherwise might have shut down.[11] *This assertion is key to understanding the magnitude of the problem that colleges faced and how vital military students suddenly became to their very survival as educational institutions.* Also, hundreds of military bases fielded teams. Later on, the services formed teams overseas to play ad hoc schedules and all-star or special "bowl" games.

The war stringently impacted nearly every facet of American life including sports and recreation. Players and coaches volunteered or were drafted into the armed forces, or began college officer programs. In 1942 more than 60 colleges abandoned football because of enrollment problems and subpar player quantity and quality. Two-thirds of colleges waived the rule barring freshman participation. Restrictions took over. Night games ceased on both coasts, and the government forbade special buses or trains for spectators to attend games. Transportation exigencies and gas and tire rationing limited college and military teams and scouting coaches from some travel, resulting in game site transfers and cancellations and a 19 percent attendance decline.[12]

Player collegiate loyalties "came down like the Wall of Jericho" during the war, Bisher said, "sacrificed in return for loyalty to country by male athletes who found themselves campus nomads in the military system.... Many a football career was born on service fields ... and heaven only knows how many were left there, not to mention those left under white crosses in military cemeteries."[13]

The army limited its personnel assigned to more than a hundred colleges (the Army Specialized Training Program — ASTP) to intramural football only. The ASTP differed from navy and Marine Corps V-programs in that it trained officers and enlisted men in technical skills, whereas V-programs trained just officer candidates. This limitation was unnecessary, second-guessed, and ultimately proven unwise. The *Football Pictorial Yearbook*, in rhetorically asking where football fit into the war effort, chastised the army for wasting time by limiting officer cadets to intramural sports, while the navy urged intercollegiate competition and encouraged its candidates to sacrifice and absorb hardships to play varsity ball.[14] In 1943 Walter Okeson, NCAA football rules committee chairman and annual *NCAA Football Guide* editor, felt that the difference between the two policies placed navy schools at a distinct advantage in player material.[15] No doubt about that.

A leading magazine called the army's decision "one of those wrinkles wrapped in the red tape of bureaucratic Washington which will never be completely understood by a civilian mind." The Military Academy superintendent, his school a wartime varsity power, tried explaining to a congressional committee why intramural sports would give the same physical and character benefits as the rougher intercollegiate game. It was a long stretch, but "that's how prevalent the physical education miasma has become."[16] Charles Moran wrote of the army's contradictory position: "If the cadet at West Point can move on the double for 12 to 16 hours, with 40 or 50 minutes a day allowed for [intramural] grid practice, are the army men at Ohio State or elsewhere of such inferior physique that they cannot stand the gaff mixed with football?"[17]

Nevertheless, most army and air force bases competed. Air force training commands ranked among the top-flight military teams, generally surpassing weaker army base elevens. Hundreds of military bases, most constructed to train the recruit surge, also fielded teams. Enjoying flexible, liberal recruiting policies, the service academies fielded sensational teams. Army's top-rated 1944-45 elevens with All-America backs Doc Blanchard and Glenn Davis remain legendary.

## The "Lend-Lease Players"

As already mentioned, from 1942 to 1945, the navy, Marine Corps, and Coast Guard placed thousands of officer candidates in colleges for preliminary training. Many, including All-America and professional players, played on football varsity teams and at navy pre-flight schools. These trainees — called "Lend-Lease players" — often participated on multiple teams during the same season, sometimes even playing against their old teammates. Marine trainee Elroy "Crazy Legs" Hirsch, a future NFL Hall of Famer, began 1943 at Wisconsin, was transferred to Michigan, and then helped the Wolverines defeat the Badgers. The vagabond Hirsch played at Camp Lejeune in 1944 and for the loaded El Toro Marine Corps Air Station in 1945.

The football application of "Lend-Lease" came from the term describing the U.S. program to ship weapons and equipment to European Allies Great Britain and the Soviet Union before and after America's entry into the war. Repayment arrangements, overlooked for all intents and purposes, were inconsequential in light of the immediate goal of defeating Nazi Germany. Thus the term aptly fit the mechanism to provide wartime college football players: Play now to win now. Let tomorrow take care of itself.

## Great Players, Great Teams

The war years produced a "mini–Golden Age" of famous players, coaches, and games, heralded in 1945 when they returned from combat for one last hurrah game before discharge. Although some players forfeited their prime years, many resumed or advanced to stardom or renown in college or the pros.

A sobering fact: a number lost their life for our country. Camp Lejeune coach Jack Chevigny died on Iwo Jima, and Okinawa claimed a dozen Marine players, including All-America Tony Butkovich. Paul Brown, wartime Great Lakes Naval Training Center coach and future pro Hall of Famer, said, "Things like football tended to dim in importance to men who, two or three months later, might be lying dead on some beach in the South Pacific. It was something I never could reconcile myself to while coaching service football."[18]

Great players wearing both college and military uniforms included: Otto Graham, Len Eshmont, Bob Dove, Barney Poole, Charley Trippi, Les Horvath, Arnold Tucker, Bob Steuber, Buster Ramsey, Buddy Young, Glenn Dobbs, Wee Willie Wilkin, Paul Governali, Nick Suseoff, Jack Russell, Don Whitmire, Marion Motley, Dick Todd, Bruce Smith, John Mellus, Joe Stydahar, Bill Dudley, Frankie Albert, George McAfee, and John Yonakor.

Great coaches in uniform included: Paul Brown, Earl Blaik, Joe Maniaci, Tony Hinkle, Paul Schissler, Bud Wilkinson, Bear Bryant, Bernie Bierman, Jim Tatum, Hampton Pool, Dick Hanley, Don Faurot, and Jim Crowley.

Numerous great games involved military teams. In 1943, Great Lakes (Ill.) Naval Training Station defeated Notre Dame 19–14 on a last-minute touchdown pass. The Irish received the national championship award anyway. In the most heralded all-military game, Fleet City Receiving Station beat the El Toro Flyers, 45–28, before 60,000 in the Los Angeles Coliseum in 1945. Other powerhouses, some representing facilities now long disestablished, included Randolph Field Army Air Base; Iowa Navy Pre-Flight; Fort Pierce Naval Amphibious Base; Alameda Coast Guard; Fort Riley; Keesler Army Air Field; Jacksonville Naval Air Technical Training Center; and the First, Second, Third and Fourth Air Force stateside training command teams.

College varsity teams played within their conferences and against other colleges, sometimes on short notice, and nearby military teams. Military elevens concentrated on playing each other as "independents," usually confined geographically, while the major conferences attempted to maintain integrity.

## "New Vigor, New Excitement"

Besides transitioning into the Department of the Navy officer program elevens, in 1942 a number of well-coached, well-manned military base squads emerged. What might have been an otherwise "drab campaign was surcharged with new vigor, new excitement by the competition of these dynamic soldier and sailor arrays."[19]

Although his college trainees could not play intercollegiate athletics, the army's athletic and recreation head touted his 1942 version of base football as being "more versatile." He trumpeted a sturdier vitality and more ambitious schedules that matched prowess with college varsities. Because army purposes subordinated football, "play was the thing and not the moulding of super grid giants." Intramural football's primary and perhaps lone army mission was physically training the troops.[20]

Soldiers, the official further said, constructed vigorous schedules designed for one-on-one or team-on-team action rather than championships. The wartime result: the army, excluding the air forces, with more establishments nationwide and overseas, fielded more base teams than the other services, but few of their base teams achieved more than fleeting, one-season notoriety. Many, especially small ones, disbanded during the season or after one or two losing campaigns. Numerous air force training command and base elevens, however, produced exceptional records and ranked high in national polls.

The army stressed inter-unit competition between battalions and regiments, developing quick rivalries overriding previously nonexistent base football tradition and institutions. Military duties came first, and football evolved as a spectator sport. Against military squads, "the khaki elevens often held their own."[21]

America's favorite college prewar participant and spectator sport, football now needed to process and train men for combat, which radically altered the scene. The NFL continued but lost its core to military duty. Approximately 350 colleges dropped football programs for a season or the war's duration. These included entire small conferences, most of the Southeastern Conference, and such large schools as Harvard, Princeton, Mississippi State, Florida, Stanford, and Oregon.

Some observers believed 1943 was the low point. Even then schools tightened their belts and played under adverse and abnormal conditions, generating praise for flexibility and criticism for quality. Simultaneously, football began rebounding. Some who gave it up were said to be "timid souls"; some "did it sadly." Military squads replaced some lost games. The annual Street & Smith magazine emphasized the main issue which recurs as a theme throughout this book: the games nevertheless continued for all the right reasons.[22]

Those colleges retaining programs, if bolstered by experienced players, played full schedules against teams with a collegiate-military mix. Colleges without eligible trainees played only 17-year-old freshmen not facing the draft, those 18 or older awaiting a draft call, physically disqualified 4-F's, and discharged servicemen. "In almost every instance they suffered defeat after defeat," noted *College Football's Twenty-Five Greatest Teams*. So afflicted, Ohio State somehow amazingly finished No. 2 in the 1944 Associated Press poll.[23]

Military and collegiate officials and conferences quickly adjusted to gargantuan travel restrictions, rationing, transportation availability, time away from base or campus, military duties and studies, and other allowances necessary for the war effort. Flexibility prevented potential chaos. Colleges relaxed eligibility requirements, permitting freshmen and other special cases to play. Collegiate playing rules governed: there were no revisions until 1945. Military elevens competed as independents, while major conferences attempted to maintain integrity.

Both military and college programs endured weekly roster problems caused by transfers and draft inductions, and juggled practices with irregular game schedules. The military and colleges primarily played three categories of games: military vs. military, colleges vs. colleges, and military vs. colleges. Military elevens occasionally played NFL teams in exhibitions or regular games against minor league pro teams (mostly in California and Hawaii). Scheduling difficulties, cancellations, and last-minute substitutions rendered completely accurate record keeping impossible. Coaches varied offensive and defensive schemes to fit personnel. Judged with the colleges and often dominating polls, military elevens played before one thousand spectators on base or a packed Los Angeles Coliseum.

By 1943, the navy had rescued football, as hundreds of players went to college for officer or specialist training or remained at their respective schools. In the Big Ten, or Midwestern Conference, this evolved into the "haves" (Michigan, Purdue, Northwestern — plus independent Notre Dame, also navy-fortified) with their service trainees who normally would have graduated in 1944–46, and the "have-nots," who "made the best of their conditions."[24]

Mid-season trainee transfers wrecked, weakened, or strengthened teams. Transfers started in late October, and the experts experienced "a harrowing season" trying to track changes.[25] The Big Ten's civilian teams — Ohio State, Iowa, Illinois, Minnesota, Indiana, and Wisconsin — approached Saturdays uncomfortably "like lambs led to the slaughter."[26] Marine football historian John Gunn claimed that the services aggressively lured many of the nation's top 1941 coaches and players to join, a "manpower grab" equal to the preflight establishment.[27]

The draft drained rosters in 1943, the most famous draftee being Notre Dame quarterback and Heisman Trophy winner Angelo Bertelli. How drained? *Time* reported in December about one squad's 4-F's: "The tailback has osteomyelitis. Another back, the best ground gainer, has a severed Achilles tendon. One tackle has two bad knees, another has only one lung. A guard has only one arm. But somehow the team's not beaten."[28]

## Carrying On

Most colleges carried on, repeatedly proving the resilience and fortitude of wartime football participants. Schools denied the use of army personnel had it rough. Those with navy students fielded some of the sport's most fabulous teams of that day, generating substantial sports-page ink and fan attention. Young players generally acquitted themselves credibly and even shouldered the load for some major teams, a few receiving All-America recognition. Trainees completing courses in November and then transferring gave freshmen a break, as "lineups seemed a constant hodge-podge and jumble."[29]

Thanks to older, more mature and experienced military players on both varsities and bases, in 1944 the sport rebounded, albeit erratically. Intriguing matchups between established collegiate teams and new service ones posed the continuous question of who had the advantage. Would youngsters playing in ripened, traditional, top collegiate programs, with limited preparation time, hold their own versus ad hoc elevens of ex-college stars and professionals? A Los Angeles scribe believed military football was the best being played, possibly excepting the NFL, declaring that few collegiate elevens could compete with any of the services' "potent aggregations" and "escape with a whole hide." Military players, the writer said, "are thoroughly familiar with all the tricks of the trade."[30]

A number of major colleges resumed playing by reducing academic or enrollment eligibility standards. For example, six Southeastern Conference schools allowed any bona fide student except former pros to dress out. Shifting of players from one school to another by the navy and Marines confused the lot. One might see a Dartmouth back one Saturday against Yale, and the next week in the Yale backfield against another team.[31]

A popular football annual called sophomores and freshmen "the star-pretenders of '44 ... mostly make-good-quick kids," augmenting older trainee hands. Time limitations prevented arduous practices, fine-tuned coaching, and gradual breaking-in that "produces precision-geared linemen and robot-controlled backs." But "youthful vim and spirit can often be a wonder-working substitute for know-how."[23] Previously unimaginable, powerhouse military teams successfully bridged the jump between college and professional levels in talent and production and laid to wartime rest the supposition that football detracted from intensive study. "That healthy bodies make healthy minds has been fully and literally demonstrated."[24]

## Tomorrow

When college and military teams began 1945 summer drills, the war was over. Not everything returned to normal overnight, but football tried. The army, a bit tardy, allowed soldiers to participate in sports during the duty day for competitive conditioning and during leisure hours for activities and recreation.[25] A war late, and a public relations debacle short.

By 1945, wartime game attendance increased annually, the new "T" formation dominated the offenses, "normality" edged back into American life, and sportswriter chatter anxiously awaited football's post-war explosion. Famed sportswriter Grantland Rice prepared readers for a new day.

> The skies are clear, the sun rises high, the wind blows fresh and fair, and it's marvelous football weather all across the map.... The sawdust is spurting in the tackle-dummy pits, the charge-machines are creaking, the passes and plunking punts are on the wing.... For King Football, stretching outside his winter cave, there's more than autumn's music in the air. He can feel not only the pulse of new blood, the invigorating strength of extra muscle, but can sense a pervading spirit of doing an enterprise that will lead on to mighty deeds.[35]

For 1946, the NCAA looked both backward and ahead. It cited those youngsters, trainees, veterans, and coaches who persevered despite the factors of weight, age, and experience which often resulted in lopsided competition. Beginning now, teams could rebuild to prewar levels quickly, with stability, longer practices, and improved defenses. "With GI Joe back on the gridiron the major colleges again will have players old enough, heavy enough and experienced enough to delight the alumni."[36]

Football America could hardly wait.

## Helping to Win the War

That football continued to be played — and consequently contributed to victory — was a tribute to an unprecedented combination of national unity, athletics, top-level leadership, forceful personalities, and overcoming service politics.

Competitive football enhanced troop and civilian morale on the home front and overseas by providing an uplifting, entertaining, and exciting diversion from the horrors, sacrifices, and boredom of war. Football's "value on the home front and in war theaters was recognized by those who directed the war effort."[37]

Teams fostered pride in unit identification. Men who might never have attended college found collegial camaraderie on military teams of varying sizes and scope, and attached football to the normal world to which they wished soon to return. Football stirred patriotism, recruiting, allegiances, war bond sales, charitable contributions, and productivity, and thus positively affected the war effort.

The NCAA further defined the value of wartime football: "High military, government and educational authorities publicly recognized the tremendous value of football as an integral part of the war training program. Indeed, American football, as perhaps no other sport, justified itself during World War II."[38]

Midway through the war, the navy — the war's strongest proponent of football — began evaluating its demanding pre-flight and college officer programs, emphasizing mandatory sports and football in particular. The evaluation concluded that "the high state of efficiency and the remarkable records that the navy has made in this war already in gunnery and aerial warfare are ample proof that these competitive methods are very worthwhile."[39]

From contemporary accounts, it is clear that the navy and Marine Corps, of all the services, firmly attested that football aided their performance of duty. Now we can state confidently that competitive, tough, conditioning football played a sizable but little-known role in helping to win the war.

CHAPTER 1

# "A Roster Out of Football's 'Who's Who'": The Bainbridge Eleven

*"At Bainbridge, sports is big time by big-timers. In one year the center has gained top-flight importance as a sports spot, deriving its strength from the cream of the crop among the gladiators of the nation. They fought for dear ol' Siwash then. Now it's strictly for the bluejacket time, but the thirst for victory is just as keen. It's an old American custom done to the tune of Anchors Aweigh."*[1]

By 1944, from out of nowhere, the Bainbridge navy Commodores rocketed into the American football hierarchy.

Undefeated in seven games during its first season in 1943, and outscoring opponents 313 to 7, "with a roster which reads like a page out of football's 'Who's Who,'" the team and station demanded immediate national notice.

Five members won berths on the Associated Press Mid-Atlantic Service eleven. Each possessed a brilliant college or professional record except for Charlie Justice, "an amazing football prodigy fresh out of Asheville (N.C.) High," named over such stars as Bill deCorrevont of Northwestern and Dan Durdan, Oregon State's Rose Bowl whiz, both Bainbridge teammates of Justice.[2]

But let's not jump the gun.

What was Bainbridge?[3] Nothing, until the navy arrived. If the navy sought isolation on a major body of water to prepare its trainees for combat, it aptly selected the site for the Bainbridge Naval Training Station. Hastily planned from scratch, beginning in early 1942, on 1,200 acres in the Cecil County countryside in the northern Chesapeake Bay region, on the property

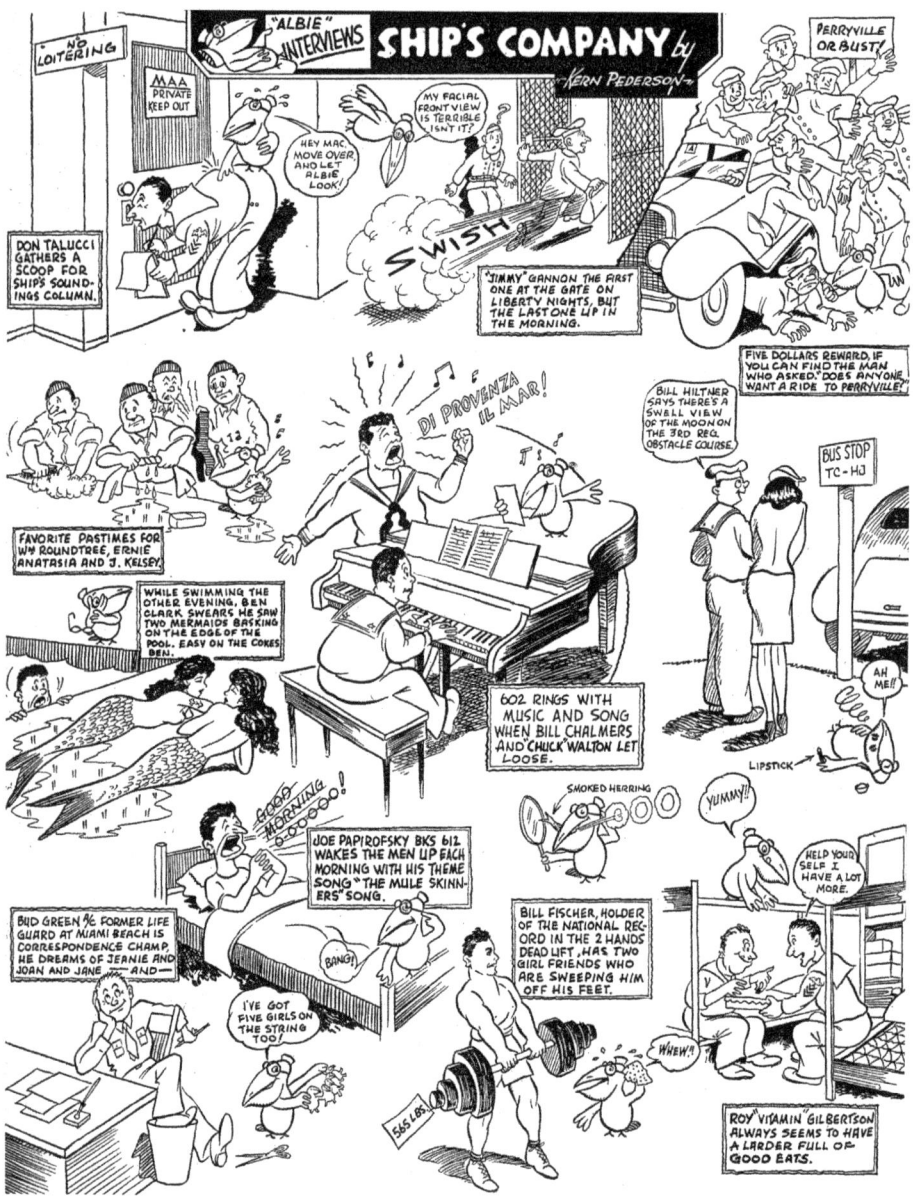

"Ship's Company." The Bainbridge (Md.) Naval Training Station *Mainsheet* weekly newspaper spiced news about the war, its sailor trainees, sports programs, and campus scenes with lots of humor (*Bainbridge Mainsheet*, ca. 1943).

of the Jacob Tome Institute, its construction overcame enormous odds while battling foul weather and mud, and coping with insufficient water and a lack of roads.

Located in northeast Maryland near the mouth of the Susquehanna River, along Route 22, and halfway between Baltimore and Wilmington, Del., essentially it was in the middle of nowhere. The topography did not fit the traditional rigid military reservation form, undoubtedly contributing to the prevailing "community atmosphere."[4] Recruits got there on the Baltimore & Ohio and Pennsylvania Railroads, through Aiken four miles away.

The navy noted that construction of Bainbridge was typical of the speed and efficiency with which the service rapidly expanded. "Where cow bells had tinkled in the spring, the sound of marching cadence echoed in October." Five months after breaking ground, Bainbridge began delivering trained seamen. In less than a year, crews built or renovated 357 buildings costing $45 million. Primarily built of wood, the complex consisted of four complete training units accommodating 4,000 men each, an officers' group, and support services structures. Each training unit contained 22 barracks housing 224 enlisted men each and a drill hall.[5]

Opened as a boot camp on October 10, 1942, Bainbridge joined similar facilities at Sampson, N.Y., and Farragut, Idaho. Recognizing its expanding role, the navy upgraded Bainbridge to a "center" in April 1944, adding it to the traditional centers at Great Lakes, Ill., and San Diego, Calif., as the three major wartime training facilities. The base newspaper, the *Bainbridge Mainsheet*, the navy's second-largest wartime paper, was published weekdays and Saturdays with a circulation of 22,000-plus.

Sampson and Farragut shut down after the war and became state-owned parks with museums. Now-deserted Bainbridge, closed in 1976, is neither. "For Bainbridge the legacy has been deliberate destruction and indifference to progressive deterioration, the whole reverting to a wild and unkept state, the orphaned sister."[6]

The first recruits found no "happy hours" or station football team. Movies were the early thirties vintage which required rewinding after each reel. "It was no uncommon sight ... to see navy personnel walking about with mud hip-high on their trousers." Sailors speculated whether rainy, muddy days at Bainbridge counted as sea duty, but genuinely accepted the blessings of water to wash with and shelter at night. The commandant characterized the station's rapid growth as a "dirty miracle."[7]

Besides the boot camp, or Recruit Training Command, Bainbridge housed service schools for shipboard ratings including gunners mate, fire controlman, radioman, electrician's mate, storekeeper, steward's mate, quartermaster, signalman, hospital corpsman, and physical instructor ("PI"), plus the Naval Academy Preparatory School, a naval hospital, and a school for WAVES. The PI school trained the trainers, enlisted men who taught physical conditioning throughout the fleet and also manned the station's football teams. Into this rating poured All-Americas, professionals, and Charlie Justice.

Captain C. F. Russell served as Bainbridge's first commandant until 1945 when relieved by Commodore William F. Behrens. Personnel assigned there averaged around 20,000. The first boot company graduated in December 1942. Bainbridge's auditorium seated 2,700 and its amphitheater 10,000. Buildings were supposed to last 25 years. Tome Field, where the gridders romped, seated 15,000. By V-J Day on August 14, 1945, the center had trained 244,277 recruits to man ships and bases, and 24,484 men in technical ratings.

"They were for getting you in and getting you out," remembered Albert Bagley. "The need was over there and not here at Bainbridge." He had quit high school as a junior. "Our whole class went to war." The base was still under construction when he arrived in December 1942. "Wasn't too much navy down there. Nothing but mud." Chief petty officers, who pushed the boots, "were physical education majors in college. They had to teach us how to poop — you were thrown into [a] long string of johns. Diets changed." Sneakers lasted only a day as the mud sucked them off feet. "We were like cattle in a barn. They kept us busy," it was said. The navy even charged sailors for their basic textbook, the *Bluejackets Manual*.[8]

President Franklin D. Roosevelt named the station after Commodore William Bainbridge, one of the navy's great pioneers and the founder of its first school. Born in New Jersey in 1774, he began a sea career at age 15 and in 1798 earned a lieutenant's commission. He commanded the frigate USS *Philadelphia* in the war against Tripoli in 1803. During the War of 1812 he led a squadron including his flagship USS *Constitution* and captured the British frigate *Java* off of San Salvador. Active in expanding sea programs, in later years he directed work on the signal code revision and construction of navy yards and docks at Boston and Philadelphia. He died in 1833 at age 59.[9]

Sailors boasted to the folks at home: "We're going to be fighting bluejackets! That is why we were sent here ... [to] transform us from civilians, unfamiliar with the ways of the sea, into sailors." They vowed to remember the experience.[10]

*Hail! Men of Bainbridge,*[11]
*Let us turn the tide,*
*March forth as one and man the guns*
*To conquer all in stride.*
*We're the navy's sons*
*Whose valor has been tried.*

*The course is rough;*
*We'll show how tough*
*They build men on this side.*

*Sing together, loud and long.*
*Pull together, stout and strong.*
*Make each day spell death to wrong.*
*Bainbridge men fight on and on.*
*Steer ships of Freedom,*
*Masters of the sea,*
*And when we're done, the battle won,*
*We'll rest in Victory.*

# 1943

Now back to serious matters, the Bainbridge eleven. On September 25, 1943, their run to fame began at the Camp Lejeune (N.C.) Marine Corps Base. "Break out the rabbit's foot mate, and keep those fingers crossed," the *Mainsheet* implored. Lejeune lost its opener to Duke, 40–0, but don't be fooled. Packing royal blue uniforms with red numerals outlined in white, the 60-man squad headed to Durham as head coach Ensign Joe Maniaci (All-America Fordham, Brooklyn Dodgers, Chicago Bears) announced, "the team's ready to shoot the works."[12] They won 9–0.

The station had decided to field a team only one month prior. Out went an urgent call for all former pigskin coaches and players to report. Quality players suddenly appeared in

**Lieutenant (junior grade) Joe Maniaci coached the Bainbridge Commodores to a 17-0-0 record in 1943-44 (game program, Bainbridge at Camp Lejeune, September 25, 1943).**

droves, but formulating a schedule proved another story. Nearby natural rivals dropped football and others had completed their schedules, but the station found ten games after numerous telegrams, telephone calls, letters, and tips.[13] Maniaci "promptly set about the organization of one of the swiftest-moving, most invulnerable teams in the East," opined the *Illustrated Football Annual*.[14]

Maniaci bemoaned the start-up task he inherited. Looking around at the odd mixture of station candidates, he found a number of well-known names and "and a kid by the name of Charlie Justice who was voted the best high school back in the South last year." Frustrated over scrambling for an eventual schedule of seven games, he realistically figured his material just happened to be stationed there and probably wouldn't remain long after completing training. Some might not finish the season. "But what a team they would have been. Oh well, *c'est la guerre*."[15]

Maniaci had starred for seven years as a running back with the Brooklyn Dodgers and Chicago Bears, with a lifetime average 5.0 yards per carry. His first assistants were Ensigns Maurice Orr (All-America, Southern Methodist University), Phil Ragazzo (Western Reserve, Philadelphia Eagles, Cleveland Rams), and Jack Williams (Texas).[16] Maniaci also coached the team in 1944.

After two weeks of practice the squad charted three backfield combos for two scrimmages. One combo included deCorrevont, Bill

Ensign Phil Ragazzo (Western Reserve, Philadelphia Eagles, Cleveland Rams), Bainbridge assistant coach and lineman, 1943 (game program, Bainbridge at Camp Lejeune, September 25, 1943).

Dutton, Tom "Knobby" Noble, and Justice. Against the Washington Redskins, the impressive sailors scored once, and Justice, "shifty Commodore back," sparkled carrying the ball. Linemen Phil Ragazzo and Garrard ("Gerry" or "Buster," All-America William & Mary) Ramsey did "a 4.0 job." Andy Farkas sparked the Redskins.[17] Over in Annapolis, Bainbridge gave No. 2–rated Navy "something to remember them by."[18]

Observers saw something special developing. Three weeks into the campaign, the *Football News* tabbed Bainbridge a "wonder team."[19] The *Baltimore Sun* said: "And if there be a cynic who believes big-time stars can be lured to play only by fame and fortune, let him look at the Commodores' roster.... Without being induced by purses or plaudits," they established cohesiveness and unity en route to a most impressive record.[20]

The *Mainsheet* updated sailors and fans. After the only team to score against the Commodores, Curtis Bay (Md.) Coast Guard, fell, 26–7, in October, the paper reported that the squad still had trouble defending against the forward pass because its backs played the receiver instead of the ball. Maniaci's efforts to install the "T" formation began developing finesse, featuring dangerous breakaway runners Durdan, Jim Gatewood (Georgia), and Justice. Fullback Harvey "Stud" Johnson (William & Mary), slowly rounding into shape, showed more power, and durable back Hilliard "Upan" Cheatham (Auburn) shined. The line showed power on defense and appeared ready for the long haul.[21]

By late October, the Bluejackets had lost seven regulars to sea duty or extra duties forcing them to give up football: backs Bill Dutton (All-America Pittsburgh), Bill Fuqua (Roanoke College), Win Siegfried (All-America Duke); quarterbacks Brick Bradford (Iowa) and Hugh Flanigan (Vanderbilt); guard Dick Kelleher (Cleveland Rams); and Hoyer Williams (Baylor). An injury placed captain and guard Len Akin (Baylor, Chicago Bears) on the sidelines for the season.

After dismantling a Philadelphia professional team 72–6 on November 6 ("more of a track meet than a pigskin session") for their fifth straight, the Commodores ranked No. 9 among the nation's 15 unbeaten and untied teams, with Purdue and Notre Dame heading the list. They led all service elevens except Iowa Pre-Flight in the prestigious Williamson military football ratings.[22]

The Commodores continued driving their point. Maryland scheduled Bainbridge twice but played them only once. "There may be easier methods of murdering a group of youngsters such as inserting them into a gas chamber or lining them up against the wall and spraying them with machine-gun slugs," a scribe wrote, branding such schedule making as "bordering on insanity."[23] By then Bainbridge led the nation in three of five game categories: passing, total defense, and rushing defense; and was second (total offense) and third (rushing) others. Maryland had "absolutely no chance of upsetting the Bainbridge outfit composed mainly of former pros and ex-collegiate stars."[24]

The scribe was correct. In its final contest, Bainbridge (46) held the Terrapins (0) to two first downs and 17 total yards, gaining 406 total yards and returning kicks for 421. Still, the team exhibited sloppy ball handling and blocking and won largely because of their brilliant backs.[25] Never mind. Bainbridge had definitely hit the gridiron map.

So, how good were they? The media went to see for themselves, as a November piece in the *Baltimore Sun* reported.[26] "Football's just an incidental at the Bainbridge Naval Training Station. But the team, incidentally, is good. Just how good, no one knows. The opposition hasn't really extended the galaxy of former college and professional football stars who comprise the Bainbridge eleven.... Yesterday's 46–0 victory of the University of Maryland was typical.... If the 8,000 seamen who witnessed the game were excited, they hid their emotions well. They beat a loud tattoo with the feet on the floorboards of the stands, but only because it was cold." WAVE cheerleader Iris Jean Moore "got more applause when she came on the field than the team did. Sixty-yard practice kicks were much in evidence, but only the few women who walked in got whistles. Not that the players mind. They're playing for the fun of it."

The Commodores, the paper reported, "are one of the peculiar phenomena of wartime: a collection of top-ranking gridiron players whose performances by necessity are comparatively unheralded. Naval duties take up all but a few hours of their time, so football must remain incidental. Only servicemen comprised the cheering section at home games." Outsiders could not attend. Both admission and game programs were free. Games were not subsidized. Away games were played on fields covered with large stones and trees bordering the end zone. Hardly any glory was involved, "but the game is played ... intensely."

The dressing-room scene "was typical of its college counterpart," according to the *Sun*. Relations between the coach ... and the players were completely democratic, in spite of the fact that only one of them is a commissioned officer and only nine are newly made chief petty officers." One difference from college ball: "Pre-game tension was completely absent. In fact, so relaxed with confidence were the players that the coach permitted an extensive interview of the squad."

DeCorrevont said, "'It's not quite as tough as college. We don't spend enough time on it. Military duty comes first, and they never let us forget it.... There's none of the do-or-die spirit, but there's always that old feeling that you'd rather win than lose any day." Justice felt "grateful to the navy for his association with 'such a flock of big boys.' He confessed to thinking he was out of place when he first joined the team but his success in action and their acceptance of him had made him much more comfortable."

Players got two hours of daily practice if their duties allowed, were subject to transfer on three days' notice once completing training, and had no idea if they would play next week or ever again. This did not diminish their interest. Team captain Akin, a four-year pro with the champion Bears ($200 per game), said, "Football is fun, no matter who or what you're playing for."

Fun, sure, and it helped to be awesome. Bainbridge topped the country in scoring average and defense, and was rated as one of the decade's greatest offensive clubs. A number of its key players notched among national leaders.[27] Powerful Duke (8–1–0; lost to Navy, 14–13) flirted with playing Bainbridge after the 1943 season. The Duke athletic director agreed, then backed off, citing severe V-12 player losses. A Commodores war bond benefit in New York or Washington never materialized either.

The navy forced Bainbridge to restrict its play to Maryland, Virginia, North Carolina, and South Carolina, and canceled its games with Pittsburgh, Villanova, Navy, and Sampson (postseason), and a second match with Fort Monroe (Va.). Observers believed it could have beaten any college or service team around.[28]

National honors accrued. The AP named them the best military team, Notre Dame the best college eleven, and Ramsey to its first-team All-America service team. Writer Grantland Rice hailed Ramsey as "the greatest lineman in college football."[29] Honorable mention included ends Howard "Red" Hickey (Arkansas, Pittsburgh Steelers, Cleveland Rams) and Carl Mulleneaux (Utah State, Green Bay Packers), tackle Ragazzo, Durdan, deCorrevont, Johnson, and Justice.

Two of Justice's backfield mates on the Mid-Atlantic All-Service squad included former National Football League players Norm Standlee (Stanford, Chicago Bears) of Camp Davis (N.C.) and Cecil Hare (Gonzaga, Redskins) of North Carolina Pre-Flight. The other was Commodores fullback Johnson. The three Bainbridge linemen were Ramsey, Hickey, and Ragazzo. Second-teamers included center Lou Sossamon (South Carolina), tackle Elwood Gerber (Alabama, Philadelphia Eagles), and backs Cheatham, and deCorrevont.

Bainbridge finished as the nation's third-highest-scoring team in only seven games, and was one of six unbeaten college-military elevens after leader Purdue. The sailors' all-opponent team included: best team, and one of the east's finest service elevens, Camp Lejeune; best back, Curtis Bay's Fred Dobler; best linemen, Camp Lee's Howie Gentry, Maryland's Pete Karangelen, and Curtis Bay's Russ Monica.

And the Bainbridge best? "Hangnail Sketches" in the *Mainsheet* spotlighted three.[30]

Ensign Phil Ragazzo, Western Reserve All-America tackle, was "quite a lad in the pro football ranks [with] the Philadelphia Eagles and the Cleveland Rams. Phil is the only officer playing with the Commodores and it's like betting on Man O' War to say that Ragazzo could make any team playing football today. One of the keenest diagnosticians of an opponents' strength, Phil pitched right in at the beginning of the season here and lent Joe Maniaci a hand with the Bainbridge line." He wants to coach "when the lights go on again," the *Mainsheet* reported.[31]

Guard and Specialist (A) Leonard "Len" Akin, team captain, born in 1916, played high school football in Oklahoma City and Dallas, Tex. He played four years for Baylor and made All-Southwest in 1938–39. He later played pro football with the Milwaukee Chiefs (American League all-stars) and in 1942 with the Bears.

Of halfback and Specialist (A) First Class Donald "Don" Durdan, the *Mainsheet* said: "Diminutive, swivel-hipped Don Durdan, one of the shiftiest and fastest scatbacks ... really knows his football." Born in 1920 in Eureka, Calif., he excelled in every major high school sport, then was Oregon State's triple-threat for four years as they won the Pacific Coast championship. There he also lettered in basketball and baseball. On New Year's Day 1942 he scored the winning touchdown in the 20–16 win over Duke when the Rose Bowl shifted to Durham, N.C. He was voted the outstanding Pacific Coast athlete in 1941. Durdan graduated from PI school and entered the V-12 program.

THE BAINBRIDGE 1943 RECORD (7–0–0)
(Scrimmaged Washington Redskins and Navy)

| | |
|---|---|
| Camp Lejeune (N.C.) Marine Corps Base | 9–0 |
| Ft. Monroe (Va.) | 57–0 |
| Curtis Bay (Md.) Coast Guard | 26–7 |
| Camp Lee (Va.) | 49–0 |
| Philadelphia Yellowjackets | 72–0 |
| Curtis Bay | 54–0 |
| Maryland | 46–0 |
| | 313–7 |

# 1944

Now promoted to lieutenant (junior grade) and heading the station's civil police, Maniaci eyed men reporting from Sampson and Great Lakes for his 1944 squad. Practice started on August 15 behind the new fieldhouse, with conditioning exercises, punting and passing drills, and light formation workouts. Player availability remained uncertain, but officials hoped enough men would report so the squad could repeat the previous year's performance. Sixty aspirants tried out.[32] The *Mainsheet* noted the normal grunts and groans of practices in Tome Quad at 1630 hours. "The telephone in coach Joe Maniaci's office has been howling like a banshee all week.... No cut will be made until each man has a chance to demonstrate his wares."[33]

Key returning players included Ramsey, Cheatham, Akin,

Bainbridge player sketches of back Charlie Justice and tackle Elwood Gerber (Alabama, Philadelphia Eagles) (*Bainbridge Mainsheet*, September 1944).

Hickey, Johnson, Durdan, Gerber, Gatewood, and Justice. One source predicted that Maniaci would carry only about 22 players because of their military duties. The previous season's big names had moved on, but the station promised to field "a fair team."[34] Thirty-eight men dotted the final roster. Assistant coaches were Chief Warrant Officer Roland Raphael (Purdue, Packers), and Specialists (A) Second Class Joe Skladany (Pittsburgh, Carnegie Tech head coach), and Ed Brominski (Columbia). And their record surpassed 1943.

"The Fighting Commodores"[35]
*Roll up the score for dear old Bainbridge,*
*Roll up the score you Commodores.*
*Down the field in Navy Blue,*
*Show your colors true.*
*Rah! Rah!*

> *Just like a Navy battle wagon,*
> *Sail on to meet and sink the foe.*
> *Fight! With might! You men of Bainbridge;*
> *Sail right on to Victory!*

Schedule conflicts continued in 1944, as contests were canceled with Richmond (Va.) Air Base, Camp Davis, Jacksonville (Fla.) Naval Air Station, and North Carolina. Travel restrictions again limited games to the same states as 1943. The Commodores played most games at home in Tome, called one of the nation's most beautiful fields.

Five top-notch guards dominated the line, including two of the finest in Ramsey and Akin. Returnee Florian Surdyk (Illinois) "has one of the most vicious charges in football." Strong reserves included Joe Petro (Muhlenberg) and "Mr. Five by Five "Rocky Rockenbock (Michigan State).[36] Transfers interrupted tempo. Hickey, who led the nation's ends in scoring with 56 points in 1943, received his commission and departed, and Ensign Ragazzo left to head the Newberry College V-12 program. Quent Klenk, Charlie Noble, and Sherry Fries also received orders. For a while it appeared Bainbridge might not be able to dress eleven players for its opener.[37]

The starting forward wall included: center Sossamon, guards Ramsey and Akin, tackles Gerber (team captain) and Lou Rymkus (Notre Dame), and ends Joe Davis (Southern California) and Al Vanderweghe (William & Mary). They "should be household names around Bainbridge by nightfall," it was

Although loaded with former college and professional stars, the Bainbridge starting lineup in 1944 usually included: front row, left to right: end Joe Davis, tackle Frank Hrabetin, guard Garrard Ramsey, center Lou Sossamon, guard Len Akin, tackle Elwood Gerber, end Alfred Vanderweghe. Back row: backs Don Durdan, Harvey Johnson, Joe Michaels, Jim Gatewood (*Bainbridge Mainsheet*, September 30, 1944).

Bainbridge back Dante Magnani explodes around left end in a 1944 home game at Tome Field (Street & Smith's *Football Pictorial Yearbook 1945*).

said. All returned from 1943 except Rymkus and Davis. The backfield starters: quarterback Cheatham, halfbacks Gatewood and Durdan, and fullback Johnson.[38]

The "bluejacket boys from the banks of the Susquehanna" traveled to Camp Peary for a 7–0 October 22 victory. "Newspaper observers — the professional pundits whose opinions influence national rankings — immediately pounced upon the win as placing the Marylanders in the upper brackets ... including not alone GI teams but colleges as well."[39]

Fans and the media anticipated certain games more than others, and the *Mainsheet* covered them enthusiastically. After outscoring their first five opponents 167–21, with two successive, grueling, close battles, the Commodores visited loaded North Carolina Pre-Flight on November 5 in a "natural" game

The Commodores prevailed against the Maxwell Marauders, 13–3, to finish the season at 10–0–0 (game program, Maxwell [Ala.] Field at Bainbridge, December 3, 1944).

that could determine the mythical eastern military service championship. The future aviators, ranked No. 7 in the AP poll and led by passing quarterback Otto Graham (All-America Northwestern) and Stan Kosloski (Holy Cross), had already torpedoed powerhouses Navy and Duke. Bainbridge prevailed, 49–20.[40]

Season Statistics to Date

Rushes: 200 for 1068 yards (5.5 yds. p/carry)
Top ground gainer: Justice, 22 rushes for 242 yds. (avg. 11.0)
　　Gatewood averaged 5.75, Johnson and Harry Hopp 4.25, Durdan 4.0
Passing: Cheatham 6 for 12, Joe Michaels 8 for 21, Justice 1 for 1
Leading punt returner: Hopp, 4 for 86; Justice 11 for 178 (16.0+)
Scoring: Johnson, 24 points, 9 on PATs

"Star-studded" Bainbridge, playing all military teams and winning 17 straight over two unbeaten seasons, took the navy championship at 10-0-0, downing the opposition 331–70. Noted for their "sheer power" along with army champion Randolph Field (Tex.), the two headed more than 100 service teams "blending in a quantity and quality of inter-camp play that fulfilled their primary mission of entertaining as many of Uncle Sam's servicemen as possible."[41]

The public sought a Randolph Field–Bainbridge meeting and flooded the War and Navy Departments with requests for postseason games. The departments waffled, then decided no, the AP reported in late November. Once more navy officials disallowed Bainbridge and other navy elevens to participate because of training responsibilities, and did not relax the rule requiring a navy team to play either on its own or its opponent's home field. The Army-Navy game in Baltimore was excepted because it was considered the normal Navy home game. No navy eleven could play on a neutral field without "special consideration." None came.[42] Bainbridge earned fifth in the AP rankings among all teams and fourth in the rankings of the respected Dr. L. H. Baker football service.

1944 record (10-0-0)
(Scrimmaged Washington Redskins)

| | |
|---|---|
| Camp Lee (Va.) | 43–0 |
| Camp Lejeune (N.C.) Marine Corps Base | 53–7 |
| Camden (N.J.) Blue Devils | 47–7 |
| Camp Peary (Va.) | 7–0 |
| Maxwell Field (Ala.) | 15–7 |

| | | |
|---|---|---|
| North Carolina Pre-Flight | 49–20 |
| Cherry Point (N.C.) Marine Corps Air Station | 50–7 |
| Camp Lejeune | 33–6 |
| Camp Peary | 21–13 |
| Maxwell Field | 13–3 |
| | 331–70 |

### 1944 Bainbridge Commodores Roster
(listed numerically by jersey number)

| Pos | Name | Ht/Wt | School |
|---|---|---|---|
| G | Garrard Ramsey | 6'1"/195 | William & Mary* |
| B | Donald Durdan | 5'9"/175 | Oregon St.* |
| B | James Gatewood | 6'½"/180 | Georgia* |
| B | Charlie Justice | 5'10"/165 | Asheville (N.C.) HS |
| B | Joe Kane | 5'8"/185 | Pennsylvania |
| G | Len Akin | 5'11"/202 | Baylor* |
| B | Frank Santora | 5'9"/166 | Garfield (N.J.) HS |
| E | John Feeney | 6'1"/200 | Scranton U. |
| B | John McTamney | 5'10"/180 | Georgetown |
| E | Bernard Kuczynski | 6'0"/195 | Pennsylvania |
| B | Jackie Field | 5'11"/195 | Texas |
| E | Charles Mehelich | 6'2"/200 | Duquesne |
| E | Alfred Vanderweghe | 5'11"/190 | William & Mary* |
| G | Joseph Petro | 6'0"/195 | Muhlenberg |
| E | Tom Vargo | 6'3"/200 | Penn St. |
| B | Joe Michaels | 5'10"/180 | Pennsylvania |
| B | Harry Hopp | 6'0"/210 | Nebraska |
| B | Dante Magnani | 6'1"/180 | St. Mary's |
| G | John Badaczewski | 6'2"/210 | Western Reserve |
| E | Joe Davis | 6'2"/200 | Southern California* |
| E | Paul Ruby | 6'2"/210 | Villanova |
| C | Lou Sossamon | 6'0"/195 | South Carolina* |
| B | Arthur Pollard | 6'0"/180 | Texas A&M |
| QB | Hilliard Cheatham | 5'11"/200 | Auburn* |
| G | Florian Surdyk | 5'11"/200 | Illinois |
| E | Joseph Schwarting | 6'0"/190 | Texas |
| B | Harvey Johnson | 6'0"/205 | William & Mary* |
| E | Carl Tomasello | 6'0"/195 | Scranton U. |
| B | Andy Pulley | 5'11"/200 | Richmond (Va.) HS |
| C | Lester Gatewood | 6'2"/200 | Baylor-Tulane |
| B | Dewey Proctor | 6'0"/195 | Furman |

| | | | |
|---|---|---|---|
| G | Lyle Rockenboch | 5'9"/205 | Michigan St. |
| T | Garvin Mugg | 6'0"/201 | North Texas St. |
| T | Frank Hrabatin | 6'4"/203 | Loyola (La.) |
| T | Elwood Gerber (captain) | 6'0"/205 | Alabama* |
| T | Jim Tharp | 6'5½"/235 | Notre Dame |
| T | Zygmont Czarboski | 6'0"/200 | Notre Dame |
| T | Lou Rymkus | 6'4"/201 | Notre Dame* |
| C | Clure Mosher | 6'1"/203 | Louisville |

HS — High school player without college experience
*Starter

# 1945

Preseason headlines predicted a sea change. "Bainbridge will not thunder the South Atlantic gridirons," the *Illustrated Football Annual* blared.[43] *The Football News* shut the door: "Undefeated Bainbridge Loses Stars Who Made It Great." After two successive unblemished campaigns, outscoring opponents 644 to 77, the nation's only team until then never to lose a game expected that record to be snapped. The Commodores, an advance obituary stated, "are not what they used to be."[44] Why not? As the war wound down, the PI school closed in June, and the marquee athletes disappeared.

Three practice weeks somehow convinced new head coach Paul Pierce (Texas State Teachers) that his unit would be good but hardly great. No superstars, no All-Americas, no NFL veterans, or All-Service standouts, the likes of Hopp, Johnson, Gatewood, Gerber, DeCorrevont, Rymkus, Akin, Mullineaux, and Ramsey. Also departed: "sensational high school back, Charlie 'Choo Choo' Justice of Asheville (N.C.) High," who trailed only Army's Glenn Davis as 1944's top scoring back.[45]

The Bainbridge candidate replacement reservoir still had thousands, mostly kids right out of high school and college freshmen averaging less than 20 years old. Therefore, Pierce's "T" formation did not figure "to be the same potent brew that the great elevens of '43 and '44 manufactured."[46]

Yet, remarkably, the unbeaten record stretched to 21 games, as Bainbridge continued outscoring opponents 140 to 13, until the Nashville (Tenn.)–based Air Transport Command halted it, 24–6. Too many outbound personnel transfers? By then the meteoric, unprecedented, startling two-plus-season run was through. But, oh, what a run.

### The Bainbridge 1945 Record (5–4–0)

| | |
|---|---|
| Atlantic City (N.J.) Naval Air Station | 14–6 |
| Aberdeen (Md.) Proving Ground | 59–7 |
| Camp Lee (Va.) | 27–0 |
| Camp Detrick (Md.) | 40–0 |
| Air Transport Command (Tenn.) | 6–24 |
| Little Creek (Va.) Naval Amphibious Base | 0–7 |
| Camp Lee | 0–26 |
| Ft. Bragg (N.C.) | 14–20 |
| Oceana (Va.) Naval Air Station | 53–14 |
| | 213–104 |

CHAPTER 2

# "Ideological Arsenal": The Impact of Football on the War Effort, Morale, and Fighting Spirit

*"The American people relied not only on their massive production of arms and material but upon an ideological arsenal. The field of organized athletics had a symbolic and rhetorical appeal.... Sport represented the moral and physical superiority of the United States."*[1]

The military firmly believed that football, "the American method of physical conditioning," provided the key to achieving such moral and physical superiority. Spectators attending the 1943 game matching Northwestern at the Great Lakes (Ill.) Naval Training Center read in their programs that "football is as American as skip-bombing" and furthermore that sports competition challenges a young man's individuality and decision-making process under all circumstances.[2]

Clark Shaughnessy, one of the era's great coaches and considered the "father of the T formation," called football "a great war game," the only field sport closely simulating battle strategy and tactics. To illustrate, he cited the tactics of British General Bernard Montgomery, almost identical with the "T" formation's fullback-counter play, in defeating General Erwin Rommel's Afrika Korps in the Battle of El Alamein on November 4, 1942. The victory saved Cairo and Alexandria and led to the German defeat in North Africa six months later.[3]

By 1942, the U.S. focus for prosecuting the war quickly manifested itself in the hardened, conditioned American boy, strongly grounded in robust athletics and competitive sports. Football as a principal mechanism naturally conformed. The *Athletic Journal* "depicted Japanese soldiers fleeing in terror from a group of uniformed football players. 'Why not battalions of football players?' stated the caption, 'they are the fightingest men we have.'"[4]

What might be the shortest way to win the war? Columbia's Lou Little, a prominent and eloquent coach, in 1942 answered for the National Collegiate Athletic Association: "'Play football. Play it hard and intensively with an even more savage will-to-win than in peacetime. Play service football as much as the military programs of the men under arms will permit." A year later Little continued rationalizing the push for football. American males love the "hard-hitting, punishing contact sport," he said, that energizes an invaluable mental approach for the combat soldier.[5] After employing the single-wing offensive formation for 20 years, in 1944 Little became one of the new "split-T" innovators.

Little also chastised peacetime America for its dull competitive spirit, physical and mental softness, and decried the prevalent de-emphasis on winning or sacrificing for victory. As one of them, he knew coaches of major college sports had done their utmost to keep the competitive spark alive and against odds to maintain the American boy in fighting trim.[6] Now the nation needed to stand up. Other critics joined Little, notably the NCAA.

Few disagreed. One college coach reflected the prevailing view, that if football hindered an all-out war effort, then cancel it for the duration. Otherwise, sup-

"Coach Morgan must've lost a lot more men in the draft than he lets on." The older players departed for military duty to be replaced by underage youngsters (Bo Brown in game program, Texas Tech at Lubbock Army Air Field, September 18, 1943).

port it and make it work. Letters he received from former players on every front pleaded to continue the game. "I am not afraid of Hitler spiking the guns in our sports set-up. The biggest danger to college football is not planning for the future."[7] Already some were thinking of the postwar.

Once America entered World War II, the military recognized that youth maturing during the pacifist, Great Depression 1930s generation required massive physical and mental makeovers. The nation's males were out of shape. Too many men flunked early-war enlistment and draft physicals because of health or mental conditions (classified 4-F). Some did end up on college grid rosters. The country's highly suspect physical fitness resulted in one of every four teenage boys being rejected for service by 1943. But by lowering standards and testing every eligible prospect, enough physically qualified fighters eventually entered the services.

For example, the author's home county, New Hanover, N.C., showed a total wartime rejection rate of 45 percent, according to a December 1945 study. The racial breakdown: 36.3 percent white, 61.1 percent black. Reasons: the lack of health care and efficient health education.[8]

The navy soon recognized this serious condition during screening for preflight schools. From a population representing "complacent obese, peaceful days" they selected only specimens who could "produce the ruggedness and sharpness of mind and body" to make a superb aviator.[9] Calisthenics and gymnastics alone could not manufacture the ideal pilot or ship officer. In 12 weeks the navy physical and mental development programs tried to surmount many mistakes of peacetime living and consequently helped to complete mission assignments and ultimately save U.S. lives. The *Chicago Daily News* added: "It was remarkable how soft we had gone mentally."[10]

The NCAA, the college sports governing organization, in 1942 promoted football's rigorous competitive tradition to indoctrinate players on the importance of the big picture — warfare, mission, victory — far larger than one man or his team. Mandatory hard drills incorporated a study of the opponent's strategy and tactics as a field or sea commander would engage the real enemy's. In diagnosing an opponent's strengths and weaknesses, the player on receiving a coach's order knew the objective would be gained if he and his comrades properly followed through.[11]

Violent, body-contact football rounded a man out by emphasizing individual and collective coordination and team play. It exposed fortitude, perseverance, resilience, the ability to play through injuries, and unit fighting spirit, while demanding self control and respect of others.[12] The overwhelming majority of players in this era wore no face mask. Those who did used a simple, basic inverted-T wire guard. Pads and helmets provided meager protection compared to today's equipment. By 1942, feedback from the combat fronts told of heroic exploits by former college athletes. The NCAA further believed the recreation advantages of football also reduced wartime stress and strain for participants as well as followers.[13]

A poignant 1944 sporting goods company advertisement in the *NCAA Football Guide* trumpeted the positive influence of competitive sports on American youth as a safeguard for democracy. "Out there, where 'the best man wins,' they develop a *will-to-win*, the *never-say-die spirit*, that makes them fight till the last man is out — till the final gun of the last quarter — the last bell of the last round — the last shot of the last long set — the last stride of the last lap." Youth playing sports in those extremely turbulent times appreciated and experienced determination, self-confidence, freedom and democracy, in addition to building strong bodies and agility.[14]

Continuing to extol the sport's virtues, coach Little believed the war returned most of the nation to its senses. He concluded that America needed football not necessarily for relaxation on Saturday afternoons, but as a team game to enhance and fuse temperament, character, and principles in the boys who played and ultimately fought for our freedom.[15]

Requiring a player to endure terrific physical punishment on the field prepared him as little else could for the emotions, mayhem, and death on the battlefield, and to sustain high morale. The American Football Coaches Association believed that when practices and games ended, the player took immense pride in showing the guts to give and take a violent pounding. It made him a better soldier, sailor, airman, or Marine.[16]

The principal proponents of military football were those officials responsible for providing adequate numbers of naval aviators (which included Marine Corps aviation) and shipboard officers for the fleet, and Marine ground officers. Naval aviation's V-5 pre-flight football conditioning program opened in 1942 snagged in intra-service politics and turf battles. Program director Commander Tom Hamilton weathered the rough beginning to create overnight a superb regimen, as much "'mental conditioning'" as physical, and unsurpassed by any service during the war. Its demonstrative motto — "'Football! Navy! War!'"— was the subject of a training manual on physical and mental strength. "Ecstatic sports journalists" lauded Hamilton's plans, methods, and organizational abilities. In a knowledgeable position, in 1943 he attributed the navy's high degree of readiness and remarkable records in gunnery and air warfare to competitive training methods.[17]

Future naval pilots learned to absorb shock and pain as football players, how to rebound from misfortune and adversity, and gain bodily skills, strength, and resourcefulness. Combined with fostering split-second reactions, these qualities, the navy believed, produced the world's toughest and finest fighting men.[18] Daily feedback in 1943 cited an "athletic ace of yesteryear" cast in a leading role at the front, praising his competitive training.[19] The *Chicago Tribune*'s prestigious sports writer Arch Ward went so far as to predict that V-5's success or failure would "determine the outcome of the war."[20] Another newspaper stated the navy saw football as molding body and mind into a winning spirit "in a game where there are no moral victories and the good loser is a dead one."[21]

A Marine with football experience made an ideal fighter on Pacific islands, wrote football historian John Gunn. "He was tough. He had stamina. He was team-oriented. And he loved action." As soon as the public became aware of Leatherneck accomplishments, adding to their lore, players flocked to recruiters,[22] Sergeant Philip "Moon" Calabrese, for example. A veteran of Guadalcanal, Bougainville, and Tarawa, who had relished his gridiron time, Calabrese credited his faith in God and ingrained mental and physical alertness for enabling him to withstand fierce combat against the Japanese.[23]

What was the payoff? The NCAA reported the combat theaters requested more football players, because those boys "could be counted on to take an assignment and to follow orders to the letter." Even the enemy favored American sports. After World War I, Germany concluded that quickly mobilized U.S. soldiers with little military background but grounded in competitive sports had outfought German veterans. Germany and Japan adopted some of our games postwar.[24] But, as one coach stated, "what the Axis could not import in one generation, however, was the American spirit of athletic competition." Athletes, they concluded, were "American weapons."[25] Two Americans stationed in Berlin — and imprisoned by the Germans later — wrote that a U.S. tank officer driving against the German panzers probably "thought back to an autumn day when he was a quarterback," and that "battle plans and football plays showed striking similarities in fundamentals of strategy."[26]

Commander (later captain) Thomas J. Hamilton, USN, head of the navy's preflight and physical training program, Bureau of Aeronautics. He was mainly responsible for developing and executing the rigorous physical conditioning programs which promoted playing football and is credited with helping to prepare flyers in winning the war (*National Collegiate Athletic Association Football Guide 1943*).

And on the home front? Regarding the 1944 game in Los Angeles between Randolph Field and the Fourth Air Force, the *Evening Herald and Express* praised military football's tremendous influence on the war effort. That kind of exhibition, matching two headline dream elevens — a setup unlikely under normal circumstances — raised money for troop athletic equipment, trained players "for the bigger game ahead," and uplifted civilian morale.[27]

Football boosted morale and the fighting spirit everywhere. Gridiron periodicals, exceptionally popular in an age with radio as its only electronic news medium, conformed to the war effort while dealing with paper usage restrictions. To the delight and appetite of participants and fans in and out of uniform, a surprising number maintained annual or weekly publication. Many of these aided my research for this book: the *Football Rule and Record Book*; *Football Prevues*; *The Football News: The American Collegiate Sports Weekly*; the *Football Review: Yearbook of the Football News*; *Illustrated Football Annual*; *Football Pictorial Yearbook*; and, extremely valuable, the *Official National Collegiate Athletic Association Football Guide*. Some of these ceased publication long ago.

*Football Prevues 1944* limited its number of pages, printed smaller type, and eliminated photographs. The editor explained why he did not suspend publication: the troops enjoyed reading it. *The Football News* promised to publish whatever interesting material it could to entertain servicemen, and liked to receive order lists from soldiers using APO mailing addresses. Naturally troops overseas thrived on sports news from home.[28] But the soldiers' popular, globally distributed magazine, *Yank: The Army Weekly*, reported lit-

**Women Marines training at the Camp Lejeune (N.C.) Marine Corps Base served as cheerleaders for their football team. How many other military teams used female cheerleaders is unknown, but likely few (game program, Bainbridge Naval Training Center at Camp Lejeune, November 19, 1944).**

2. "Ideological Arsenal": The Impact of Football on the War...    49

Players from white-jerseyed Randolph (Tex.) Field, one of the war's strongest military elevens, stop a Texas back in the 1944 Cotton Bowl. The battle ended tied 7–7 (Street & Smith's *Football Pictorial Yearbook 1944*).

tle of the military games to troops overseas, concentrating on college games and other sports "so as not to upset the fighting men about all these uniformed GI's frolicking about on the playing fields back home."[29]

Sports brought various college campus elements together and provided a relief from an arduous study week or weekend academic restrictions, all campus morale boosters. Young trainees needed football's diversion. At the Great Lakes boot camp, it linked home to the transition period.[30] Great Lakes, it was said, "played as thoroughly as it worked.... Sailors took great pleasure in crashing into each other, and pounding the daylights out of each other.... [Great Lakes] even made soccer into a raucous contact sport, turning that rather gentle game into all-out football without helmets or pads."[31] The 1943 game of Camp Lejeune (N.C.) Marine Corps Base at Jacksonville (Fla.) Naval Air Technical Training Center, Marines and sailors playing against each other, but together, in a way exemplified the cooperative interservice spirit that would lead to victory overseas.[32]

Cooperation and conditioning aside, military elevens zealously played to win, particularly in 1945. Overnight rivalries developed between services and bases. Fans attending the game pitting Fleet City (Calif.) Naval Receiving

Station and El Toro (Calif.) Marine Corps Air Station in San Francisco's Kezar Stadium prepared for a "civil war" and "old fashioned family football quarrel." Those "blood brothers," it was said, "like to cut each other's throats occasionally."[33] No kidding. Further motivation required? Dartmouth All-America and Chicago Bears pro Bob MacLeod stated the coach of his 1944 El Toro eleven gave pep talks that included a "fake telegram from the commandant of the Marine Corps." The telegram "told the players flatly, 'The next time (you mess up) you'll catch the next boat to the next action place.'"[34]

With the national elation of victory, 1945 produced classic, star-filled matchups, and sports scribes reached for superlatives. They billed the December game between unbeaten Fleet City (23) and the Pacific Fleet All-Stars (7), a once-in-a-lifetime display of powerful combinations of top players, as one that "may well live in football history as one of the greatest games of all time."[35] The following week Fleet City whacked El Toro for the second time, 48–25, in what is remembered as the war's best all-military game.

If wartime restrictions could cripple college football, it would have been by 1944, the *Football Rule and Record Book* stated. Public attention and support accelerated, producing record crowds in many sections. Big Ten attendance exceeded 1943 by 300,000; Ohio State broke its record, aided by 83,627 in Cleveland for the Illinois contest; and Notre Dame played before half a million. The caliber of play improved or held its own with 1943 and courageous college men carried on.[36]

Buy Bonds! While service personnel attended all-military games free, civilians often gained admission only by buying a war bond. Game programs and pregame publicity urged support of the government's bond drives to finance the war's staggering costs. Into late 1945, after V-J Day on August 14, the final drive solicited funds. "We haven't finished the job yet" until all financial obligations are finished, and bills have to be paid, the *Brooklyn (N. Y.) Eagle* shouted at the Brooklyn Bond Bowl Game on Nov. 11, 1945. The First Air Force from Mitchell Field, N.Y., defeated the Army Air Forces Training Command from Texas, 24–6. "The firing may have ceased officially; victory parades have been held; bonfires have been lit; some of our boys are home — but THE JOB remains unfinished."[37]

Purchasing a bond admitted a spectator for the Brooklyn tilt. Sports "sent its stars and its money to the far reaches of the earth to bring victory. But sports must not bog down now." Those who had already bought a bond needed to do it again, the *Eagle* reminded fans. "Do you remember Waddy Young and Don Wemple? They played football at Ebbets Field several seasons for the (National Football League) Brooklyn Dodgers. They will never play football again. They're dead, lost in action with the Air Force. Their job is done. But not yours."[38]

Foremost among the myriad postseason and bowl games involving military teams was the 1945 Brooklyn Bond Bowl Game played at Ebbets Field, Brooklyn, N.Y. Purchasing a war bond admitted a spectator. The First Air Force team from Mitchell Field (N.Y.) downed the Army Air Forces Training Command (Tex.), 24–6 (game program, First Air Force vs. Army Air Forces Training Command, November 11, 1945).

The War Department appointed famed sportswriter Grantland Rice to head the civilian War Football Fund, Inc., to raise money for Army Relief, a service charity. It organized eight games between professional and army all-star teams, coached by the well-known Colonel Bob Neyland (Tennessee) and Major Wallace Wade (Duke), which netted $241,292.[39] Gate receipts from the 1944 annual game matching the College All-Stars and the NFL champion Chicago Bears earned $78,000 for the Army Air Forces Aid Society and Chicago Service Men's Center.

The 1944 Army (23)-Navy (7) war-bond game in Baltimore, Md., drew 66,566 fans who paid scalpers as much as $35 per ticket. War bonds sold: $58,637,000 to ticket buyers, including 15 box seats at $1,000 each. The game claimed history's largest sports radio audience, with shortwave relays to the entire globe for every G.I. Joe and Jane.[40] That night Cadets coach Colonel Earl "Red" Blaik received a telegram from the Philippines: "'The greatest of all Army teams — STOP — We have stopped the war to celebrate your magnificent success. [General Douglas] MacArthur.'"[41]

In December 1944, despite horrible weather and snow flurries, before a "hardy gathering" of 8,356 in New York's Polo Grounds, the "vaunted ground offensive" of Randolph Field defeated the Second Air Force, 13–6, to win the Army Air Forces championship. Nevertheless, the "bone-crushing battle between super-charged lines and ever-running backfields" in the Treasury Bowl game brought $79.5 million in war bond sales.[42]

Cartoon showing football fan saddened by the 1943 season's end following great games between Army (0) and Navy (13), and Notre Dame (14) and Great Lakes (Ill.) Naval Training Center (19). The war's gloomiest season nevertheless produced some of its most exciting military games (*The Football News*, December 4, 1943).

## 2. "Ideological Arsenal": The Impact of Football on the War... 53

Navy's back Hillis Hume (32) carries against Army in the Midshipmen's 13–0 victory in 1943, their fifth straight win over the Cadets, before 15,000. President Franklin D. Roosevelt ruled the game be played "in the comparative privacy" of West Point, N. Y., under strict travel limitations to prevent outsiders from attending (*National Collegiate Athletic Association Football Guide 1944*).

Officials formed the powerful March Field, Calif., Fourth Air Force "warborn aggregation" to raise funds to buy athletic equipment, cigarettes, candy and magazines for overseas forces, and for the Red Cross and army charities. The merchants, service clubs, and Riverside Chamber of Commerce assisted.[43] Midway into the 1944 season they raised $138,000 for army charities and the All-Pacific Recreation Fund, headed by celebrity Joe E. Brown, that shipped recreation and comfort items to the Pacific and other theaters. Servicemen in hospitals and their dependants received priority.[44] The "GI Juggernaut" went 32–7–3 during the wartime seasons, essentially as a part-time, off-working-hours activity, with men sometimes practicing on their own.[45] By August 1944, 90 percent of all sports equipment being made headed for the armed forces, costing $38 million annually — the equivalent of outfitting 30,000 football, 65,000 baseball, and 110,000 softball teams. Colleges had enough to go around and husbanded theirs.

Attendance at college games in 1944 "leaped upward" to approximately 5,555,000 for 333 home games played by 67 colleges, according to the Associated Press's annual canvass. Low ticket prices spurred attendance. This increase of about 1.5 million over the 273 games by 57 schools charted in 1943 did not result from additional schools resuming play. Pennsylvania led with 379,000 for seven games at Philadelphia's Franklin Field.[46] By 1945, with the end of gasoline rationing and wider sports interest, zooming attendance broke existing records before the end of November. Penn led again with 478,000. Military all-star games played in Hawaii in 1944 drew crowds exceeding 45,000 service personnel.

The principal customers for military games remained the troops. In 1943 Great Lakes used football to encourage enlistments and as entertainment. The 1942 team (8–3–1) played all 12 games on the road including in Chicago, St. Louis, and Cleveland, and at Big Ten schools Michigan, Iowa, and Illinois, energizing recruiting drives and showing the navy flag to young people from landlocked states.[47]

By November 1945, magical Notre Dame awaited its third sellout crowd versus Navy in Cleveland's Municipal Stadium. The Irish played before sellouts at Georgia Tech and Pittsburgh, and no tickets remained for upcoming games with Army in New York's Yankee Stadium and at Northwestern. On December 1 Army walloped Navy, 32–13, before 102,000 in Philadelphia. How conditions had changed. The president ruled that the 1943 contest would be played "in the comparative privacy" of West Point under the same travel restrictions as the 1942 game at Annapolis, to prevent outsiders from obtaining tickets. Only persons on duty there or living within a 10-mile radius could attend, and tickets were sold only on game day.[48] Navy won its fifth straight over Army, 13–0, on November 27, 1943, before 15,000.

As the 1945 football season approached, the services shifted thousands of personnel to the West Coast for the war against Japan. Many talented football players transferred, including to Fleet City, for games considered essentially good for morale. By season's end, Fleet City expected to perform before nearly a half-million, mostly sailors and soldiers.[49]

Because the NCAA strongly believed the sport's paramount contribution to the war effort was the training of men for combat, it accordingly cooperated with the armed forces. According to John L. Griffith, when victorious America "sits down to analyze the place of football in wartime, the game will be remembered first and foremost for its training values." But football also gave sports-conscious men and women lighter, refreshing entertainment, whether in a stadium or by radio.[50] Reviewing 1945, the fourth and final wartime season, the NCAA reemphasized football's place and tremendous value in wartime, and cited military, the government, civilians, and educators for making it work. "Indeed, American football, as perhaps no other sport, justified itself."[51]

Fleet City's December Victory Bond Drive game reminded fans that such a game normally would be a dream, as the shadow of war and death hung over the nation. According to the game program, "We Americans who prayed so long for peace must now continue to work to pay for the victory we have won. It is the least we can do in keeping the faith with those who laid down their lives for the ideals we hold in common and the flag we love."[52] A state university coach predicted the country would "get militant" about athletics and physical fitness so as to avoid a repeat of prewar conditions.[53] For the moment that seemed plausible.

The future arrived quickly. In 1945, with the war about to be won, Grantland Rice reflected that sports created the "happy links" joining battlefields and Main Street. "The interest created, the skills acquired, will not be left behind when Johnny comes marching home."[54] But not all soldiers did.

> *They hit the line — and they hit it hard —*
> *And they ran the ends of same.*
> *They passed and kicked to the distant goal,*
> *When they starred in the college game.*
> *But they heard the bugles of war that called*
> *To a rougher and tougher test.*
> *And now they sleep under foreign soil,*
> *The stars who have earned their rest.*
> *They played the game in the good old way*
> *That led to the bayonet's thrust.*
> *They led the charge to the final goal*
> *Which covers their golden line.*
> — Grantland Rice, 1945[55]

CHAPTER 3

# "Lend-Lease Football": Navy and Marine Corps College Officer Training Programs

*"'Lend-lease' huskies, wearing navy blue or the khaki of naval aviation trainees, turned the Longhorns into a team that the rest couldn't touch."*[1] — Weldon Hart

Once-beaten Texas — and that loss was to a team unheard of before or since — ran roughshod over the Southwest Conference in 1943. How? Coach Dana X. Bible fortunately got and kept a solid cadre of good V-12 boys for the entire season. Only Texas A&M's beardless, all-civilian "Kiddie Korps" presented any obstacle.[2]

No stretch or play on words, the "Lend-Lease" moniker applied to temporarily loaned star football players and linked directly to the successful U.S. program to provide weapons and equipment to our allies. It resonated and stuck because essentially it was correct.

In a year when Baylor dropped out, Texas walloped all-civilian Arkansas, Rice, Southern Methodist, Texas Christian, Texas A&M, and Blackland Field, edged Oklahoma, and tied Randolph Field (Tex.) 7–7 in a classic Cotton Bowl showdown on New Year's Day 1944, in what became the highlight military post-season game. Its only loss was to Southwestern University, 14–7. Southwestern? Yes. The Georgetown, Tex., Pirates, stocked with activated Marine Corps reservists (33 of their 37 players) formerly on the Longhorns, compiled a 10–1–1 mark against a mixture of service and big-name college teams. Now playing in Division III, the team soon achieved mediocrity once Marine trainees departed, and fell to 2–6–1 by 1945.

Southwestern's regional "Cinderella" sisters included the Southwestern Louisiana Institute (SLI) Ragin' Cajuns and North Texas Agricultural College. Those schools, "lifted from athletic obscurity by the V-12 program, found that if the navy giveth, the navy also taketh away." Like other 1943 Southwestern Conference teams, they lost many of their stars by November first.³ Also called "the mushroom teams ... such sudden growers" the Cinderellas "sprouted quickly in '43 under a heaven-sent rain of veteran Marine trainees."⁴

Meanwhile, through the "recruiting coup of the century," SLI enrolled 175 two-year college starters — including two Marine trainees, quarterback Alvin Dark (future major-league baseball player) of Louisiana State and Rice All-America guard Weldon Humble (future pro Hall of Famer). On January 1, 1944, in the first Oil Bowl, SLI (5–0–1), now Louisiana-Lafayette, avenged an earlier tie with "Cinderella" team Arkansas A&M, 24–7.⁵ SLI won "despite losing a raft of players to Marine boot camps November 1. The team had a 'pocket full of refunds' from teams unwilling to play. For polling purposes, one can imagine the problem of trying to make known to the sports desks of the *New York Times* and the Associated Press the background of a team from Lafayette, La., that had played five games."⁶

Marines dominated the one-shot, 1943 Arkansas A&M Boll Weevils (5–2–1)

A Marine Corps "Lend-Lease" trainee, back Spot Collins was among the many former Texas players who helped Southwestern University's "Cinderella" team defeat the Longhorns, 14–7, in 1943. Southwestern recorded a 10–1–1 mark but soon settled into mediocrity when trainees departed (Street & Smith's **Football Pictorial Yearbook 1943**).

who defeated Arkansas 20–12 wearing borrowed uniforms and sneakers sent by the Naval Air Technical Training Command in Tennessee, a team disbanded because of disobedience of orders. Now Division II Arkansas-Monticello, the Weevils also lost to Southwestern. The Cinderellas beat up on each other.[7]

## The V-Programs

Why and how did these "lend-lease" players get there? Through the Department of the Navy's college officer-training programs, called the V-Programs.

The department knew it required thousands of junior officers to man the projected number of ships and aircraft, and lead hundreds of infantry rifle platoons. At the war's outset and throughout, the department determined and adjusted the fluctuating number of officers and recruited and administered accordingly. When the draft age was lowered to 18 in November 1942, that drastically reduced the potential college enrollment pool. Traditionally demanding that its officers be college graduates, the service established the V-12 program to provide undergraduate educations for selected candidates, assisted in the start-up by the American Council on Education.

The pre-commissioning V-Programs, that substantially produced a continuous pipeline of officer candidates, originally were designated:

V-1, for college freshmen and sophomores (begun in 1942);
V-5, pre-flight, for potential aviation cadets;
V-7, for college juniors and seniors (instituted in 1940) and
V-12, for general line and staff officers — the largest program.

The successful Naval Reserve Officer Training Corps, already on many campuses, and the V-1 and V-7 programs integrated into V-12 in 1943.

The single purpose of the V-Programs was to give prospective naval, Marine, and Coast Guard officers a college education in areas the navy most required. They were "not intended to protect young men from the fighting, to save colleges from closing, or to achieve any of the other ends often ascribed to it by admirers and critics," wrote James G. Schneider, who studied V-12 in depth.[8] But "a passing mark means as much to the navy as a well-aimed shell," ribbed the campus magazine at North Carolina, a V-12 school.[9] Furthermore, the National Collegiate Athletic Association believed V-Programs in 1943 supplied the backbone of American football.[10]

Of note, in December 1942 the army established the Army Specialized Training Program in some colleges to provide specialized technical training of men already on active duty, but did not allow them to play varsity football. Consequently, no army or army air forces trainees on any college campus played varsity football, only intramurals.

## V-12

The V-12 program commenced on July 1, 1943, six months after being announced. The navy intended it as a college course, from planning to recruiting to operation, and deferred to the schools—within broad outlines and requests—regarding course content, textbooks, academic credit, and awarding of degrees. The active-duty candidates attended classes along with civilian students, wearing enlisted uniforms, while those attending medical, dental, and theological schools wore midshipmen's uniforms. Their academic load and expectations exceeded those of civilians.

The matter of jurisdiction, discipline, and administration necessitated joint agreements. Officer procurement personnel selected the candidates, shipped them to schools, and then connected with them again at commissioning time. Meanwhile, an active duty support staff administered the programs at each institution.[11]

Successful curriculum completion qualified a student for further training at midshipmen's schools or the Marine Corps officer candidate school before commissioning as an ensign or a second lieutenant.[12] Some 60,000 students of the 125,000 who enrolled completed the V-12 regimen. Many returned to college after the war to complete undergraduate or graduate degrees under the GI Bill. More than 40 future navy admirals and 18 Marine Corps generals began their careers in V-12.

"The unprecedented democratic nature of the selection process" provided educational opportunities for many young men, James G. Schneider found. Officers successfully completing V-12 training and its follow-up courses assumed enormous responsibility and leadership loads. Those commissioned at age nineteen at once commanded dozens of men up to twice their age.[13] Candidates and cadets included reservists and men fresh off the streets. The World War II "90-day wonder," referring to officers commissioned via compressed training, did not come from V-12. The minimum was eight months for those with seven previous college semesters (the "irregulars"), and approximately two years for men with no college ("regulars").

Colleges and the navy soon bonded in this major contribution to the war effort. Offered an opportunity to participate, hundreds of colleges jumped, particularly small ones fearing a dearth of students would create the loss of revenue and therefore faculty, necessitating an indefinite shutdown. Additional students, the primary motivator, became a godsend. As a result, from the 500 schools that qualified, 131 were chosen in 43 states and these eventually hosted navy training programs in some manner under government contracts.

Asked not to pursue a unit aggressively, schools nevertheless began their "political tactics." Schneider determined "life in college America was getting too difficult for institutions to use less than their maximum efforts to secure one of the very desirable college training contracts." With their schools' existence at stake, college officials nevertheless also derived patriotic satisfaction from participating in the war effort. Secretary Frank Knox said in December

Former Oregon back Roy Dyer played at Southern California as a Marine Corps V-12 officer candidate trainee. The Trojans, but not the Ducks, were one of only four Pacific Coast Conference (now PAC-10) schools fielding teams in 1944. Using mostly Marine "Lend-Lease" players, USC perfected the T formation and won its eighth straight Rose Bowl (Street & Smith's *Football Pictorial Yearbook 1943*).

1942 that the navy would give special consideration to small colleges but refused to offer priorities to self-supporting colleges.[14] Then the navy responded to political pressure. According to Schneider, a member of Congress "was not doing his duty to his constituents if he didn't actively support their 'most reasonable' request to land a navy contract." A school's selection was reason for celebration, "with a flurry of planning, purchasing, remodeling, and hiring."[15]

Participants came from the Ivy League, state universities, teachers' colleges, and private and church-aided colleges. For example, Duke, which owned an NROTC unit, offered Marines basic, engineering, premedical, and predental curricula. The number of students ranged from 2,000 (660 Marines) at Dartmouth to 68 at Webb Institute of Naval Architecture in New York. Besides helping achieve victory, the schools reaped benefits and prestige, and drew institution and community closer together. Some gained more national attention with their V-12-dominated athletic teams than before.

To facilitate transfers between schools, the program operated on a year-round schedule of three four-month terms, beginning on July 1, November 1, and March 1, with five and a half work days. Every student carried a minimum of 17 hours of academic work plus physical training. The end of V-12 terms did not coincide with the completion of football schedules, causing some squads winning their first few games to lose their last few because of October 31 departures.

V-students were males and nearly unanimously white. The navy stated that no racial barriers existed, but because a person's race went unnoted on his V-12 application, the number of blacks accepted is unknown. Schneider believed the program originally enrolled a dozen, 36 by mid–1945, and probably 75 overall. This exceptionally bold, pioneering step to integrate the navy officer corps paved the way to commissioning of black officers at Great Lakes Naval Training Center.[16]

The V-12 program commenced when 70,000 men already in V-1 or V-7 programs reported. Marines eventually numbered 11,460, but by mid–1945 that number decreased to only 1,902. Both services contended "with the morale problem that arose from the sense of urgency to get out to the 'real war,'" an attitude pronounced in the Marines because of their fighting reputation and macho image.[17] Marine V-12 attrition was eight percent, about the normal college rate.

For their 40 V-12 detachments (units), the Marine Corps recruited a sizable number of candidates who happened to play football. College campuses recognized "that most of the 'jocks' were enlisting in the Marines," and coaches encouraged players to sign up.[18] One football historian equated the Marines' "manpower grab in 1943 [as] comparable to the navy's establishment of its pre-flight programs in 1942" when it induced top coaches and players. The

Corps actually believed that the president was trying to save small colleges. Furthermore, historian John Gunn reasoned, "a football player made an ideal Marine.... He was tough. He had stamina. He was team-oriented. And he loved action." Marine V-12 players received two Navy Crosses, seven Silver Stars, three Bronze Stars and other decorations for valor on Iwo Jima and Okinawa.[19]

Soon the leading football schools coincidentally hosted Marine units: Notre Dame, College of Pacific, Duke, Northwestern, Georgia Tech, Michigan, North Carolina, and others, including eight of the 1943 Associated Press top 20 teams. Other colleges lifted into temporary powers by navy and Marine trainees included Franklin & Marshall, Rochester, Purdue, and unbeaten Colorado College. The navy refused to let its schools play in the Sun, Grape, and Raisin Bowls, and other postseason games, because of gas rationing and training conflicts.

Using seven navy and twenty-six Marine trainees, Purdue turned a 1–8–0 1942 season into 9–0–0 Big 10 championship in 1943 and a No. 5 AP ranking. "Any doubts about the wartime strength of Purdue's 1943 football team were convincingly dispelled. They were a great team that would never have been, but for the course of world events far away from college football."[20]

By 1944, hundreds of Marine trainees who'd propped up college elevens transferred to advanced training, permanent duty stations, or headed overseas, depleting V-12 ranks in some schools. Iwo Jima loomed only four months away. Mounting casualties created an urgent need for marines in the Pacific, and those failing to qualify for a commission shipped out to combat duty. Incoming 1944 V-12 ranks included men with combat experience, and wounded on Guadalcanal or in other Pacific campaigns, who'd recovered and returned to civilian life and football, despite carrying pieces of shrapnel. The Corps consolidated some units, anticipating a reduced officer need, leaving 13 active.[21]

An annual football magazine stated some 1943 V-Programs backfired unintentionally, in spite of navy cooperation in providing material to smaller colleges. Small schools depending on navy or Marine students faced a large disadvantage when competing with those with large enrollments, except the few Cinderellas. The two outbound student transfer-moving dates of July 1 and November 1 meant July transferees wasted the previous spring's team practice, and fall transferees left in mid-season. Players learning one school's system might switch to a rival in the same conference.[22]

The V-Programs started phasing out in June 1945, but some schools continued offering NROTC. By October, with the war ended in August, "everyone had the 'short-timer's attitude.' ... The bold wartime educational experiment had done its job."[23]

# V-5

The V-5 pre-flight program launched prospective naval aviators toward earning commissions and wings. Three officials devised the regimen: Undersecretary James Forrestal, Captain Arthur Radford, commander of aeronautic training, and Lieutenant Commander Thomas J. Hamilton, a carrier pilot, former Navy head football coach, and director of overall flight training. Soon promoted to commander, Hamilton retired as a rear admiral. The Naval Academy football stadium locker room bears his name.

Hamilton's determination, organizational genius, and cheerleading led the way. He demanded physical conditioning and competitive team sports to meet the prospective pilot's need for special indoctrination and "hardening," and "to generate desirable psychological attitudes and group loyalties [that] placed particular emphasis on football and hand to hand combat. In short, these men were trained for war through sport," wrote Donald J. Rominger, Jr., in *The Journal of Sport History*.[24]

The Bureaus of Aeronautics and Personnel conflicted over the emphasis on football. Former heavyweight boxing champion Commander Gene Tunney, a Roosevelt favorite who headed Personnel's physical section, strongly disagreed that V-Programs should play a national college schedule. Tunney's rebuke fueled a smoldering internal debate of "sports versus calisthenics." He opposed the commissioning of "fat football coaches," and viewed pre-flight training as "elitist collegiate play" that slowed combat training, "thereby forcing an unfair share of the war's burden on less fortunate enlisted personnel." To Rominger, however, Hamilton's persistence regarding "toughening" to rid students of "socially developed sanctions against aggression" was "social engineering at its zenith."[25] Besides, those "fat football coaches" exposed to V-5 training procedures included prominent names: Bear Bryant, George Halas, Paul Brown, Jim Crowley, Ray Morrison, Tex Oliver, Don Faurot, Jim Tatum, Raymond Wolf, Matty Bell, Woody Hayes (who commanded a destroyer escort), Bud Wilkinson (on carrier USS *Enterprise* [CV-6]), and Gerald Ford (on carrier USS *Monterey* [CVL-26]).

Hamilton prevailed and deserves singlehanded credit for making the program work. A football writers' association named him 1942 "Man of the Year." After long deliberations, Knox permitted participation in intercollegiate athletics, subject to eligibility rules, and limited athletes to traveling 48 hours away from school. Lacking adequate practice time, coaches squeezed three hours into one and a half on the field, requiring sharp focus at the end of an arduous duty day.[26]

Before formal authorization and without staff or facilities, Hamilton announced his plan in December 1941. In early 1942 the navy opened three pre-flight schools at state universities in Athens, Ga.; Chapel Hill, N.C.; and Iowa City, Ia., and a fourth at St. Mary's College in Moraga, Calif. Each operated through the war and fielded impressive elevens. The fifth operated only in 1943 at the Del Monte Hotel, Monterey, Calif. Minnesota coach and Marine reserve Major Bernie Bierman in March 1942 commanded the first cadre of V-5 instructors, who began training the first cadet class in May 1942.

Cadets had to be unmarried and between 18 to 27 year of age, and received $75 per month. Hamilton insisted that everyone learn football mechanics and be required to play either varsity or intramural football or soccer, "especially those [sports] that were fast, explosive, and violent were regarded as laboratories in which to develop strength, courage, and concentration under pressure."[27]

Lieutenant Commander Jim Crowley, member of Notre Dame's famed "Four Horsemen" backfield, was one of the high-profile wartime military coaches at North Carolina Preflight in 1942 and Sampson (N.Y.) Naval Training Station in 1943-44 (Street & Smith's *Football Pictorial Yearbook 1944*).

Navy "birdmen" endured the most stringent, strenuous, and complete conditioning routines of any service or college for one purpose: "To master the fastest, most vicious machines in the world — fighting aircraft."[28] To Bierman, Iowa Pre-Flight's first coach, the regimen incorporated physical and emotional conditioning and qualities, and developed strength, skill, maturity, stamina, and the "will to win."[29] Football's experienced mentors turned out cadets who would not merely enter battle, but would react quickly, remain alert, and aggressively and fearlessly accomplish their missions and return to base, disregarding fatigue, discomfort, or wounds.[30]

"A Navy Flyer's Creed"[31]

"I am a United States Navy flyer.

"My countrymen built the best airplane in the world and entrusted it to me. They trained me to fly it. I will use it to the absolute limit of my power.

"With my fellow pilots, air crews, and deck crews, my plane and I will do anything necessary to carry out our tremendous responsibilities. I will always remember we are part of an unbeatable combat team — the United States Navy.

"When the going is fast and rough, I will not falter. I will be uncompromising in every blow I strike. I will be humble in victory.

"I am a United States Navy flyer.

"I have dedicated myself to my country, with its millions of all races, colors, and creeds. They and their way of life are worthy of my greatest protective effort.

"I ask the help of God in making that effort great enough."

Both navy and Marine cadets trained in the same categories over 26 weeks: flight, ground, military, and physical. Academic work consisted of mathematics, physics, celestial navigation, aerology, essentials of naval service, nomenclature, and navigation signals. Students did no actual flying. On completion, most cadets entered heavier-than-air primary training at the Pensacola, Fla., Naval Air Station.

The Chief of Naval Operations in 1943 issued a training manual for playing football the naval-aviation way. "We are facing enemies who are careless of life because they are so steeped in a fanatical nationalism," it said, enemies to whom the common rules of war meant nothing. "It is our duty to train the cadets to be superior to that enemy, mentally and physically." Within, detailed explanations and diagrams showed men and coaches the numerous positions, skills, formations, and strategies leading to gridiron victory, instruction not left to chance.[32] *The Football News* reported that pre-flight football was no luxury or extra-curricular recreational activity. Virtually every officer attached to units acted as either football coach, instructor, supervisor, or official. The squads went directly to and from their game sites to minimize time away from cadet duties.[33]

In 1944 Hamilton's successor reiterated that V-5 was producing aviators superior to any enemy mentally and physically. He insisted on accommodating intramural competition as well as varsity, and approximately 10,000 cadets played football, 60–65 percent without previous experience. "We are definitely on the offensive now. In football we always have been."[34]

Pre-flight school football flourished with big names and big games. The schools agreed to use no more than five officers (permitted in 1942 only) and to seek cadets available for up to five games before graduation. At St. Mary's, the navy changed the campus only to meet military purposes, such as adding more housing and specialized structures, but not its personality. Civilian classes continued but with only 200 students and a faculty-staff of 50. The navy averaged 200 officers and 1,900 cadets. "It all depended upon how fast we were losing pilots."[35]

Player material in 1942 turned over so rapidly that St. Mary's Air Devils coach Lieutenant Commander Tex Oliver faced continuing player availability uncertainty. During three weeks in October, 15 cadet players graduated, but gloom, if any, stayed under wraps. The coaching staff actually appreciated the loss of stars at mid-season and were glad to see them go into advanced training. Fortunately, Stanford All-America quarterback Frankie Albert (future College Hall of Famer, San Francisco 49ers) and end Eddie Erdeletz (St. Mary's College coach, future Navy coach), who led the team, already had their commissions. Some officers who had been out of football for several years reported for practice "with all of their old enthusiasm of college days."

**All-Americas such as back Bruce Smith (Minnesota) rushed into both military and football uniforms, often playing with multiple elevens during the war or over the same season. Here Smith, previously with the Great Lakes (Ill.) Naval Training Center Bluejackets, runs for St. Mary's (Calif.) Pre-Flight Air Devils against Fourth Air Force in 1943 (*National Collegiate Athletic Association Football Guide 1944*).**

Military football game programs, although limited in size because of wartime paper shortages, publicized their service or unit's activities to the benefit of game attendees and ultimately historians. Naval aviation received enormous attention (game program, Camp Lejeune at North Carolina Pre-Flight, November 13, 1943).

The Air Devils peaked at 5-3-1 in 1942 and never achieved the prominence of other V-5 elevens.[36]

Almost all the 45 players at Iowa Navy, in April 1942 the first V-5 school, came from Big Ten schools, including Michigan quarterback Forest Evashevski (future Iowa coach). En route to fame as the nation's premier V-5 football program over 1942-44, the Seahawks amassed records of 6-4-0, 9-1-0 (a November loss to Notre Dame, 14-13), and 10-1-0 (an opening loss to Michigan, 12-7) versus primarily Big Ten and Midwest universities.

Military training took up 80 percent of the Iowa Field House, and varsity teams struggled to find facilities, disadvantaging them within the Big Ten. In 1943 coach Don Faurot's staff included future heavyweights Bud Wilkinson and Jim Tatum, who later won national championships at Oklahoma and Maryland using his split-T offense. Their typewritten, mimeographed press guide noted tickets at $2.75 for the home Nebraska game, and the "absence of special concessions to varsity participants" for road trips — going directly there and directly back.[37]

For eleven months, the navy rented the Del Monte Hotel resort in Monterey, "where the sporty rich used to cavort, and in the salons where the wealthy idle gathered to kill time, selected groups of the youth of the land [were] taught to kill the assailants on the United States and liberty." The Navyators, who practiced on the hotel's polo field, went 7-1-0, beating UCLA and California and losing only to loaded College of Pacific, 16-7. Stars included All-Americas Len Eshmont (Fordham, New York Giants), Paul Christmas (Missouri, Chicago Cardinals), Jim McDonald (Ohio State, Detroit Lions), Parker Hall (Mississippi, Cleveland Rams), Bowden Wyatt (Tennessee player and future coach, College Hall of Famer), and Ed Cifers (Tennessee).[38] The resort is now the U.S. Naval Postgraduate School.

Each room housed four to eight cadets in double-decker bunks. Cooks turned out balanced meals of 5,000 calories. The stores where "debutantes" and "young bucks" bought furs, nylons, and dancing pumps became offices. An observer noted: "One accustomed to the fastidiousness of the old idle hour Del Monte hotel hardly would recognize it.... There is still grappling in the famed Bali Room where society danced and the arty groups put on world noted dress parties. But it is the honest grappling of the wrestling mat ... by eager youth ... in hand to hand combat. And the taproom? The beer taps are gone. The display of liquors and liqueurs in fancy bottles has long since been removed.... They're making men where once men made fun."[39]

The Georgia Pre-Flight Skycrackers posted a solid 12-2-1 record under coaches Lieutenants Raymond "Bear" Wolf (North Carolina coach) in 1942 and Rex Enright (South Carolina coach) in 1943, before slipping to 4-5-0 in 1944. The 1942 highlight: A 23-hour, 40-minute train ride to Philadelphia for their opener to beat Pennsylvania, 14–6, with a flat 24-hour return.[40] Stars included Frank Filchock (Indiana), Jim Poole (Mississippi), Charlie Timmons (Clemson), Don Hightower (Texas A&I), Billy Patterson (Baylor), Noble Doss and Orban Sanders (Texas), and Bob Suffridge, Art Edmiston, and Bobby Foxx (Tennessee).

Cadets began arriving at North Carolina in May 1942 until reaching a quota of 1,875.[41] The first class graduated in October. Two hours of daily participation in competitive sports was compulsory. "The militarization of Carolina" caused academic turbulence and physically modified the campus, the alumni magazine remembered. The navy appropriated the dining halls, employing Italian and German prisoners of war and prohibiting coeds and civilians from eating there, and used dormitories and fraternity houses for lodging. "The university was navy."

Scuttlebutt abounded concerning cadet tenures in Chapel Hill. Word was that cadets tolerated the layover as "an annoying delay" before "the real game" in Pensacola. At a 1943 UNC football game, cadets cheered for the opponent. Since V-5

After a rigorous daily routine of classes and military drills, navy V-5 aviation trainees suit up for football practice in the late afternoon at North Carolina Pre-Flight. The author played varsity lacrosse on this Navy Field, 1952–55 (monograph, "U.S. Navy Pre-Flight School, Chapel Hill, N.C., 1942-1943").

OFFICIAL SOUVENIR PROGRAM
**U.S. NAVY PRE-FLIGHT SCHOOL**
ST. MARY'S COLLEGE, CALIFORNIA
vs.
**FLEET CITY BLUEJACKETS**
★ ★ ★ ★ 4 NOVEMBER 1945 ★ ★ ★ ★
KEZAR STADIUM • SAN FRANCISCO, CALIF.

St. Mary's, a weak 2–4–1, was the lone pre-flight school among the five still playing football after the war ended on August 14. Still, it tied the mighty Bluejackets, 7–7, its only blemish on a perfect season (game program, St. Mary's [Calif.] Pre-Flight vs. Fleet City, Kezar Stadium, San Francisco, November 4, 1945).

trainees remained on campus longer than V-12s, most early pre-flighters were Carolina students who viewed this training as extending regular student life. But they expressed relief and unease when reviewing the alumni casualty reports, and "were trying to pack a little college into their lives before the Big Fight." (The army sent nearly 500 students there in special training programs.)[42]

The Carolina program involved two future U.S. presidents, Gerald Ford and student George H. W. Bush, plus student Ted Williams, the Red Sox ballplayer, and coach Bear Bryant. After finishing instructor school, Ford stayed to teach naval subjects and coach nine sports, including football, before being ordered to sea duty. When Bryant took the Maryland head coach position after the war, he recruited a number of V-5 players. Bush, the most famous V-5 graduate, entered the navy on his eighteenth birthday and was its youngest pilot just before turning 19. He flew 58 Pacific combat missions, was rescued at sea after being shot down in his torpedo bomber in 1945, and received the Distinguished Flying Cross, three Air Medals, and the Presidential Unit Citation.

The 1942 season (8–2–1) began with "Lieutenant Commander [Jim] Crowley's North Carolinians, handsomely uniformed and handsomely outfitted with cluster of stars at every post."[43] In their best season, 1944 (6–2–1), the Cloudbusters downed powerful Duke, 13–6, and Navy, 21–14. Coached by Lieutenant Commander Glenn Killinger, that eleven included quarterback Otto Graham (Northwestern, future pro Hall of Famer), selected on most all-service squads.

Cadets studied and played hard. With a campus male to female ratio of 6:1 (800 coeds), dances continued showing off "glamorous satin ball gowns, but crisp naval uniforms replaced tuxedos on the dance floor." Harry's served beer and the student union juke box serenaded with "I'll Be Seeing You" and "Don't Sit Under the Apple Tree." Coeds got pinned in the arboretum, quick engagements followed, "wedding fever" spread. Boys "with uncertain futures were anxious to add a little permanence to their lives."[44]

From 1943 on the navy restricted pre-flight grid roster eligibility to cadets only, no officers, which tended to lower their level of competition equivalent to college civilian elevens. With the war over, and aviator needs diminished, only St. Mary's among the V-5 schools played in 1945. Officials canceled the other schedules as well as for many bases.

Disestablished in June 1946, V-5 trained 80,000 cadets and 2,500 instructors. Naval aviation expanded from seven to more than 100 carriers, from 4,500 to 60,000 pilots, and from 3,500 to 41,000 aircraft. At the end, Hamilton credited his pilots with superior performance records. Undoubtedly the V-Programs indoctrinated and prepared colleges of varying sizes for the onslaught of veterans descending in the late 1940s to pursue educations under the GI Bill. Rominger concluded: "The war saw a thorough permeation of the country's social and ethnic fabric with military-athletic euphemisms and philosophies, and V-5 played a redoubtable role in defining that fabric. It was only a short distance from the idea of sports training for national defense to sports training for national welfare.... Whether [it] ... merely revived the older concept of character development through play, or whether it broke new ground in motivation, research and mass athletics, it stands as a unique bench mark in the history of sport and war."[45]

## Chapter 4

# "A War Game in Miniature": Reacting, Adjusting, and Playing the Game

*"Within the letter and spirit of the rules, of course, every football game this fall should be a war game in miniature."*[1]— Lou Little

Famed Columbia coach Lou Little, a stern proponent of the sport as a combat conditioner, staked out the upcoming 1942 season. Drive harder, run faster, and use deception and a strong defense. Every lesson football teaches the American college athlete prepares him for actual combat.[2] For a country at war experiencing new and severe sacrifices and adjustments to its way of life for survival, the sport of football required immediate changes if it, too, was to exist within the framework of upheaval.

College football reactions and adjustments to wartime began immediately after the Japanese struck Pearl Harbor on Sunday, December 7, 1941. The day before in Honolulu, the University of Hawaii defeated Willamette University of Salem, Ore., 20–6. Another mainland team present, San Jose State, had its game with Hawaii on December 13 canceled, "the first time in our history that American college football teams have been under hostile attack." The Spartans remained several days and volunteered for blackout duty before leaving with a ship dispatching wounded. Willamette also stuck around and provided guard services before sailing for San Francisco.[3]

By then the regular college season had ended but several bowl games were yet to come. The first major adaptation to wartime relocated the 1942 New Year's Day Rose Bowl away from Pasadena, Calif., for the first and only time. Officials feared the 100,000 spectators presented an inviting bulls-eye for Japanese bombers. Led by halfback Don Durdan, later a Bainbridge Navy star, Oregon State upset Duke, 20–16, before 54,000 in Durham, N.C., in the "Transplanted Rose Bowl Game."

Approaching 1942, the National Collegiate Athletic Association believed collegiate and high school coaches would expand their programs, figuring that a lengthy war meant combat service for even the day's youngest high school boys. Some programs did, some contracted, and some disappeared. Fortunately a multitude of necessary adjustments kept football alive and allowed boys to play for conditioning as well as recreation and competitive school spirit.

Colleges nationwide waived the freshman eligibility rule which generated dire predictions of diminished player and game quality. Freshmen immediately impacted the game, particularly at schools without navy and Marine students. Those schools depended entirely on the student body for material, recognizing "there will be no opportunity to augment this basic group by any devious method as which might have been used heretofore."[4] Undergraduate players enrolled in army and navy special courses which deferred them as long as they met leadership and scholarship basics.[5]

One lesson learned was that "17-year old college boys ... are not the inept dumbjohns they were very often accused of being [and] can give an excellent account of themselves in gridiron action."[6] For example, in 1943 Notre Dame's young sophomore

Former Duke back Jasper "Jap" Davis played for an army all-star team against the Washington Redskins in Los Angeles (Calif.) Coliseum on August 30, 1942. Davis, a member of the Blue Devils' 1939 Rose Bowl team, helped coach the 1942 Duke squad in the "Transplanted Rose Bowl Game" in Durham, N.C., where Oregon State prevailed, 20–16. After serving in Europe, after the war he became a coaching legend at the author's New Hanover High School in Wilmington, N.C. (provided by John Gunn).

Johnny Lujack stepped in to replace Heisman Trophy quarterback Angelo Bertelli, since departed for Marine Corps duty. A quick coaching adjustment worked, and Notre Dame and Lujack excelled. After World War II navy service, Lujack earned All-America honors twice, won the Heisman Trophy in 1947, and was later enshrined in the College Football Hall of Fame.

Authorities shelving football regretted being forced to do so while admitting the utility of gridiron competition to prepare our fighting men. Georgetown, fielding a team for 45 straight seasons, faced 1942 without a holdover. Most 1941 players had either entered active duty or joined the reserves and the Reserve Officers Training Corps, and ended up elsewhere. Yet they manufactured a 5–3–1 campaign, losing to powerful North Carolina Pre-Flight, 23–7, before dropping out for 1943.

Teams said farewell to peacetime travel arrangements, comforts, and accommodations (e.g., missing classes), and then played with abandon regardless of preparations. Harry Wismer wrote in *Football Pictorial Yearbook 1944*, "Call it pent up energy, call it American resourcefulness, call it wartime fever or what you may, college football asked for no quarter and gave none."[7] To cite one league, the Big Ten expanded schedules from eight to ten games to accommodate service teams. In a game displaying scheduling flexibility and ingenuity, played five days after booking, North Carolina snapped Duquesne's 11-game winning streak, 13–6. Keeping options open and immediately handling demanding changes, athletic directors, coaches, military officials, and players eventually underpinned the resilience of college football.[8]

Wartime conditions obligated football administrators and coaches, both civilian and military, to reach into heretofore unexplored reservoirs of

"Now get out there and show them you're worth being deferred till the end of the season." (Bo Brown in game program, Texas Tech vs. Lubbock Army Air Field, September 18, 1943).

resourcefulness, set aside any permanent illusions, maintain flexibility, and react positively to the unexpected. Success in reaching ad hoc, temporary objectives depended to an extent on such resourcefulness. If an exception existed, it would have been the navy pre-flight programs.

Some athletic directors found reasons for playing, others did not. In a day when they often worked alone or with limited assistants, particularly at small schools, they dealt with mounting problems and difficult decisions besides who to schedule and where to play. Problems included finding and hiring coaches and staff, arranging transportation and other logistical support, eliminating or curtailing intersectional games, utilizing all facilities competing with burgeoning intramurals, limiting practices to short daily periods (military teams practiced about an hour), and cooperating and coordinating with military officials on campus. Plus, football could not interfere with accelerated academics. But "the colleges [would] suffer any difficulties cheerfully in order to play."[9]

## Conferences and Schools Adjust by Season

The college conferences abandoning football in 1943–44 included Missouri Valley, Pennsylvania State Teachers College, West Virginia Athletic, North Central Intercollegiate, Central Intercollegiate, Nebraska Intercollegiate Athletic, Oklahoma Collegiate, South Dakota Intercollegiate, Kansas College Athletic, Texas Collegiate Athletic, Lone Star, Border Intercollegiate Athletic, Mountain States (Big Seven) Athletic, Rocky Mountain Athletic, New Mexico Intercollegiate, Central Intercollegiate Athletic, Interstate, California Collegiate Athletic, Far Western, Washington Intercollegiate, Pacific Northwest Intercollegiate, Iowa Intercollegiate Athletic, and Missouri College Athletic Union.

Mid-Atlantic colleges, for example, completed schedules with no apparent decline in interest, but experienced a drop-off in football quality and attendance, alarmingly so where games were unreachable by train. For the moment, manpower and transportation obstacles could be ameliorated by switching games from sparsely populated locations to metropolitan centers. Thereby potential spectators need not anguish over driving in the face of severe tire and gasoline rationing.[10] Black colleges achieved this.

All Southern Conference schools kept playing. Freshmen became eligible in 1942, diluting form and substance while balancing competition. Seventeen- and eighteen-year old freshmen played throughout collegiate football and compensated for squad shrinkage. Player attrition hit Duke hard. When coach Wallace Wade left for army service, replaced by Eddie Cameron, the nominally powerful Blue Devils failed to match the Duke Rose Bowl team. Conference coaching ranks shrank as mentors and their assistants joined the military, including Rex Enright (South Carolina) and Jim Tatum (North Carolina). Seven of the 16 schools started with new head coaches.[11]

College football overseers continued optimistic, looking for silver linings anywhere to sustain it. Colleges in 1942 lost a plethora of players, freshmen to seniors, to the military—"youthful spirits attuned to attack by the flame of war."[12] These depleted ranks nevertheless generated new season records for yards gained and scoring. All told, the madly scrambled and harrowing season perplexed experts trying to monitor the changes.[13]

Reviewing the 1942 season, and with mobilization accelerating, the NCAA rules chairman and *Football Guide* editor forecast "less time to devote to meticulous coaching, to say nothing of poorer and poorer material to work with and ... a decided falling off in the caliber of college teams." Interest would not waver, however, he predicted. He proved correct on each account.[14]

By the end of 1943, approximately 190 colleges had abandoned football. The NCAA noted a developing uncertainty for military teams, that could force the sport to the sidelines or curtail it as the nation at war mobilized for victory. Predictions depended upon how manpower had shifted around and what college stars were now trainees.[15]

Postcard of Camp Lejeune (N.C.) Marine Corps Base team playing at home, ca. 1943 (provided by John Gunn).

The Southeastern Conference, which temporarily lost members Florida, Auburn, Tennessee, Vanderbilt, Kentucky, Mississippi, and Mississippi State, relaxed eligibility rules for servicemen but not civilians. Only Georgia Tech and Tulane had navy units. Contingent on his commanding officer's approval, any serviceman could play regardless of professional or college experience and without an academic mark to maintain. Civilians could not transfer and had to pass their courses.[16] Football prospects for 1943, however, remained "in a state of almost astronomical nebulosity" employing mostly 17- and 18-year-old freshmen, "4-Fs with loose eardrums," and some naval reserves. "*C'est la guerre.*"[17]

In the Southern Conference, *Football Pictorial Yearbook* reported that Clemson's coach Frank Howard lost all regulars and started from scratch with plenty of uniforms. He pined for suggestions as to where he could find someone to fill them. N.C. State's Doc Newton, with no returnees, fretted that all his prospects had emigrated to Duke as Marines.[18]

Wartime eliminated the Southwest Conference's usual balance. Trainees needed to reserve stamina for classes and night studies. Long chartered Pullman train trips became memories. The league revoked the freshmen (and most other) eligibility rules, allowing participation by any military student, including transfers, graduates, and professionals, turning the 1943 chase into a guessing game. A leading sports writer lamented: "Big business football is out. Newspaper headlines belong to a bigger game," but fans still attended games for relaxation and diversion.[19] Without trainees, Tulsa's 42-man varsity went 6–0–1 using 24 4-F and nine underage players, and Texas Tech fielded 27 freshmen and five sophomores on their 34-man roster.

The Pacific Coast in 1943 will be remembered as "Mr. Amos Alonzo Stagg's Season," recognizing the 83-year old College of Pacific's national coach of the year. He lost only to the Fourth Air Force.[20] California schools played within the state and Northwest teams played within that region. In the Western Plains, revamped schedules eliminated intersectional games until feasible. Their lone eligibility rule required a player to be duly registered and approved by faculty. Like other sections, few older head coaches — such as Oklahoma's Dewey Luster — stayed, as many joined the military's physical training branches. Understudies carried on and firings after poor seasons for those remaining appeared impracticable.[21]

After the strong 1942 showing by navy-strengthened squads, the Midwest figured to experience talent leveling because of calls to active duty, a narrowing of the gap with all-civilian elevens. But 1942 fortunes reversed. Reigning No. 1 Ohio State lost repeatedly while dressing kids and physically disqualified men. Wisconsin and Minnesota watched former players beat them in 1943. Michigan (8–1–0) picked a varsity from 1,000 navy and 300 Marine students. One was ex-Gopher All-America Bill Daley who led the Wolverines to victory over Minnesota, 49–6, before his navy transfer. Northwestern, using eight Gophers, whipped Minnesota, and Michigan's 10 Badgers helped the Wolverines defeat Wisconsin, 27–0.

Notre Dame, which canceled its traditional series with Southern California and Stanford, employed mostly V-12 and NROTC trainees en route to the 1943 national championship. While trainees comprised all of Muhlenberg's team, two enlisted men assisted its civilian coach. After its naval battalion finished in October, tiny William Jewell College in Missouri (4–3–1) had one center and one end remaining.

Army and Navy ruled the Mid-Atlantic, Army by stockpiling promising youngsters and Navy by collecting college veterans. Neither academy had a man drafted. Lacking trainees, Temple lost money maintaining a full schedule, with attendance about one-third of 1942. Princeton joined schools playing unofficial, informal games.[22] In the Rocky Mountains, conference races were canceled.[23] "This year ... gives you mines, mountains and befuddlement," noted one prognosticator, the promise of unpredictable football at best with almost all teams starting over with new personnel, requiring "the magic of a soothsayer" to figure out who would do what.[24]

The NCAA praised former high school stars, now freshmen, for projecting themselves through varsity competition. On the trainee campuses, graduations and transfers often opened positions and playing time. Fans anticipated and followed trainee moves bearing directly on their schools' prospects. As stars departed, their former teams sometimes spiraled downward, and stars arriving often boosted their new teams' fortunes. With coaches also entering active duty in numbers, professors and alumni coaches stepped in to assist, including an increase in women coaches. (Although the NCAA raised the matter, the author found no evidence that women coached college football varsities, but some may have.) Home-and-home games fit travel restrictions.[25]

Sportscaster Harry Wismer surmised that schools quitting the game could not stand experiencing or anticipating defeats after years of thumping once weaker clubs for warmups. Some returned to the gridiron for 1944. The Southeastern Conference, for instance, resumed play with 11 of their 12 programs. The other SEC member, Vanderbilt, played "informal" games with other schools or clubs, as did Harvard, Boston College, and Princeton.

NCAA Guide won-lost records do not always delineate whether a school's season was official or informal. Some Stanford players played for hated rival California. When some conferences folded, a team or two might continue to play varsity games as independents. Athletic directors revised plans, believing football must either bounce back or die, and cited the number of discharged servicemen as potential players.[26]

The Big Ten commissioner went further: schools abandoning football recognized "the error of their ways ... that young men will play the game with or without the sanction of college administrators."[27] Only four of ten Pacific Coast Conference schools fielded 1944 teams, and Southern California, using mostly navy and Marine students, perfected the "T" formation to win its eighth straight Rose Bowl. Other coast teams lacked prewar talent. Sailors and Marines helped Georgia Tech (Southeastern), Duke (Southern), and Oklahoma (Big Six) win conference championships.

Besides the Southeastern Conference programs, other big names reinstating football in 1944 included Michigan State, Princeton, Syracuse, Southern Illinois, Utah State, and Boston College. Tennessee rebounded from a year off by going 7–0–1 before losing to Southern Cal in the Rose Bowl, 25–0. Discharged veterans began making a difference, including Joe Saia at Mississippi State, Buzzy Gher at Yale, George Savitsky at Pennsylvania, and Bon Turner at Rice. Veterans comprised 19 members of the powerful Second Air Force Superbombers. The Melville (R.I.) Naval Patrol Torpedo Boat outfit dominated New England with its "beribboned, cited veterans of the PT fighting with the Japs," edging out the Coast Guard Academy.[28]

Transfers continued complicating rosters and affecting game outcomes. Rutgers' Howard Bernstein played every minute until an army induction notice removed him from the Lehigh game six minutes before the end so he could report to Fort Dix, N.J., at 6:00 P.M. Tackle Thad Ellis started at North Carolina, played a few games at Duke, then returned to Carolina in time to play against the Blue Devils. Bucknell's Harold Swenson became eligible on Monday, played on Saturday, and transferred out on Wednesday, ending history's shortest varsity football career (to that time).[29] No player came close to matching the vagabond record of end George Barney Poole of the famed Pooles of Ole Miss. The future College Hall of Famer played seven varsity seasons: three at Mississippi, one at North Carolina, and three at Army.

Because of September player availability uncertainties, some schools traded the usual spring practice for an extra summer month once freshmen enrolled. Others resumed spring practices. A broadened 1944 season appeared after officials revoked the 25-mile travel rule. Coaches realized that diminished standards required continued flexibility with players and schedules. A squad need not be three-deep at every position to survive; day coaches sufficed for Pullmans; no team ever starved on a road trip despite rationing; athletics bonded lonely trainees with the rest of the campus; and fans would pay to see good games regardless.[30]

The Mid-Atlantic, although experiencing 1944 with balanced competition and increased interest, notably a 25 percent rise in attendance, slumped to a wartime low in player quality and numbers. In the Rockies,

"Warplanes purr over the snow-capped peaks of the skyline country, dimming the din of the football throngs. The players pause in the practice sessions to look up into the clouds, as if to recognize an old teammate up there."[31] That was understandable. As the war progressed, casualty lists including football players increased. Fewer experienced players around created a younger average age and decline in the caliber of play. For example, Stagg welcomed 30 prospects but only one returnee.

By now, "green" vis-à-vis experience and maturity became the catchword. Compared to prewar standards, southern football nosedived. Big-name college trainee players had long since departed for combat zones, high schoolers answered the draft, military teams said good-bye to too many quality players going overseas, and leftovers were too green. A casualty: North Carolina's greenies struggled for one victory in nine games, 20–13 over the Cherry Point (N.C.) Marines. Naval trainees kept the Southwest Conference from struggling even more. Texas Christian's coach Dutch Meyer patched together a championship team fielding "comparatively green and not particularly talented ... small rugged band of opportunists."[32]

Because of lenient wartime eligibility rules, end George Barney Poole set a fixed modern college football record. The College Football Hall of Fame honoree played seven varsity seasons: three at Mississippi, one at North Carolina, and three at Army, for which he is best remembered (Street & Smith's *Football Pictorial Yearbook 1944*).

As the postwar era arrived, college football prospects for 1945 brightened immediately, spurred by the release of thousands of servicemen and the new GI Bill, which paid for veterans' college educations. Many would be recruited heavily regardless of whether they played during wartime. Charlie "Choo Choo" Justice of Bainbridge-Hawaii by North Carolina and Clyde

"Smackover" Scott of Navy by Arkansas sparked such exciting headlines. Most teams now returned to action, including Vanderbilt, Colorado A&M (now State), Baylor, Utah, and Carnegie Tech. The SEC reenacted the prewar ineligibility of "migratory athletes," permitting only those transfer students who played on 1944-45 teams, upsetting plans of some coaches.[33]

## Offensive and Defensive Formations

Most colleges began wartime play using the winning offensive formations of the previous decade, the single wing and double wing. But by 1943, the formations' college triple-threat tailback began fading out. "The actual extent to which grid specialists are replacing the run-pass-kick stars of yesteryear is easily discernible" in their absence from rankings among the nation's top ten 1942 offensive leaders, the NCAA reported. The principal exception was back Frank Sinkwich (All-America Georgia), "Flat-foot Frankie," the virtually unanimous player of the year and the first ever to gain 2,000 yards. His marks: total yards 2,187 on 795 passing and 1,392 rushing.[34]

In 1943 teams began switching to the relatively new and more potent basic "T" offensive formation, using a balanced line, with the principal ball-handler quarterback taking the snaps from under the center. The straight T was a radical change from the popular prewar single and double-wing sets where the tailback was the principal runner and passer, and differed from the Notre Dame T which shifted into a box formation.

In the T, which emphasized speed and innovative imbalance rather than sheer power, the quarterback was the principal passer but not the runner, and handed off to the ball-carrier halfbacks and fullback. A main reason coaches switched to the T, if they had a good ball-handling quarterback, was because individual line assignments called for simple blocking. Variations included a flanker and man-in-motion, Iowa Pre-Flight's split-T, Pittsburgh's and Brown's offset T, Dartmouth's double-splits, Yale's triple-split line, and an unbalanced line (two linemen on one side of the center). Possessing abundant manpower depth, some military and collegiate powerhouses such as El Toro Marine Corps Air Station in 1944-45 deployed separate T and wing-offense units. Ohio State, Michigan, and Colgate also ran both offenses. Thus the eventual postwar multiple platoon system began.

In 1944 on its 150th anniversary, Army (23) used the T to beat Navy (7), which used the single wing: "a perfect game of contrast." The previous season coach Colonel Earl Blaik scrapped the single wing, Army's hallmark, and introduced brush blocks, flankers, man-in-motion, streamlined fullbacks, fleet flankers, and a clever passer "who can flip 'em to the bucket." Blessed

Back Charley Trippi (Georgia) played for the Greensboro (N.C.) Army Air Forces Overseas Replacement Depot Tech Hawks in 1943. The 1942 Maxwell Award winner later earned membership in the college and professional halls of fame ("Army Town: Greensboro, 1943–1946," Greensboro [N.C.] Historical Museum, 1994).

with "mercury gaited carriers," the Cadets utilized a "precision-geared line" with a passing game that spread the defense for long gainers.[35]

Fans enjoyed the fascinating and exciting T, and popular players such as Sid Luckman described "How to Watch the T Formation."[36] His former coach at Columbia, Lou Little, called Columbia's version the split-T. Little refined what coach Clark Shaughnessy is credited with developing. During the late 1930s, Shaughnessy worked with Chicago Bears coach George Halas to modernize the primitive new offense, and the Bears' Luckman, a pro football Hall-of-Fame member, became the first modern T quarterback in both college and the pros. After the 1940 season saw Shaughnessy lead Stanford to a 9–0–0 record and Halas, Luckman, and the Bears whip the Washington Redskins for the National Football League championship, 73–0, the T became a fixture.

By 1944, manpower limitations forced coaches to switch to the T because individual line assignments revolved only around a good quarterback and simple blocking. Teams varied the combinations of the T with other formations and the flanker and man-in-motion. By 1945, a football yearbook observed that the T was set as today's offense. "It's easier to teach unseasoned hands how to advance the ball than it is to coordinate them on defense. Most coaches ... are proceeding on the theory that if you can't stop the other fellow you had better try to outscore him."[37]

The most widely used offensive formations:

**T-formation**— Seven linemen; backfield composed of quarterback (primary ball handler and passer) taking snaps under center, two halfbacks (running backs, No. 1 ball carriers and also receivers), fullback (blocker and No. 2 ball carrier); usually a balanced line masking the point of attack; ends split away from tackles a few yards, halfbacks four yards deep, and fullback five yards behind center; man-in-motion added variety; excellent passing and deceptive formation.

Weakness: difficult to develop a mass power attack; quarterback should be an excellent ball handler and passer; halfbacks, fast and clever ball carriers, and good receivers.

**Single wing**— Seven linemen; backfield composed of tailback (primary ball handler, runner, and passer), fullback (blocker and No. 2 runner), blocking back (primary blocker), and wingback (receiver and No. 3 runner); similar to modern shotgun formation; balanced or unbalanced line; strong running game to strong side.

Weakness: weaker running game to weak side and for passing and punting plays.

**Double wing**— Similar to single wing with two wingbacks spread in backfield as blockers or receivers (blocking back became wingback), tailback handling the ball as principal runner and passer, and fullback (No. 2 runner); unbalanced line with wingbacks flanking each offensive end one yard behind the line; optimum for spinners, reverses, and multiple pass patterns; strong for running through tackle.

Weakness: lacks power up the middle; plays slow getting to the line; plays require intricate maneuvering and precise timing (a handicap when teaching new players with short practice times).

The single- and double-wing tailback had to be a good runner, passer, and punter.

For the 1946 season, experts predicted more variations of the T formation, even combining it with the single wing. Other formations included the "QT," "5–1," and single wing with quarterback close to center.

Authorities supposedly agreed that play selection was the most important game factor, and that poor selection could nullify teamwork and harm morale (as well as the final score). A brilliant quarterback could raise a mediocre eleven. He should have "courage, initiative, brains, vocal command and the complete confidence of his teammates."[38] Ergo, for the navy, prime leadership qualities for the Pacific War.

Conversely, changing or shifting defensive theories, maneuvers, and schemes proceeded gradually. Teams insisted on kicking the ball out of bounds, "a strategy much criticized because of the failure to use it as a psychological tactic in fine offense technique, and the preference for using it rather as a simple preventative against spectacular runbacks."[39] Coaches soon changed this tactic, as seen below.

Coaches also weaned themselves away from the old-school, "hold-that-line" defensive strategy and switched to a more fluid scheme designed to bend but not give, to slow a play rather than stop it cold at the start, and retard the long-gainers. But by war's end, ends still rushed the passer and "bull-butting linemen" charged through, whether caught in a mousetrap, to block kicks. "The fans do not want safety-first football. The players are not geared for it, mechanically or by temperament. The coaches ... can shoot the works with what they've got."[40]

Generally, player experience and talent, weather conditions, and sometimes the opponents' offense, dictated defensive formations. Five or six men played on the line. Linebackers were important because they got into practically every play after linemen stripped a ball carrier of his blockers.

The 6–2–2–1 was the most widely used and best balanced defense. It fielded six linemen, two linebackers, two halfbacks, and one safety. Effective against running, passing, and kicking games, its weakness was lack of strength against line plunges. Other standard defensive formations included the 7–1–2–1 diamond; 7–2–2 box; 5–3–2–1; and 6–3–2.

## Rules, Coaching, and Strategies

Military teams played by prewar collegiate rules. The NCAA and military officials by mutual consent deferred "official" changes until 1945. Midway through the war, however, a gentlemen's agreement among coaches introduced some national and regional modifications. They eliminated the out-of-bounds kickoff. Henceforth teams kicked off again to keep the ball in play for a return. Passing from anywhere behind the line of scrimmage, as in the pros, was permitted. It "upjacks the attack of teams that cannot rely on straight power." A fumble recovered by the defense could be advanced. And certain penalty rulings were modified governing forward laterals and offense within the ten-yard line.[41]

One major rule change in 1941 had essentially introduced what evolved into the postwar two-platoon system. It allowed substitutes to enter except during last two minutes of the first half as long as that sub and the replaced player stayed put for at least one play. Unrealized at the time, this new rule eventually helped reduce player exhaustion and injuries and improve quality of play in accommodating college manpower shortages.

The NCAA in 1945 codified earlier unofficial changes for the out-of-bounds kickoff and a legal forward pass from anywhere behind the line. The first such kickoff was without penalty, a second resulted in the receiving team taking the ball at the kicking team's 40. Also, substitutes could enter by reporting to any official, and the center in snapping the ball could not have any part of his body ahead of the ball and his feet had to be behind the ball.[42]

Most games employed four field officials: a referee, linesman, umpire, and field judge. They wore a striped shirt, white knickers-pants, long black socks, bow tie, and usually no cap. Field dimensions, goal post location, and markings were the same as today's except for the end zone which was marked with diagonal stripes.

In its 1942 preview, the NCAA saw the decline of "old-fashioned generalship" in coaching and stated that "games, no less than wars, are won by teams bearing the stamp of master technicians employing the highly complicated offensive and defensive tactics" of the modern game.[43]

New concepts and tactics adapted, improved, and refined included the forward pass and pass protection, man-in-motion, shifting defenses, numerous defensive sets, the quick kick, lateral-forward pass, high tackling, flankers, offensive sets to spread the defense, and free substitution. The navy's "Rules of Generalship" advised coaches on successful formulae: (1) A rush of more than 40 yards is rarely worth it because something bad or unforeseen happens; (2) Don't lose the ball on downs, and always kick the ball forward when necessary; (3) Push the kicking game; (4) "Make and play for the breaks"; (5) Beating a weak team is simple, but beating an equal or better one generally depends on (4). In summary, the winner usually wins by making fewer mistakes.[44]

Coaching routines never settled but adapted to reality. The 1944 *Illustrated Football Annual* forecast not enough time "in these world-shaking days" for lengthy drills, preparations, meticulous coaching, and developing "precision-geared linemen" and "robot-controlled backs." The makeup of college elevens full of "star-pretenders" and "mostly make-good-quick kids, sophomores and freshmen," along with a handful of older trainees still around, would be vastly different. Could youth and desire offset know-how for another season?[45]

First of all, coaches tried to whip players into shape. In the initial wartime season the NCAA bemoaned the lack of physical fitness throughout the population. "In fighting a Japanese army, toughened by five years of warfare, and a German nation, which even before 1939 had spent years in developing physical fitness throughout Germany," executive director Walter Okeson noted, "we are sadly handicapped." Modern football is offensive, not defensive, "a combat game ... teaching teamwork, the will to win and the determination not to lose no matter how tough the going," all to train American boys to fight. To train and "toughen the moral fiber, you need the nearest thing to warfare you can find. There is little doubt that thing is intercollegiate football."[46] Those going into action thanked football fitness for their survival. One told a Marine major serving as secretary of the American Football Coaches Association that he always felt the same coolness and competitive urge as when a football game started.[47]

The navy pre-flight schools stressed rigorous physical training as a factor in evaluating students competing as naval pilots. Kansas State basketball coach Jack Gardner in 1942 joined the navy and oversaw athletic and physical programs at 42 Midwest naval flight and training schools. Since most civilians reporting as V-12 officer candidates were out of shape, the navy spent more time on meeting high fitness standards than on pure military training.

Physical training demands could work against pre-flight teams. The venerated Grantland Rice noted that 1942 pre-flight elevens abounded in player material but were handicapped by a strenuous, near body-wrecking regimen and a constant personnel ebb and flow as the brand-new schools settled into operation. Generally they were "weary and battered, worn down, and ... far from any football sharpness" after a 10-hour daily training regimen. They lost when running out of gas, as did Georgia and Iowa Pre-Flight, from sheer physical and mental lapses and weariness, against Louisiana State and Notre Dame. Still, even while concentrating on a much bigger task ahead and with football a diversion, they defeated many solid collegiate elevens that season.[48]

And what about the nation's physical fitness for the postwar? It needs to "get militant" about athletics and fitness, wrote a major college coach in 1944, or risk fumbling the ball and making no more progress than was seen after World War I which precipitated the 1941 prewar malaise.[49]

*Football: The Naval Aviation Physical Training Manuals*, issued in 1943 by the Chief of Naval Operations and a valuable textbook for all levels, said

Del Monte (Calif.) Pre-Flight pummeled Alameda Coast Guard, 34–7, en route to a 1943 7-1-0 record in their lone season. Here the Navyators' end Fred Stanford gains yardage (Street & Smith's *Football Pictorial Yearbook 1944*).

the country faced desperate enemies, steeped in "a fanatical nationalism," who cared nothing about human life or conventional rules of warfare. It stated the navy was duty-bound to train future aviators "to be superior to that enemy, mentally and physically" and be prepared to run through and demolish "a broken field of Axis planes." The manual directed that everyone receive football instructions, such as tackling using the best body blow, and compete for a position on a team, whether college varsity or intramurals.[50] Other manuals included additional sports and hand-to-hand combat instruction. However, it was acknowledged, "The most physically fit soldier in the world is worthless if he does not have in his mind and heart the will to win."[51]

Postscript: Created on the spot, the team ranked No. 2 in the nation in 1943 bore the unfamiliar name of Iowa Pre-Flight. The next season, the Associated Press Top 10 ranked such new names as Randolph Field, Bainbridge Navy, and March Field (Fourth Air Force). "And just as swiftly, they vanished from the scene."[52]

# World War II Military Teams (Partial)

Many military teams played full schedules for the four-season duration. Most played one, two, or three seasons or folded after a few games in their only attempt to field a team.

Nicknames: "Very few of the service teams were without one, and with many of the teams the necessary title was much emphasized. Use was made of every kind of publicity to popularize the name."[53]

Abilene AAB Flyers, Tex.
Aberdeen Ordnance School, Md.
Aberdeen Proving Ground, Md.
Air Transport Command, Nashville, Tenn., Rockets
Alameda CG, Alameda, Calif., Sea Lions
Alaska Air Transport Command Clippers
Albuquerque AB, Alb. N.M., Colin Kellys/Flying Kellys
Algiers, La., Navy
Amarillo AAF, Tex., Sky Giants
Army Air Forces TC, Randolph Field and Fort Worth, Tex., Skymasters
Army Air Forces Personnel Distribution Command, Louisville, Ky., Comets
Atlantic City NAS, N.J., Flyers/Corsairs
Bainbridge NTS/NTC, Md., Commodores
Barksdale AAB, Shreveport, La., Skyraiders
Beaumont Hospital, El Paso, Tex., Raiders
Bergstrom AAF, Tex.
Berry Field, Tenn.
Blackland AAF, Waco, Tex., Eagles
Bogue Field, N.C., Marines
Bowman Field, Ky., Flyers
Bryan AF, Tex., Raiders
Bushnell General Hospital, Brigham City, Ut., Medics
Bunker Hill NTS, Ind., Blockbusters
Camp Ashby, Calif., Stevadores
Camp Barkeley, Tex.
Camp Beale, Marysville, Calif., Bears
Camp Butner, N.C.
Camp Campbell 220th Armored, Ky., Engineers
Camp Davis, N.C., Blue Brigade/Fighting AA's
Camp Detrick, Md.
Camp Gordon 3rd Armored Division, Ga., Tankers
Camp Grant, Rockford, Ill., Warriors

Camp Hood-North, Fourth Army, Gatewood, Tex., Maroons
Camp Hood-South, Gatewood, Tex., Doughboys
Camp Kilmer, N.J., Eagles
Camp Lee, Va., Travelers
Camp Lejeune MCB, N.C., Marines/Leathernecks
Camp Mackall, Hoffman, N.C., Chutists
Camp McCoy, Wisc., Engineers
Camp Peary, Williamsburg, Va., Pirates
Camp Pendleton, Calif., Marines
Camp Polk, La.
Carlisle Barracks-Medical Field Service, Carlisle Barracks, Pa., Medicos
Charleston CG, Charleston, S.C.
Chatham AAB, Savannah, Ga., Blockbusters
Cherry Point MCAS, N.C., Marines/Leathernecks
CG Receiving Station, Berkeley, Calif., Pilots
Colorado Springs AB, Colorado Springs, Colo.
Coronado, Calif., Amphibs
Corpus Christi NAS, Tex., Comets
Curtis Bay CG, Md., Cutters
Daniel Field AB, Augusta, Ga., Fliers
Del Monte, San Francisco, Calif., Navyators
Deming AAF, N.M., Dusters
Drew AAF, Fla.
Eagle Mt. Lake, Fort Worth, Tex., Rangers
Eastern Flying TC, Maxwell Field, Ala., Eagles
Edgewood Arsenal, Md.
Ellington Field, Houston, Tex., Flyers
El Toro MCAS, Irvine/Santa Ana, Calif., Flying Marines
Fairfield-Suisun AAB, Fairfield, Calif., Skymasters
Farragut Naval Training Station, Id.
First Air Force, Mitchell Field, N.Y., Aces
Fleet City NTC/Naval Receiving Station/Naval Personnel Training and Distribution Center, Shoemaker, Calif., Bluejackets
Fort Bliss, El Paso, Tex., Anti-Aircrafters/Commandos
Fort Bragg Field Artillery Replacement Training Center, N.C., Cannoneers
Fort Benning, Ga., Doughboys
Fort Benning 1st Student Training Regiment, Ga., Panthers
Fort Benning, Ga., 4th Infantry Raiders
Fort Benning, Ga., 300th Infantry, Sabres
Fort Benning, Ga., 124th Infantry, Gators/Tigers
Fort Benning, Ga., 176th Infantry, Spirits/Rockets

Fort Bragg, N.C.
Fort Bragg 3rd Field Artillery Replacement Training Center, N.C., Canoneers
Fort Crook, Neb.
Fort Douglas, Ut.
Fort Knox, Ky., Armoraiders
Fort MacArthur, Calif.
Fort Monmouth, N.J.
Fort Monroe, Va., Gunners
Fort Ord., Calif.
Fort Pierce, Fla., Amphibs
Fort Riley Replacement Training Center, Kan., Centaurs
Fort Sheridan, Ill., Comets/GI's
Fort (Francis E.) Warren, Cheyenne, Wyo., Broncos/Fighting Quartermasters
Fourth (4th) Air Force, March Field, Riverside, Calif., Flyers
Galveston AAF, Galveston, Tex.
Georgia PF, Athens, Ga., Skycrackers
Godman AAF, Fort Knox, Ky., Bombers
Goleta MCAS, Goleta, Calif., Marines
Great Lakes NTS, Great Lakes, Ill., Bluejackets
Great Falls AAB, Great Falls, Mont., Bombers
Greensboro, N.C., Army Air Force Overseas Replacement Depot, Tech Hawks
Greenville AAB, N.C., Bombers
Gulfport AAF, Gulfport, Miss.
Gulfport NAS, Gulfport, Miss.
Gulfport NS, Gulfport, Miss., Seabees
Hill Field, Ogden, Ut., Flyers
Hondo AAF, Hondo, Tex., Comets
Houma AB, Houma, La.
Hutchinson NAS, Hutchinson, Kan., Navalairs
Iowa PF, Iowa City, Seahawks
Jackson AB, Jackson, Miss., Bombers
Jacksonville NAS, Jacksonville, Fla., Flyers
Jacksonville Naval Air Technical Training Center, Jacksonville, Fla., Air Raiders
Keesler Field, Biloxi, Miss., Keeslerites
Kearney AAF, Kearney, Neb., Raiders/Flyers
Kearns AAB, Salt lake City, Ut., Eagles
Kinston, N.C., Marines
Kirkland Field, Albuquerque, N.M., Flying Kellys
Klamath Falls, Ore., Marines

Knoxville, Tenn., Engineers
LaGarde Hospital, New Orleans, La.
Lake Charles AAF, Lake Charles, La.
Lakehurst NAS, Lakehurst, N.J., Blimps
Lincoln AAF, Neb., Wings
Logan NTS, Logan, Ut.
Lowry Field, Denver, Colo., Bombers/Bombardiers
Manhattan Beach CG, Brooklyn, N.Y.
Maxwell Field, Montgomery, Ala., Marauders
Mayport NAS, Mayport, Fla.
McClellan Field, Sacramento, Calif., Rangers
McCook AAB, McCook, Neb.
Melville Patrol Torpedo Base, R.I., Night Raiders
Memphis Naval Air Technical Training Center, Tenn., Blues
Miami AAF, Miami, Fla.
Miami NTC, Miami, Fla., Navaltars
Minter Field, Calif., Flyers
Montford Point, Camp Lejeune, N.C., Panthers
Moore General Hospital, Swannanoa, N.C.
New River Marine Corps Air Station (Peterfield Point), N.C., Devil Dogs
New London Submarine Base, New London, Conn., Diesels
Norfolk Fleet Marines, Norfolk, Va.
Norman NAS, Norman, Okla., Zoomers
North Carolina PF, Chapel Hill, N.C., Cloudbusters
Olathe NAS, Olathe, Kan., Zippers/Clippers
Ottumwa Naval Air Station, Ottumwa, Ia., Skyers
Parris Island Marine Corps Recruit Depot, S.C.
Patterson Field, Oh., Stars
Pearl Harbor Navy All-Stars, Pearl Harbor, T.H.
Pensacola NAS, Pensacola, Fla., Goshawks/Goslings/Air Cadets
Pleasanton Naval Personnel Distribution Center, Calif., Bluejackets
Pocatello, Id., Marines
Pomona Army Ordnance Base, Calif., Gunners
Portsmouth Fleet
Randolph Field, Tex., Ramblers
Reno AAB, Nev., Flying Wolves/Flyers
Richmond AAB, Richmond, Va., Thunderbirds
Rome AAF, N.Y.
Rosecrans AAB, St. Joseph, Mo., Flyers
Salt Lake AAB, Salt Lake City, Ut., Wings
Sampson NTS, Sampson, N.Y., Sailors/Bluejackets

San Diego NTS, San Diego, Calif., Bluejackets/Tars
San Francisco Bay CG Receiving Station, San Francisco, Calif., Pilots
Santa Ana AAB, Orange County, Calif., Flyers
Santa Barbara MCAS, Santa Barbara, Calif., Marines
Second (2nd) Air Force, Colorado Springs, Colo., Superbombers (formerly of Spokane, Wash.)
Selman AAB, Monroe, La., Cyclones
South Plains AAF, Lubbock, Tex., Winged Commandos
Spokane Air Service, Spokane, Wash., Commandos
St. Mary's PF, Moraga, Calif., Air Devils
Stockton AAB, Stockton, Calif., Commandos
Third (3rd) Air Force, Morris Field, Charlotte, N.C.; later Drew Field, Tampa, Fla., Gremlins
Tonapah Fourth Air Force, Tonopah, Nev., Flyers
Tulsa AB, Tulsa, Okla., Bombers
U.S. Coast Guard Academy, New London, Conn., Bears
U.S. Military Academy, West Point, N.Y., Cadets
U.S. Naval Academy, Annapolis, Md., Midshipmen
U.S. Submarine Base, New London, Conn., Undersea Raiders
Will Rogers AAB, Oklahoma City, Okla.
Wilmington Army Engineers, Calif.
Wilmington CG, Wilmington, N.C.
Wilmington Engineers, Amarillo, Tex.
Yuma AAB, Ariz., Gremlins

**Black teams:** Tuskegee AAF, Tuskegee, Ala., Warhawks; Columbus AF, Columbus, Ga.; Bryan AF, Tex.; Camp McKall, N.C., Paratroopers; Fort Benning, Ga.; Fort Riley, Kans.; Norfolk NTS, Norfolk, Va., Brown Bombers; Aberdeen Proving Ground, Md.; Selman AAB, Monroe, La.; Randolph Field, Tex.; MacDill and Daniel Fields, Ala.; 56th Engineers Training Battalion, Wash.

## CHAPTER 5

# "Shifty and Smart, Harder to Stop Than Superman": Charlie Justice, Glamor Prodigy

*"The heat was on," wrote Shirley Povich in the* Washington Post *in 1944. "Choo Choo Justice and his marauding on the gridiron amounted to a home front for the navy—Halsey, Nimitz and Justice shared the headlines."*[1]

This "Choo Choo" was no National Football League star or college All-America singled out by the esteemed sportswriter. On the contrary, this smallish, teenaged boy, right out of high school, through talent, determination, and wise coaching, bolted onto the military football scene and soon became the glamor football prodigy of World War II.

His new navy family at the Bainbridge Naval Training Station recognized in a flash the enormous gridiron potential once he arrived in 1943. "He didn't have a big college or pro reputation. He didn't even have a press books full of clippings, but this high school kid is holding his own with the cream of the crop in the Commodores' ball-carrying department."[2] The impact had only begun, and for two remarkable football seasons he played a key, memorable role in Bainbridge's rapid ascendancy to wartime greatness.

"You've probably seen him in action," the station newspaper boasted about 18-year old Seaman 2nd/Class Charlie Justice, "so you know that he's fast, shifty and smart. Fact, once he gets past the line of scrimmage, he's harder to stop than Superman." In the first six games Justice rushed 25 times for 302 yards and scored two touchdowns. "Not bad for a high school kid."[3]

Justice graduated in 1943 from Lee H. Edwards High School in Asheville, N.C., also known as Asheville High. According to biographer Bob Terrell, his desire to play football overcame physical difficulties and ill health as a boy.

As a single-wing quarterback and halfback, he led the Edwards offense to undefeated seasons in 1941–42, as Edwards outscored opponents 487–7, scoring a point a minute in 1942 against mostly out-of-state foes. Justice made the All-Southern and All-State teams both times, and led the South with 172 points. On the state's 1942 Shrine Bowl team, he scored three touchdowns against South Carolina preps.

Football was natural and expected in the Justice family. Three brothers preceded him in the sport and a fourth wore his jersey number in 1943. At Edwards he still found time to fall in love with his future wife Sarah. "From that point on Charlie and his loves [football and Sarah] would not be separated."[4] Justice later reflected, "It was destined that I was going to play football and be an athlete."[5]

If the nation were not at war he would have accepted one of some 12 college scholarship offers. But he was drafted into the navy, passed the tests for aerial gunnery, and headed for Bainbridge for training. His eventual rating was petty officer specialist (physical education instructor) second class (SP(A)2c), a rating established during the war and equivalent to today's petty officer second class, but disestablished thereafter. He taught physical education and "pushed boots" through recruit training, coincidentally to allow adequate time for athletics.

Fresh out of high school in Asheville, N.C., 18-year-old Charlie Justice practices punting during Bainbridge (Md.) Naval Training Station drills in 1943, after convincing coaches he could kick as well as receive. Justice wore three jersey numbers at Bainbridge in 1943–44, 3, 9, 23, and number 12 in Hawaii. Postwar at North Carolina, his jersey (22) would become the most famous athletic number in state history (game program, Bainbridge at Camp Lejeune, September 25, 1943).

## 1943

Justice reported to Bainbridge in the summer of 1943, and as a baby-faced, raw apprentice seaman joined 99 others in trying out for the team. Coach Lieutenant Joe Maniaci (Fordham, Brooklyn Dodgers, Chicago Bears) issued him a ragtag uniform and no football shoes. Their introduction took on a "Knute Rockne–meets–George Gipp overtone," wrote famed sportswriter Furman Bisher. Maniaci instructed him to stay out of the way and only field punts. "You won't get hurt that way, kid."[6]

Tar Heel football historian Ken Rappoport credited the navy for bringing Justice "down to earth." "'What do you want?'" snapped Maniaci. "'I'm a halfback,'" Justice responded. After checking out the young, rather undersized applicant, Maniaci dismissed him to other end of the field for punting drills, with Justice wearing only sweat socks.[7]

Bored with just shagging, it didn't take long for Justice to turn this around. One practice he booted the ball 65 yards back up the field, without shoes. 'Who kicked that ball?' Maniaci bellowed. 'The kid over there.' Maniaci called to Justice. 'You kick like that all the time?' 'I do it better when I'm wearing football shoes,'" Justice said, pointing to his sneakers.[8] That did it. Maniaci told him there was no way he would make the club, with all their pros and All-Americas. But if he wanted to hang around and kick, fine. After two weeks Justice got cleats and made the squad.

Impressed with his practice runs, Maniaci inserted him into the Washington Redskins scrim-

By now nicknamed "Choo Choo," Charlie Justice scampers at home at Tome Field in 1943. "He runs like a runaway train." Sportswriters pounced on it and it stuck forever (Street & Smith's *Football Pictorial Yearbook 1944*).

mage. All he did was intercept two passes, make four tackles, average five yards per carry, and race 45 yards for the sailors' lone touchdown. His four punts, however, averaged only 20 yards. "'It's a good thing you can do something else besides kick or you'd be headed for sea duty,'" an admonishing coach said. "It seems that every time I needed a break I got the break," Justice recalled.[9]

"I went out for football primarily for one reason," Justice told Rappoport, "to get out of KP. I knew just enough to know that if you played football you were automatically jerked from KP duty." He had heard of Maniaci but until reporting for practice nothing about the array of professionals with whom he would compete and ultimately play alongside. "Justice was lost in this forest of talent."[10]

Justice, who stood 5'10" and weighed between 165 and 170, eventually thought that being the only high school boy worked to his advantage. "Nobody would believe it." When asked why he didn't attend college, he answered, "Well, I'm not old enough. I didn't get out of high school in time."[11] Realizing his place in the pecking order, and deploying his charm and personality, he soon established himself with coaches, teammates, and the media. To the latter, he became a "darling": great player, great copy. It would last his entire football career.

The pros quickly liked the kid, "who had a great competitive flair and an even and controlled temperament mixed with his natural talents." Terrell discovered Justice practiced enthusiastically with an "attitude of total cooperation and self-sacrifice. His good nature and fine spirit were always present." Justice noted the pros often operated on the field independently from coaching instructions, including changing called plays in the huddle. "'Aw hell, he don't know what he's talking about,' someone would say." Do what we say, they told Justice. Maniaci allowed them to freelance a bit because he knew it worked.[12]

Maniaci finally provided the opportunity. Bob Quincy and Julian Scheer, in their Justice book, called it "a battlefield promotion." Maniaci said, "He's got everything. He can run, tackle, block, and boot that ball a country mile." The coach then had to determine how to utilize him most effectively as a spot player.[13]

So how did he get the nickname "Choo Choo"? At one game a naval officer watching from the stands reportedly said, "'Say, that Justice kid runs just like a choo choo train.'" Sportswriters immediately pounced and it stuck, forever. While starring at North Carolina later, he received mail addressed only to "Choo Choo, N.C.,"[14] or his jersey number "22, Chapel Hill, N.C." Justice later added his version to *Touchdown Illustrated* in 1988. He said an officer was sitting with Paul Menton, sports editor of *The Evening Sun* of Baltimore, and said: "Look at that guy run. He looks like a runaway train.

We ought to call him Choo Choo." Menton picked it up and used it in the paper.[15] Coincidentally, Justice's father worked for a railroad. Even today young North Carolinians recognize the name and know the legend.

With two weeks of practice "under their skivvies," Bainbridge fielded three backfield combinations. One included Bill deCorrevont of Northwestern, Bill Dutton of Pittsburgh (All-America), Charlie Noble of Marquette, and Justice "of North Carolina." Justice never started. By the second game, Hilliard Cheatham (Auburn), Jim Gatewood (Georgia), Don Durdan (Oregon State), and Harvey Johnson (William & Mary) comprised the first team.[16]

Here are some seasonal games, facts, and numbers of note.

**Bainbridge 26, Curtis Bay Coast Guard 7, at Bainbridge, October 16.** Justice scored the final touchdown by returning an interception 32 yards.

**Bainbridge 49, Camp Lee 0, at Camp Lee, Va., October 23.** "AP: With Bill deCorrevont, of Northwestern fame, pitching and Al Vanderweghe [William & Mary] and Charlie Justice catching, the Sailors unleashed a devastating aerial attack." Before 12,000, Justice, "fleet 18-year old speedster," ran "the spectacular play of the day," took a deCorrevont lateral and raced 60 yards through the entire Lee team for a 20–0 halftime lead. Justice also scored a fourth quarter touchdown.[17]

**Bainbridge 54, Curtis Bay 0, at Curtis Bay, Md., November 6.** Bainbridge "steam-rollered a hapless" Curtis Bay team. In the fourth quarter "the fleet-footed" Justice, in "the standout run of the day," took a Cheatham 72-yard touchdown pass, "bobbing and dancing his way the last 45 yards."[18]

A week later Justice did not play against Maryland because of a bad back. He told the *Baltimore Sun* he felt "grateful to the navy for his association with 'such a flock of big boys.' He confessed to thinking he was out of place when he first joined the team but his success in action and their acceptance of him had made him much more comfortable."[19]

The AP named Justice Mid-Atlantic Rookie of the Year, but he was still unknown nationwide, wrote Quincy and Scheer. "A back with only a high school background had no right to out-point proven pro and college stars."[20] The *Bainbridge Mainsheet* observed, "Justice seems to be the surprise package of '43. You'll hear more of him."[21]

"The Guy Doesn't Do Justice to Himself," the *Mainsheet* wrote.[22] "Leaving his foes / In clouds of dust is / Asheville's pride / One Charlie Justice."

# 1944

All of a sudden, plaudits and superlatives rained down upon Justice. The NCAA in its 1944 preview reminded readers that "Charley [*sic*] 'Choo Choo'

Justice, extraordinary youngster of Bainbridge ... ran wild in every game."[23] That season he finished second nationally (14 touchdowns for 84 points) to All-America halfback Glenn Davis of Army (20 touchdowns for 120 points) in scoring. Soon even the first name would be correctly spelled: Charlie.

In mid–September the Commodores scrimmaged powerful Navy. "According to the reports it ended up all even with Charlie Justice dashing 60 yards to tally a Bainbridge score. The guys here [at Bainbridge] aren't talking about it."[24]

**Bainbridge 43, Camp Lee 0, at Bainbridge, September 30.** Justice "picked up where he left off last year" for the Commodores in their eighth straight win, by scampering for two 50-yard touchdown runs on an interception and punt return without a hand touching him.[25]

**Bainbridge 53, Camp Lejeune 7, at Bainbridge, October 7.** In the second quarter, Jackie Field (Texas) and "the fleet-footed, shifty" Justice, a "high school phenomenon," "each hit pay dirt from 32 yards out." Both gigantic lines battled fiercely, and Bainbridge was penalized 105 yards, mostly for unnecessary roughness.[26] The AP reported the 19-year old Justice "already has made a down payment on a backfield spot on the 1944 all-service team." He handled the ball seven times and scored on runs of 83, 51, 50, and 32 yards. The other three carries were for 34, 26, and 12 yards.[27] What running, and what blocking.

Justice supplied the coup d'etat. "Standing on his own 17, 'Choo Choo Charlie' took [a] lateral and headed for the western sidelines. Apparently stopped on the line of scrimmage, he suddenly reversed his field and, sidestepping a half dozen enemy tacklers, broke into the clear and swept 83 yards for the day's longest scoring jaunt.... Don't get the idea that this Lejeune team is any pushover even if the score was monstrous."[28] So was the Asheville phenom.

"The Fighting Commodores"[29]

*Roll up the score for dear old Bainbridge,*
*Roll up the score you Commodores.*
*Down the field in Navy Blue,*
*Show your colors true.*
*Rah! Rah!*
*Just like a Navy battle wagon,*
*Sail on to meet and sink the foe.*
*Fight! With might! You men of Bainbridge;*
*Sail right on to Victory!*

**Bainbridge 47, Camden (N.J.) Blue Devils 7, at Bainbridge, October 14.** Unbeaten Camden, atop the eastern professional football league, scored first on a 42-yard fumble recovery return. Then the sailors poured it on. "Youthful Charley Justice again stole the show offensively" by scoring twice on a 3-yard end sweep and a 36-yard off-tackle gallop.[30] Bainbridge "continues to be a high handicap team," the *Mainsheet* reported, with 300 penalty yards in three games. Justice booted three extra points but each time the team committed a penalty, nullifying the kicks.[31]

**Bainbridge, October 17.** "AP — 'He's the greatest natural football player I've ever seen,' says Bainbridge coach Joe Maniaci of 19-year old Charley Justice, while Duke coach Eddie Cameron chortles at them kind words and rubs his hands in glee." In the sailors' first three games Justice scored six touchdowns and averaged 25 yards per carry. The *Baltimore Sun* reported, "Cameron is sleeping well despite his unsuccessful Duke team because he apparently has the inside track on the kid's services after the war. Justice has told intimates, 'It's Duke for me.'"[32] His numbers: nine rushes for 186 yards, total (counting runbacks of kicks and interceptions), 16 for 399.

The *Sun* continued[33]:

> The part they don't tell is his fire-eating love of football — he has been dressed and waiting in an empty dressing room three hours before a game — his ability to learn quickly from mistakes, his vicious blocking, good kicking and ability to shift directions bewilderingly on the dead run. Last year he was a surprise David — weighing 165 — among a flock of giants.... Back of a tremendous line that has given its opponents this year minus 84 yards from rushing, he outshines such proven ball carriers as Harvey Johnson ... Don Durdan ... Jim Gatewood ... Jackie Field ... Harry (Hippety) Hopp ... Joe Kane ... and a flock of others. Because of the Commodores' triple deep backfield strength, he has played just 58 minutes ... but when he's in, there ain't no justice in Charley Justice.

**Bainbridge 7, Camp Peary 0, at Williamsburg, Va., October 22.** Prior to the game that the media billed as an early-season service championship, Coach Maniaci expected trouble. "'The only thing we know about Peary is that they can field 15 professional ballplayers against us. We don't know whether they use the 'T,' the single wing or what. All we know is they've got an awfully tough ball club." They sure were. Hopp (Nebraska) ran back a punt 65 yards for the only score as the Commodores took their eleventh straight victory.[34]

Dr. William Friday, president emeritus of the University of North Carolina system and a close postwar Justice friend, watched that game in the William & Mary stadium. Friday was stationed at the naval ammunition depot in Norfolk and later remembered[35]:

> His club won, and he put on quite a show. I believe he was wearing tennis shoes. To see him out there running among all those big fellows was amaz-

To the delight of a multitude of fellow Bainbridge navy white hats, Choo Choo Justice roars down the sidelines for another Commodore touchdown (*Bainbridge Mainsheet*, October 21, 1944).

ing. If I recall [correctly] his main contribution was punting. He kept the opposition on the defensive all day. He was so different, and that was why he stood out. There are some people you can't coach, like Michael Jordan and David Thompson. You just let them go. There was a quality of grace in their performance. He was one of those. He was given a gift. I can't ever remember Charlie being called for any kind of penalty. He was a gentleman, a unique person."

In their hard-fought return engagement on November 25, Bainbridge prevailed 21–13. Peary kept Justice "bottled up throughout the afternoon," holding him to two rushing yards, his only bad game.[36]

**Bainbridge 15, Maxwell Field 7, at Montgomery, Ala., October 29.** "AP — About five minutes were left when flashy Charlie Justice ... took a lateral and galloped around right end" to score from six yards out. Justice passes set up the drive, his 35-yarder to Charlie Mehelich (Duquesne) taking it to the six. Bainbridge tied the score 7–7 in the second quarter when Justice sped 17 yards for a touchdown and Harvey Johnson kicked the extra point. Bainbridge added a late safety.[37] Visiting Maxwell lost a second game to Bainbridge on December 2, 13–3, and was the only military team playing both Bainbridge and their air force powerhouse equivalent Randolph Field in 1944.

"Justice Thorn in Maxwell Field's Side," blared the *Mainsheet*. You can't tell Maxwell "'there isn't any Justice,'" as he engineered the scoring plays for the team's twelfth straight win. He stopped Maxwell's second scoring drive by hauling down Johnny Clements (Southern Methodist, Chicago Cardinals) from behind, and "did about everything else but tote the water bucket during time out. Until the fleet 20-year old former Asheville, N.C., schoolboy and his mates settled down to playing football after a ragged first period, the 12,000 fans in the shirt-sleeved crowd thought they saw an upset in the offing." Five army bands entertained. The field sent three bombers to rescue the Commodores from bus trouble to bring them to Maxwell. Justice booted one of the season's longest punts, 71 yards, which rolled dead on the Maxwell six. His longest run of the day was 20, which almost went for a score but he slipped at midfield in the clear and fell. Justice now ranked second among East scorers with eight touchdowns for 48 points, and trailed Army's Glenn Davis who had 60.[38]

**Bainbridge 49, North Carolina Pre-Flight 20, at Chapel Hill, November 5.** "Joe Maniaci's rugged (with a capital 'rug') Bainbridge football team can beat any college eleven of the American gridiron," the *Greensboro Daily News* trumpeted. "Carolina fans were treated to their first view of pro football as it is, and should be, played." The "big bruisers" from Maryland averaged 209 pounds on the line and 195 in the backfield. "That was just the starting team, the rest of the personnel got bigger." Bainbridge scored 41 points in the second quarter. Justice tallied on a 42-yard screen pass. Reserved seats cost $2 each.[39]

This marked his first game in Kenan Stadium in Chapel Hill, where ultimately Justice would become the state's all-time premier college football player. Playing only 10 minutes against the No. 1-ranked military eleven, he scored on a 65-yard "Sally Rand" naked reverse and led the team in yards gained.[40] "The Bainbridge team whooped onto the field, hoisted Charlie on to big shoulders, and carried him off the field to admiring cheers from the crowd."[41]

**Bainbridge 33, Camp Lejeune 6, at Camp Lejeune, N.C., November 18.** Justice highlighted the game with a dazzling 83-yard run during which he outfoxed the superback Elroy "Crazy Legs" Hirsch. "'I was having a hot day. We ran a sweep to the right ... and I twisted around John Yonakor, a big end from Notre Dame, cut back across the field and found no opening there, so I cut across to the right sideline again and when the way closed up there

I cut back across the field for the third time, found a lane over there, and went on in for the touchdown." Untouched, he faked out Hirsch, the last man he passed.[42]

The Lejeune newspaper piled on the plaudits: "Justice Leads Way as Commodores Win." Justice, "the boy among men ... sprinted to his 12th, 13th, and 14th touchdowns of the season.... National reputation on professional and collegiate gridirons faded into nothing as Justice, the high school star from Asheville, N.C., more than lived up to his pre-game ballyhoo. The kid handled the ball seven times from scrimmage for 145 yards and three touchdowns."[43]

Justice paced his team in scoring (21 touchdowns for 126 points) and yards rushing (80 carries for 1,011 yards) for the unbeaten two years, while playing only 10 minutes per game. He fit in

In what might have been the war's classic one-on-one matchup, the great back Elroy "Crazy Legs" Hirsch [Wisconsin, Michigan, Camp Lejeune (N.C.) Marine Corps Base, El Toro (Calif.) Marine Corps Air Station], a former V-12 trainee, was outfaked and outrun by Charlie Justice on his way to a score in Bainbridge's 33–6 victory on November 18, 1944, at Lejeune (Street & Smith's *Football Pictorial Yearbook 1943*).

perfectly with a much older veteran group of players, including many All-Americas, National Football League pros, and postseason bowl participants. Recognizing something special in this young man, they opened holes for him to run through, and exploited his superb defensive savvy. Those were the days when a team's best players played on both sides of the ball as much as they could. Other: team leaders: Justice, 84 points; Hopp, 52; Johnson, 18 (PATs); Vanderweghe, six touchdown passes caught; Justice, 629 yards rushing. Justice later credited his Bainbridge career as two years of pro ball.

Justice earned a spot on the AP All-Service second team along with backs "Indian" Jack Jacobs (Fourth Air Force), Glenn Dobbs (Second Air Force), and Bill Daley (Fort Pierce). Eight Commodores made the 1944 Mid-Atlantic All-Service team:

| First team | Second team |
| --- | --- |
| E Al Vanderweghe | T Lou Rymkus |
| G Garrard Ramsey | G Leonard Akin |
| HB Justice | QB Hilliard Cheatham |
| FB Harvey Johnson | FB Harry Hopp |

After marrying Justice on November 23 in Asheville, Sarah moved to Washington, D.C., to be closer to him, and ultimately worked at the station, making recruit portraits. "Sarah thinks we got married so I wouldn't have to go to Annapolis," he said about the navy's offer to send him to the Academy. "That wasn't it." The navy tore up his orders once they wed because married students were against regulations.[44]

## 1945

After the Bainbridge physical education instructors school closed in 1945, Justice joined other East Coast athletes shipped to Hawaii to prepare for the pending invasion of Japan. Naturally they were expected to play a little organized football in their spare time, for bragging rights, of course. Quincy and Scheer went further. Justice's fame on stateside shore duty embarrassed a navy at war, they said, precipitating his transfer to Honolulu during the period when civilian officials were prodding the armed forces to "get their big-name athletes out of the country."[45]

Justice played several games with a group of navy all-stars in the Honolulu area against similar teams from the Marines and air force. By then he graduated into a starting backfield position along with old Bainbridge colleague Cheatham, Bob Sweiger (Minnesota), and Bob Morrow (Illinois Wesleyan, Chicago Cardinals), the nemesis quarterback when Bainbridge beat Camp Peary in 1944. A November game against the air force stars ended a wartime football rivalry which "[bid] aloha to Hawaiian servicemen and women ... with the final game of a thrilling series.... These games, scheduled ... as a means of recreation [have] succeeded admirably in [their] purpose."[46]

Playing before crowds of 45–50,000 service personnel in the Honolulu-Pearl Harbor area, the air force all-stars went 4–0, Justice's squad 2–2, and the Marines 0–4. Justice, who earlier leaned toward attending Duke, played alongside former Duke backs George McAfee and Steve Lach. His final game in uniform was a losing effort against the Marines in San Francisco. For those who wonder about his wartime naval service, he led trainees in physical education — and he played football.

## Postwar

More than 250 colleges wanted Justice after the war. The Philadelphia Eagles, Chicago Bears, Boston Yanks, and Redskins offered him professional contracts. He settled on college at North Carolina, but on one condition. They struck a deal. I'll attend on the GI Bill, he told Carolina, and you give my scholarship to my wife, Sarah. That worked. She attended classes for two years before leaving to care for their first child. After Charlie died, Sarah related this story to the author about how she went to Carolina on a football scholarship, hardly a secret to the media.

What about his service to our country, and his maturity and growth? Among others, Carolina teammate Robert H. Koontz said that the navy positively influenced Justice and "gave him a tremendous amount of experience that served him well."[47] Teammate Joe Augustine remembered, "Everyone was looking for something to rally around after World War II," and in North Carolina Justice became the man.[48] Justice remembered what really mattered. "They tell us we [football players] contributed to morale. I hope so. I'm no hero. I'm lucky. Most of the guys I started with for gunnery school were lost in the Pacific.'"[49]

Back Charlie Justice (then 5'10"/175) on the navy's Pacific All-Star squad out of Hawaii in his final game in a military uniform in 1945. Justice and other football players had been shipped there to prepare for the invasion of Japan. He never saw action or got farther west than Hawaii (Game program, Fleet City vs. Pacific All-Stars, Kezar Stadium, San Francisco, December 2, 1945).

A coach said as Justice left the navy: "'Calling him a freshman football player when he enters college is like calling Joe Louis a promising young fighter.' Charlie thus became the most highly discussed talent ever to pass from high school to college, via a three-year layoff."[50] Learning lessons in the school of hard knocks "armed [him] with the experience of a professional football player and the exuberance of a college freshman."[51]

At Carolina, the triple-threat (run, pass, punt) halfback wearing jersey number 22 gained 4,883 yards running and passing, a school record that lasted 45 years, scored 234 points, and ran or passed for 64 touchdowns. Justice finished second in the Heisman Trophy balloting in successive years, 1948–49, one of only three players (Army's Glenn Davis, 1944-45, and Arkansas' Darren McFadden, 2006-07 being the others) thus accorded runner-up finishes. A member of the College Football Hall of Fame, Justice earned first-team All-America honors in 1948-49 and was named national player of the year in 1948.

The Tar Heels during the "the Justice era" went 32–6–2 and played in three major bowls including the Sugar and Cotton (when bowls were far fewer and more prestigious than today), finished in the AP Top Ten for three seasons, and reached No. 1 for a while in 1948. Justice received the most valuable player award for the 1950 College All-Star game in leading the post-collegians to a 17–7 victory over the NFL champion Eagles. Music created a special place for him in the Orville Campbell-Hank Beebe hit song, "All the Way Choo Choo." Tar Heel Andy Griffith penned the ditty, "What It Was Was Football" about the team.

Justice fashioned a solid but unspectacular career with the Redskins until retiring from football in 1954 to become briefly the "color man" in their radio broadcasting team, perhaps the first ex-player to do so. He returned to North Carolina in 1955.

## Postscript

On October 17, 2003, Choo Choo died in his Cherryville, N.C., home at 79. The statement of Carolina Athletic Director Dick Baddour resonated for all Tar Heel friends and fans. "Charlie Justice was one of the most beloved people in the history of this great University. He was a true Carolina icon. There was only one Charlie Justice, not only because of his football feats, but because of his humility, devotion to his family and teammates and his love for Carolina. His passing is a great loss to so many people who loved and admired him."[52]

## CHAPTER 6

# "All Hail to the Navy": Great Lakes, Fleet City, Pre-Flights, and Midshipmen

*Two years into the war, the NCAA lauded the service for the "collegiate game's very existence" as "the 'plasma' for the lifeblood of football.... 'All Hail to the Navy'" became the playing theme for 1944.*[1]

The National Collegiate Athletic Association kicked off the first postwar football season by continuing to heap praise upon the navy and Captain Thomas J. Hamilton for playing the key role in "recognizing football's value and keeping the game alive." Football in the navy was a "training 'must.'"[2]

The navy responded by fielding numerous powerful teams at the Naval Academy, five pre-flight schools, and at naval stations, in addition the its "Lend-Lease" officer candidate training programs at some 131 colleges. Because the navy did and the army did not allow its students to play varsity football, colleges with navy and Marine Corps officer candidates had a huge leg up on talent and coaching, and consequently better won-lost records. Yet the navy after 1942 disallowed commissioned officers with collegiate or professional experience from playing pre-flight varsity football, placing those schools "on approximately the same footing as their college opponents" who would dress mostly freshmen.[3]

The Great Lakes (Ill.) Naval Training Station/Center, playing the sport since World War I, vied with the brand-new Bainbridge (Md.) Naval Training Station/Center as best base team. Fleet City (Calif.) Naval Receiving Station bolted into the spotlight in 1945, producing what some observers rated as the finest single-season wartime service eleven. At 25–6 for their

Great Lakes (Ill.) Naval Training Center Bluejackets starters, 1942 (8–3–1, military champions, seven shutouts, all games on the road). Linemen, left to right: Carl Mulleneaux, Jim Barber, Bill Radovich, Bob Nelson, Ken Robesky, Jim Daniell, Fred Preston. Backfield: Pete Kmetovic, Rudy Mucha, Bob Sweiger, Bruce Smith. Smith received more wartime service honors than any other player, including the Washington (D.C.) Touchdown Club's trophy as top service player (*Illustrated Football Annual 1943*).

three campaigns against mostly college competition, Iowa Pre-Flight also deserved No. 1 consideration and surely topped the pre-flights. Great Lakes and Bainbridge were so evenly matched in many eyes that the better team sometimes boiled down to a personal opinion (if one had seen them play).

To Bainbridge's advantage, its holdover 1943 players competed the following season, whereas Great Lakes players could participate only one season. From the start Great Lakes played mostly college teams, predominantly from the Big Ten, some of which used naval and Marine Corps trainees and some not. Bainbridge, primarily playing military schedules, won 21 consecutive games over two and a half seasons.

Below is a look at some formidable navy elevens. Only the Naval Academy, Great Lakes, Jacksonville, and San Diego still operate today.

## Camp Peary (Williamsburg, Va.) Naval Training and Distribution Center Pirates

The 1944 eleven coached by Lieutenant Commander Norman P. "Red" Strader (St. Mary's), finished fourth in the Williamson service poll after twice battling Bainbridge Navy.

| 1944 Camp Peary (5–2–0) | | 1945 Camp Peary (4–4–0) | |
| --- | --- | --- | --- |
| Washington Redskins | 33–17* | Amphib Trng Base | 6–0 |
| Cherry Point MCAS | 20–0 | Camp Lee | 0–13 |
| Camp Lee | 38–0 | Fort Monroe | 40–0 |
| Bainbridge NTS | 0–7 | Fort Bragg | 12–0 |
| Camp Lee | 41–0 | Cherry Point MCAS | 27–0 |
| North Carolina PF | 19–7 | Camp Lee | 6–7 |
| Bainbridge NTS | 13–21 | Pers Dist Comd | 14–21 |
| *Scrimmage | | Cherry Point MCAS | 0–7 |

## Del Monte Pre-Flight (Monterey, Calif.) Navyators

Del Monte played only one season and closed 11 months after opening. Coach Lieutenant Bill Kern (All-America Pittsburgh, coach Carnegie Tech and West Virginia) wanted "to play his cadet group as much as possible while still getting some mileage from the highly touted officer corps," particularly his All-America "dream backfield" of Leonard "Len" Eshmont (5'11"/180, Fordham, New York Giants), Parker Hall (Mississippi, Cleveland Rams), Jim McDonald (All-America Ohio State, Detroit Lions), and Paul Christman (Missouri).[4] Tackle Ray Bray (225, Western Michigan, Chicago Bears) received a direct commission as an ensign and instructed at Del Monte and Chapel Hill, Glenview, Ill., and Jacksonville, Fla. He recalled that Del Monte was "like living in a resort. The place was beautiful — everyone loved it…. The time went by so fast and we were really sorry to leave."[5]

Featuring a "devastating" single-wing with unbalanced line, Kern raised eyebrows with delayed bucks, double reverses, flankers and pass-laterals. The line and backfield averaged 210 and 195 pounds respectively.[6] They ranked No. 8 in the final AP poll and fourth among military elevens.

| 1943 Del Monte PF (7–1–0, 252–65) | |
| --- | --- |
| Alameda CG | 34–7 |
| St Mary's College | 33–7 |
| Pleasanton Navy | 34–6 |
| College of Pacific | 7–16 |
| San Francisco U | 34–0 |
| UCLA | 26–7 |
| St Mary's PF | 37–14* |
| California | 47–8 |
| *at Kezar Stadium, San Francisco; 49,000 | |

## Fleet City Naval Receiving Station, aka Pleasanton and Shoemaker Field (Shoemaker, Calif.) Bluejackets

Fleet City was the nickname for the world's largest receiving station, located 40 miles east of San Francisco in the Amador Valley. Together with a Seabee (naval construction battalion) replacement depot, hospital, disciplinary barracks, and personnel separation center, it was part of the U.S. Naval Training and Distribution Center. An observer wrote that the Bluejackets "inhabit a thriving, modern city at Shoemaker, replete with theatres, bowling alleys, ship's service stores and refreshment counters."[7]

Lieutenant Jack Malevich coached the 1944 squad which finished ranked No. 9 among service teams and No. 18 overall. Linemen Joe Stydahar (West Virginia, Chicago Bears) and Bob Suffridge led the way.

The 1945 Fleet City T-formation eleven, under Lieutenant Commander William J. Reinhart (coach Oregon), "was regarded by a majority of the servicemen as the best football team anywhere," according to the NCAA.[8] The schedule included three minor-league professional/semi-pro teams. Major news services did not rank military teams that season, but the Williamson poll named them No. 1. Its two battles with the El Toro Marine Corps Air Station were considered classics. The Bluejackets entertained a quarter of a million "football-loving servicemen." Thousands of men "are now being channeled through the separation center back to civilian life," a game program read.[9] Its meeting with the Fourth Air Force before 50,000 in San Francisco's Kezar Stadium for the Pacific Coast championship generated thousands for the War Wounded Fund.

Stars included HB Claude "Buddy" Young (5'5"/160, All-America Illinois), No. 10 in the Associated Press voting for male athlete of year; HB Steve Juzwik (5'8"/195, Notre Dame), named Washington Touchdown Club 1945 outstanding service player in the country; HB Edgar Jones (5'10"/195, Pittsburgh); FB Harry Hopp (6'0"/210, Nebraska, Bainbridge); and QB Charles O'Rourke (5'11"/185, Boston College).

*Opposite:* Super-powerful 1945 Fleet City (Calif.) may have been the most potent single-season wartime eleven (11–0–1), with two wins over mighty El Toro (Calif.) Marine Corps Air Station. Its biggest star was fleet-footed back Buddy Young (Illinois), shown with backs Curtis Sandig and Steve Juzwik, and linemen Al Forte, Frank Kinard, and Quentin Klenk (game program, Fleet City vs. Fourth Air Force, November 25, 1945).

| 1943 FLEET CITY (1-4-1) | |
|---|---|
| San Francisco U | 13-0 |
| St Mary's PF | 0-43 |
| Del Monte PF | 7-34 |
| Modesto JC | 6-20 |
| Alameda CG | 6-46 |
| Modesto JC | 6-8 |

| 1944 FLEET CITY (6-4-1) | |
|---|---|
| College of Pacific | 7-6 |
| El Toro MCAS | 7-13 |
| Alameda CG | 7-7 |
| St Mary's PF | 12-0 |
| 4th AF | 0-39 |
| San Francisco CG | 27-6 |
| California | 19-2 |
| CG Pilots | 27-6 |
| El Toro MCAS | 0-14 |
| St Mary's College | 26-0 |
| Nevada | 19-2 |
| St Mary's PF | 0-3 |

| 1945 FLEET CITY (11-0-1) | |
|---|---|
| San Joaquin Cowboys | 77-0 |
| 2nd AF | 7-0 |
| El Toro MCAS | 21-7 |
| Camp Beale | 88-0 |
| Hollywood Rangers | 16-0 |
| Fort Warren | 21-9 |
| St Mary's PF | 13-13 |
| Los Angeles Broncos | 41-6 |
| San Jose St | 26-0 |
| 4th AF | 20-10 |
| Pearl Harbor All-Stars | 23-7 |
| El Toro MCAS | 48-25 |

## Fort Pierce (Fla.) Naval Amphibious Training Base Amphibs

Located near Port St. Lucie and Vero Beach, the 1944 Fort Pierce team ranked No. 18 in the AP poll and No. 9 in the Williamson service poll. Stars included B Bill Daley (All-America Minnesota, Michigan). The 1944-45 coach was Ensign Hampton Pool (Stanford), who also played end. In 1945 QB Johnny Lujack (Notre Dame) joined the team.

| 1944 Fort Pierce (9–0–0, 385–22) | | 1945 Fort Pierce (3–9–0) | |
|---|---|---|---|
| Miami NTC | 40–7 | Air Trng Cmd | 10–13 |
| Chatham Field | 74–0 | 1st AF | 7–19 |
| Miami | 38–0 | Air Trng Cmd | 7–19 |
| Mayport NS | 53–0 | Jacksonville NAS | 6–13 |
| Miami NTC | 70–0 | 3rd AF | 26–12 |
| Mayport NS | 48–2 | Jacksonville NAS | 7–35 |
| Jacksonville NAS | 21–0 | Pers Dist Ctr | 7–16 |
| 3rd AF | 7–6 | Fort Benning | 14–13 |
| Keesler Field | 34–7 | Amph Trng Base | 7–27 |
| | | Keesler Field | 21–7 |
| | | Fort Benning | 6–40 |
| | | Amphib Trng Base | 0–20 |

## Georgia Pre-Flight (University of Georgia, Athens) Skycrackers

The 1942 Georgia Pre-Flight eleven finished at No. 4 nationally under two coaches named "Bear": head coach Lieutenant Raymond "Bear" Wolf (coach North Carolina), assisted by Paul "Bear" Bryant (Alabama, coach Alabama, Vanderbilt). Back Frank Filchock (5'10½"/190, Indiana, Redskins) headed the 48-man, half-officer roster. Georgia and other pre-flight squads often curtailed or canceled practices because of intense study periods or military duties. Lack of game preparation for these talented, experienced players tended to help balance the youth and inexperience of their opponents.

Starting in 1943 the navy disallowed commissioned officers and former professional from playing. New classes of cadets came and went every two weeks. Coach Lieutenant Rex Enright (Notre Dame, coach South Carolina) turned to FB Pat Harder (200, Wisconsin) and HB Steve Filipowicz (195, Fordham).

Adhering to navy policy of changing coaches annually, Lieutenant Raymond W. "Ducky" Pond (Yale) came aboard for 1944 and found Harder the only returning regular. The 1945 schedule was canceled.

### 1942 Georgia PF (7–1–1)

| | |
|---|---|
| Pennsylvania | 14–6 |
| North Carolina PF | 14–14 |
| Duke | 26–12 |
| Pensacola NAS | 26–0 |
| Louisiana St U | 0–34 |
| Jacksonville NAS | 20–6 |
| Auburn | 41–14 |
| Tulane | 7–0 |
| Alabama | 35–19 |

### 1943 Georgia PF (5–1–0)

| | |
|---|---|
| Daniel Field | 19–13 |
| Georgia Tech | 7–35* |
| Newberry | 53–0† |
| North Carolina PF | 20–7 |
| Tulane | 14–13 |
| Clemson | 32–6 |

*12,000 at Atlanta
†10,000 at Athens

### 1944 Georgia PF (4–5–0)

| | |
|---|---|
| South Carolina | 20–14 |
| Cherry Point MCAS | 38–0 |
| 3rd AF | 7–19 |
| North Carolina PF | 0–3 |
| Georgia Tech | 7–13 |
| 3rd AF | 12–34 |
| North Carolina PF | 19–33 |
| Daniel Field | 30–0 |
| Daniel Field | 53–12 |

## Great Lakes (Ill.) Naval Training Station/Center Bluejackets

Principally a boot camp for initial training, Great Lakes is located north of Chicago on Lake Michigan. Right after Pearl Harbor, a mammoth, two-year, $120-million station expansion began during an extremely frigid winter, utilizing 26 architectural firms, 14 general contractors, and 13,000 workmen. By September 1942, acreage swelled from 172 to nearly 1,600 and trainee numbers from 6,000 in January to 68,000 in 17 separate training camps. By mid-1943, the station employed more than 700 instructors.

Lieutenant Commander Paul D. "Tony" Hinkle (Chicago, coach Butler), who coached the Bluejackets during 1942-43, instituted a platoon system of "commandos" as shock troops, a unit using a basic single-double wing and the Notre Dame box, and another employing the straight T. Led by FB Steve Belichick (Western Reserve, Detroit Lions), HB Bruce Smith (6'0"/185,

Heisman Trophy 1941, All-America Minnesota), and B Bob Sweiger (Minnesota), the sailors captured the Associated Press top service ranking and their third straight military championship. Two players, B Bill deCorrevont (Northwestern) and E Howard "Red" Hickey (Arkansas), moved to Bainbridge for 1943.

"The Lakes" powerhouse posted seven shutouts (six consecutive), allowed only 91 first downs, and finished eleventh among all college-military elevens. They played all games on the road to stimulate recruiting, but because of transportation restrictions and rationing comparatively few watched. The Michigan game at Ann Arbor drew 17,000. No other wartime player matched or exceeded Smith's numerous honors. These included both the Grantland Rice (*Collier's*) and United Press All-Service teams, and the Lieutenant Robert B. Smith Trophy of the Washington (D.C.) Touchdown Club as Best Service Player. Smith ranked seventh nationally with 1,335 total yards on 5.9 yards per carry.

Hinkle's 1943 repeat armed-forces champion Bluejackets fielded as solid a backfield as any wartime squad: QB's Steve Lach (6'1"/200, All-America Duke, Chicago Cardinals) and Paul Anderson (5'11"/200, Western Reserve), who also played halfback, and backs Dewey Proctor (5'11"/190, Furman, and later Bainbridge), Emil Sitko (5'8"/175, Notre Dame), Steve Juzwik (Notre Dame, Washington Redskins), and Ray Jones (Texas). The team suffered numerous injuries and player shortages. Anderson, the only back to start all games, played all 60 minutes in four. Proceeds from

**All-American at Great Lakes Again Shines**

Great Lakes (Ill.) Naval Training Center quarterback Steve Lach, Duke All-America and former Chicago Cardinal, threw the last-minute touchdown pass to Paul Anderson to defeat Notre Dame, 19–14, in 1943 in the war's greatest military game. Lach later teamed with Charlie Justice on a Hawaii navy all-star squad (*The Football News*, October 16, 1943).

the welfare and recreation fund covered costs for the center's athletic program, at no expense to the government, said to be the world's largest. Switching from recruiting to entertainment, the eight home games attracted some 170,000 naval personnel. Only about one-quarter of assigned personnel could attend each game. In the finale, Great Lakes downed unbeaten Notre Dame on a last-minute Lach-to-Anderson touchdown pass in certainly its greatest wartime victory and probably military football's finest game of all-time.

By 1944, the Midwest accounted for approximately 35 percent of the navy's personnel. Nearly all finished boot camp at Great Lakes, the world's largest naval training base. The 40-man roster contained players from 27 colleges and averaged 20.4 years of age, the youngest among known military elevens. One-third were undergoing boot camp, the rest were recent graduates. Officers and professionals could not compete. Six WAVE cheerleaders and the Center band excited home crowds of 25,000.

Future National Football League Hall of Fame coach Lieutenant (junior grade) Paul E. Brown (Ohio State, Miami (Oh.), coach Ohio State) assumed coaching duties in 1944, relieving Hinkle, who departed for Southwest Pacific duty. Brown divided his 38-man squad, representing 20 colleges, into three working combinations. Six had only high school experience. Because the Center played predominantly colleges, the commanding officer banned ex-pros. Three rookie backs, part of the Center's youngest-ever backfield, shined in the shutout of Northwestern.

The unexpected Japanese surrender triggered immediate demobilization of key players.

Lieutenant (junior grade) Paul E. Brown, USNR, athletic officer and head coach at Great Lakes (Ill.) Naval Training Center, 1944–45 (15–6–2). Brown, former Ohio State coach, became a National Football League legend with the Cleveland Browns and resides in the NFL Hall of Fame (provided by John Gunn).

6. "All Hail to the Navy": ... Pre-Flights, and Midshipmen

Brown had only two practice weeks prior to the 1945 opener against Michigan, a "man-sized task." Michigan was coached by Fritz Crisler, who invented the two-platoon system that season. Future NFL Hall of Fame member FB Marion Motley (6'0"/210, South Carolina State, Nevada), one of the few visible blacks playing military football, sparkled. Fullback Jim Mello (Notre Dame) led scorers with 67 points. Starless and with three losses, the Bluejacket high schoolers and former reserves stunned football (the AP sports surprise of the year) by thrashing Notre Dame a week before Pearl Harbor Day. By then recruits being trained decreased from 60,000 to 10,000. With such obvious signs, the glory days of military football faded quickly.

1942 GREAT LAKES NTS (8–3–1)

| | |
|---|---|
| Michigan | 0–9 |
| Iowa | 25–0 |
| Pittsburgh | 7–6 |
| Wisconsin | 7–13 |
| Michigan St | 0–14 |
| Missouri | 17–0 |
| Purdue | 42–0 |
| Camp Grant | 33–0 |
| Marquette | 24–0 |
| Illinois | 6–0 |
| Northwestern | 48–0 |
| Notre Dame | 13–13 |

1943 GREAT LAKES NTC (10–2–0)

| | |
|---|---|
| Fort Riley | 20–19 |
| Purdue | 13–23 |
| Iowa | 21–7 |
| Pittsburgh | 40–0 |
| Ohio St | 13–6 |
| Northwestern | 0–13* |
| Marquette | 41–7 |
| Western Michigan | 32–6 |
| Camp Grant | 12–0 |
| Indiana | 21–7 |
| Marquette | 25–6 |
| Notre Dame | 19–14 |

*at Evanston, Ill.; 36,000

1944 GREAT LAKES NTC (9–2–1)

| | |
|---|---|
| Fort Sheridan | 62–0 |
| Purdue | 27–18 |
| Illinois | 26–26 |
| Northwestern | 25–0 |
| Western Michigan | 38–0 |
| Ohio St | 6–26* |
| Wisconsin | 40–12 |
| Marquette | 45–7 |
| 3rd AF | 12–10 |
| Marquette | 32–0 |
| Fort Warren | 28–7 |
| Notre Dame | 7–29 |

*at Columbus; 73,477

1945 GREAT LAKES NTC (6–4–1)

| | |
|---|---|
| Michigan | 2–27 |
| Wisconsin | 0–0 |
| Purdue | 6–20 |
| Fort Benning | 12–21 |
| Marquette | 37–27 |
| Western Michigan | 39–0 |
| Illinois | 12–6 |
| Michigan St | 27–7 |
| Fort Warren | 47–14 |
| Notre Dame | 39–7 |
| College All-Stars | 0–35 |

## Iowa Pre-Flight (University of Iowa, Iowa City) Seahawks

The Seahawks, originally known as Iowa Navy, in 1942 played all but one game against major Midwest colleges. Coach Lieutenant Colonel Bernie Bierman, USMC, who had led Minnesota to five Big Ten championships, was called to active duty in 1941 to help organize naval aviation physical training. Almost all of his 45 players were from Big Ten schools, such as QB Forest Evashevski (Michigan), a future University of Iowa coach. Starting strong, the team collapsed indifferently and dropped its last three games. Losing cadets and stressful regular duties got the blame. All wartime home games were in Iowa Stadium.

The Seahawks started with great personnel, including end Mal Kutner (All-America Texas), Jim Langhurst (Ohio State), and Dick Fisher, a half dozen former Minnesota stars, and other nationally known players. Notre Dame stopped the Seahawks' four-game streak, from which they never fully recovered after losing many early-season personnel.

The 1943 club, coached by Lieutenant Don Faurot (coach Missouri), returned only one player, but still the Seahawks gained national prominence and finished No. 4 in the AP poll and No. 1 among service teams. Its 324.4 yards rushing per game set a new intercollegiate record, and its 3,244 total yards surpassed national champion Notre Dame by 107. Halfback Richard Todd (Texas A&M, Redskins) received the Robert L. Smith Memorial Trophy as the outstanding service player and gained first-team All-Service honors. Other pros included center Vince Banonis (All-America Detroit University, Cardinals) and Perry Schwartz (California, Brooklyn Dodgers).

Fifty-seven of the more than

Iowa Pre-Flight halfback Richard "Dick" Todd (Texas A&M, Washington Redskins) received the Washington (D.C.) Touchdown Club's 1943 trophy as the best military player and all-service first team honors in leading the Seahawks to a 9-1-0 record against primarily Midwestern college elevens (*Illustrated Football Annual 1944*).

100 prospects who reported for summer drills in 1944 made the squad. Under coach Jack Meagher (coach Auburn), this team "arguably could have been the strongest of the three." Unlike most military elevens, Iowa Pre-Flight had an unusual continuity in material.[10] Leading football analyst Dr. L. H. Baker ranked it third overall and second among service teams. The Seahawks placed their center on the AP All-Service first teams all three years: George Svendsen (All-America Minnesota, Green Bay Packers) in 1942, Vince Banonis in 1943, and George Strohmeyer (Texas A&M) in 1944.

| 1942 Iowa PF (6–4–0) | | 1943 Iowa PF (9–1–0) | |
|---|---|---|---|
| Kansas | 61–0 | Illinois | 32–18 |
| Northwestern | 20–12 | Ohio St | 28–13* |
| Minnesota | 7–6 | Iowa St | 33–13 |
| Michigan | 26–14 | Iowa | 25–0 |
| Notre Dame | 0–28 | Missouri | 21–6 |
| Indiana | 26–6 | Fort Riley | 19–2 |
| Fort Knox | 13–7 | Marquette | 46–19 |
| Nebraska | 0–46 | Camp Grant | 28–13 |
| Ohio St | 12–41 | Notre Dame | 13–14 |
| Missouri | 0–7 | Minnesota | 32–0 |
| | | *23,496 | |

Bunker Hill (Ind.) Naval Training Station Blockbuster defenders surround Iowa Pre-Flight back Art Guepe (Marquette), one of the few bright spots in its 33–7 loss in 1944 to the Seahawks (Street & Smith's *Football Pictorial Yearbook 1945*).

1944 Iowa PF (10-1-0, 313-96)

| | |
|---|---|
| Michigan | 7-12 |
| Minnesota | 19-13 |
| Olathe Navy | 45-12 |
| 2nd AF | 12-0 |
| Purdue | 13-6 |
| Fort Warren | 30-0 |
| Marquette | 26-0 |
| Tulsa | 47-27 |
| Bunker Hill Navy | 33-7 |
| Missouri | 51-7 |
| Iowa | 30-6 |

## Jacksonville (Fla.) Naval Air Station/Naval Air Technical Training Center Flyers/Air Raiders

The Jacksonville (Fla.) Naval Air Station facility opened in February 1941 and trained skilled machinists mates, metalsmiths, ordnancemen and radiomen. The NAATC was a separate command subordinate to the NAS commandant. The team, originally known as Jacksonville Navy, played numerous colleges in the first three seasons and ranked sixth among service teams in 1942 under coach Lieutenant Hobbs Adams (coach Kansas State). Triple-threat back George McAfee (6'0"/180, All-America Duke, Chicago Bears), the kingpin and inspirational leader, threw a crucial touchdown pass in defeating his alma mater.

The 1943 linemen averaged 201 pounds, the backs 184, husky for that era. By the season's finale, the Raiders, coached by Marine Captain Fred F. Frink (Illinois), found themselves. "No locker room orations or touches of sentiment" for the "swan song" were necessary to fire up the Center for their game against Camp

Back Bobby Tom "Bob" Jenkins (Alabama), a "human dynamo," "190 lbs. of fluid force," with "marlinspike legs" and "virtually unstoppable," spearheaded Navy's (6-3-0) 1944 squad (Street & Smith's *Football Pictorial Yearbook 1944*).

Lejeune. "All the dope portends a super-duper contest," it was said.[11] But Jacksonville lost. Future College Hall of Famer Lieutenant Jim Tatum (North Carolina) coached the 1945 eleven.

1942 JACKSONVILLE NAS (9–3–0)

| | |
|---|---|
| Florida | 20–7 |
| Georgia | 0–14 |
| Miami | 14–0 |
| Spence Field | 33–0 |
| Daniel Field | 55–0 |
| Tampa | 26–0 |
| Georgia PF | 6–20 |
| Rollins | 6–13 |
| Clemson | 24–6 |
| Pensacola NAS | 16–10 |
| Duke | 13–0 |
| Spence Field | 19–6 |

1943 JACKSONVILLE NAS (3–4–0)

| | |
|---|---|
| Fort Benning | 13–7 |
| Miami | 0–6 |
| North Carolina | 0–23 |
| Camp Lejeune | 7–20 |
| Miami | 20–0 |
| Daniel Field | 44–0 |
| Camp Lejeune | 6–13 |

1944 JACKSONVILLE NATTC (4–3–0)

| | |
|---|---|
| Florida | 20–27 |
| Miami NTC | 39–13 |
| North Carolina PF | 13–14 |
| Fort Benning 3rd Inf | 35–13 |
| Fort Benning 4th Inf | 26–19 |
| Cherry Point MCAS | 33–0 |
| Fort Pierce | 0–21 |

1945 JACKSONVILLE NATTC (9–2–1)

| | |
|---|---|
| Miami NTC | 35–6 |
| Cherry Point MCAS | 26–0 |
| Corpus Christi NAS | 35–7 |
| Fort Pierce | 13–6 |
| Miami NTC | 61–0 |
| Fort Pierce | 35–7 |
| Fort Benning | 33–7 |
| Corpus Christi NAS | 13–14 |
| Pensacola NAS | 48–0 |
| Fort Benning | 7–14 |
| Pensacola NAS | 48–0 |
| Camp Johnson | 0–0 |

## Navy — a.k.a. the Naval Academy or Annapolis (Annapolis, Md.) Midshipmen

Captain Johnny Whelchel, the Naval Academy's coach in 1942-43, had a way with words. He described football as "a war without guns, and who in hell wants to lose a war?" and his star, "will-'o-the-wisp" 150-pound HB Hal

Hamberg, as a "PT boat amid a squadron of dreadnaughts." Late in the war Whelchel commanded the heavy cruiser USS *San Francisco* (CA-38) in the Pacific.

The 1944 eleven, mentored by Commander Oscar Hagberg, who had just returned from Pacific submarine command, won the Eastern championship Lambert Trophy. Several scribes mailed their votes before the Army-Navy game kickoff "with the wisdom-streaked comment" that their choice would be the winner.[12] The three-year eligibility expired for four of Hagberg's best players, including Hamberg and All-America center Jack Martin, but all could practice. Superb talent abounded nonetheless. Colorful journalism followed back Bobby Tom "Bob" Jenkins (Alabama), a "human dynamo," "190 lbs. of fluid force," "virtually unstoppable" with "marlinspike legs," and "the piston-legged personification of power." Receiver Bill Barron was called a "speedy stepper," their "breakaway boy [who] buzzes hither and yon."[13]

Academy officials in 1944 reversed the previous eligibility rule because of the NCAA's "'Four Year' wartime rule" and allowed four players another season. The Middies disappointed fans and never reached their full potential. They lost to Georgia Tech, "a team which they would have beaten nine times out of ten," and then came the Army debacle when they were pregame favorites. A leading football magazine wrote that the 1943 players believed in the preseason "drumbeating that ushered them into the hall of champions" before playing a down.[14] Another periodical called them "the riddle of 1944."[15]

Again in 1945 Navy possessed a galaxy of talent equal to or perhaps greater than Army's, to the delight of sportswriters. They fielded the best backs in the country. To accommodate the talent, Hagberg switched to the T formation. His problem became who to play and for how long. "The joint is jumpin'," as in the popular swing song, "with swivel-hipped halfbacks with buggywhip arms." Jenkins, now the "Talladega Thunderbolt," shredded "rivals asunder with berserk plunges." Returnee Clyde "Smackover" Scott was raring to go at his new wingback position. Other big names galore: Bobby Hoernschemeyer (Indiana), Bob Kelly (Notre Dame), Tony Minisi (Pennsylvania), Dub Jones (Tulane), and Dick Duden.[16] But Navy never jelled and tailed off at season's end with a controversial and sluggish 6–6 tie with Notre Dame and a 32–13 shellacking by the Cadets.

---

*Opposite:* Superback Len Eshmont (Fordham, New York Giants) played and starred on more teams during World War II than any known player: North Carolina Pre-Flight (1942), Del Monte (Calif.) Pre-Flight (1943), Norman (Okla.) Naval Air Station (1944), and St. Mary's (Calif.) Pre-Flight (1945) (provided by John Gunn).

1942 NAVY (5–4–0)

| | |
|---|---|
| William & Mary | 0–3 |
| Virginia | 35–0 |
| Princeton | 0–10 |
| Yale | 13–6 |
| Georgia Tech | 0–21 |
| Notre Dame | 0–9 |
| Pennsylvania | 7–0 |
| Columbia | 13–9 |
| Army | 14–0 |

1943 NAVY (8–1–0)

| | |
|---|---|
| North Carolina PF | 31–0 |
| Cornell | 46–7 |
| Duke | 14–13 |
| Penn State | 14–6 |
| Georgia Tech | 28–14 |
| Notre Dame | 6–33 |
| Pennsylvania | 24–7 |
| Columbia | 61–0 |
| Army | 13–0 |

1944 NAVY (6–3–0)

| | |
|---|---|
| North Carolina PF | 14–21 |
| Penn State | 55–14 |
| Duke | 7–0 |
| Georgia Tech | 15–17 |
| Pennsylvania | 26–0 |
| Notre Dame | 32–13 |
| Cornell | 48–0 |
| Purdue | 32–0 |
| Army | 7–23 |

1945 NAVY (7–1–1)

| | |
|---|---|
| Villanova | 49–0 |
| Duke | 21–0 |
| Penn St | 28–0 |
| Georgia Tech | 20–6 |
| Pennsylvania | 14–7 |
| Michigan | 33–7 |
| Wisconsin | 36–7 |
| Notre Dame | 6–6 |
| Army | 13–32 |

## Norman (Okla.) Naval Air Station Zoomers

The 1944 team, coached by Lieutenant Commander John Gregg, ranked fifth among service elevens. The 1945 season was canceled. Key players: B Emil Sitko (Notre Dame, Great Lakes 1943, St. Mary's Pre-Flight 1945) in 1944; and HB Leonard "Len" Eshmont (Fordham, New York Giants). The Zoomers downed Big Six champion Oklahoma and handed Sugar-Bowl bound Oklahoma A&M its only loss. Eshmont played for more military teams than any known player: North Carolina Pre-Flight in 1942, Del Monte Pre-Flight in 1943, Norman Naval Air Station in 1944, and St. Mary's Pre-Flight in 1945.

1943 NORMAN (4–3–0)

| | |
|---|---|
| Oklahoma | 6–22 |
| 49th Army | 40–0 |
| Fort Riley | 0–33 |
| Oklahoma A&M | 20–0 |
| Oklahoma JV | 19–0 |
| Lubbock AAB | 0–13 |
| Will Rogers AAB | 33–6 |

1944 NORMAN (6–0–0)

| | |
|---|---|
| Oklahoma | 28–14 |
| Arkansas | 27–7 |
| Amarillo Field | 19–13 |
| 2nd AF | 13–6 |
| Oklahoma A&M | 15–0 |
| Lubbock AAB | 42–0 |

## North Carolina Pre-Flight (University of North Carolina, Chapel Hill) Cloudbusters

In 11 games in 1942 the Cloudbusters, coached by Lieutenant Commander James H. "Sleepy Jim" Crowley (one of the Notre Dame Four Horsemen, coach Fordham), allowed only 142.8 yards per game and 842 rushing yards, fifth and eighth nationally. Halfback Len Eshmont carried the load. Lieutenant Frank Kimbrough (coach Baylor) succeeded Crowley in 1943, and Lieutenant Commander Glenn Killinger (Penn State) replaced him the next season, assisted by Lieutenant Commander Bear Bryant.

The 1944 roster featured star quarterback Otto Graham (6'0"/190, All-America Northwestern). After beginning with three wins, including successively over Navy, 21–14, and Duke, 13–6, they faded. Stan Koslowski's (Holy Cross) runs split the Midshipmen defense and led the momentous upset. Graham keyed the game winner, lateraling to HB Frank Aschenbrenner (5'10"/180, Marquette) after a 50-yard scamper to complete the 74-yard touchdown.

Both the varsity and Pre-Flight elevens were known as "Carolina," sometimes causing confusion. The varsity played only college teams except two against the Cherry Point Marine Corps Air Station.

1942 NORTH CAROLINA PF (8–2–1)

| | |
|---|---|
| Catawba | 13–2 |
| Harvard | 13–0 |
| Georgia PF | 14–14 |
| N.C. State | 19–7 |
| Boston College | 6–7 |
| Temple | 34–0 |
| Syracuse | 9–0 |
| Georgetown | 23–7 |
| Manhattan | 17–0 |
| William & Mary | 14–0 |
| Fordham | 0–6 |

1943 NORTH CAROLINA PF (2–4–1)

| | |
|---|---|
| Navy | 0–31 |
| Duke | 0–41 |
| Camp Davis | 23–18 |
| Georgia PF | 7–20 |
| Wake Forest | 12–20 |
| Camp Lejeune | 14–14 |
| N.C. State | 21–7 |

North Carolina Pre-Flight at Chapel Hill, one of five naval aviator officer candidate wartime schools. Candidates took preliminary training there to qualify for advancement to flight training at Pensacola, Fla. (game program, Camp Lejeune vs. North Carolina Pre-Flight, November 13, 1943).

1944 NORTH CAROLINA PF (6–2–1)
| | |
|---|---|
| Cherry Point MCAS | 27–14 |
| Navy | 21–14 |
| Duke | 13–6 |
| Virginia | 13–13 |
| Georgia PF | 3–0 |
| Jacksonville NAS | 14–13 |
| Bainbridge NTS | 20–49* |
| Georgia PF | 33–18 |
| Camp Peary | 7–19 |

*at Chapel Hill; 22,000

## St. Mary's Pre-Flight (St. Mary's College, Moraga, Calif.) Air Devils

The Air Devils played primarily college opponents, more than the other pre-flight teams. Their 1942 squad, mentored by Lieutenant Commander Tex Oliver (coach Oregon), all had college experience, mostly from western schools. The team leader, QB Ensign Frankie Albert (5'10"/170, All-America Stanford), "scintillated every time Pre-Flight shifted to the T formation." As with all pre-flight teams throughout the war, frequent personnel movements, causing availability uncertainties, deterred St. Mary's, which bogged down in mid-season, keeping the team from achieving its potential after strong early-season expectations.[17]

Former Minnesota All-America and Heisman Trophy recipient HB Bruce Smith transferred from Great Lakes for 1943 and joined E Ed Manske (All-America Northwestern, Chicago Bears), G Joe Rentz (Notre Dame), and B Vic Bottari, who led California over Alabama in the 1938 Rose Bowl.

Lieutenant Jules Sikes (Texas A&M, coach Georgia) coached the 1944 season, assisted by Lieutenant George Svendsen, a carrier pilot who participated in strikes on Tarawa, Truk, Wake, Makin, Saipan, Tinian, Guam, the Palaus, and Yap.

Lieutenant Commander George "Potsy" Clark (Illinois, coach Illinois, Kansas, Minnesota, Butler, Brooklyn Dodgers, Detroit Lions) coached in 1945. He enjoyed a star backfield of Jim McDonald, Parker Hall, Emil Sitko (his third navy team), and Len Eshmont (his fourth). Clark's otherwise inexperienced team developed a strong line but seriously lacked reserves. Albert returned from carrier duty to help for a few games. For the final game, the pros did not play, including linemen Bob Titchenal (San Jose State, Redskins), John Kuzman (Fordham, Chicago Cardinals), Ray Riddick (Fordham, Packers), and John Woudenberg (Denver, Pittsburgh Steelers).

1942 ST. MARY'S PF (6-3-1)
| | |
|---|---|
| College of Pacific | 38-9 |
| Oregon | 10-9 |
| UCLA | 18-7 |
| Alameda CG | 40-0 |
| Santa Ana AB | 59-0 |
| Washington | 0-0 |
| Santa Clara | 13-6 |
| Stanford | 13-28 |
| California | 6-12 |
| USC | 13-21 |

1943 ST. MARY'S PF (4-4-1)
| | |
|---|---|
| Alameda CG | 13-13 |
| College of Pacific | 7-13 |
| USC | 0-13 |
| California | 39-0 |
| 4th AF | 6-7 |
| San Francisco U | 41-0 |
| Del Monte PF | 14-37 |
| Modesto JC | 19-6 |
| Pleasanton Navy | 48-0 |

1944 ST. MARY'S PF (4-4-0)
| | |
|---|---|
| College of Pacific | 6-14 |
| Fleet City | 0-12 |
| USC | 0-6 |
| UCLA | 21-12 |
| 4th AF | 0-7 |
| Alameda CG | 32-13 |
| Fleet City | 3-0 |
| California | 33-6 |

1945 ST. MARY'S PF (2-4-1)
| | |
|---|---|
| College of Pacific | 69-0 |
| USC | 14-26 |
| 4th AF | 7-20 |
| UCLA | 13-6 |
| Fleet City | 13-13 |
| El Toro MCAS | 0-7 |
| California | 0-6 |

Besides allowing participation on college varsity and V-5 preflight squads, as part of its demanding physical conditioning regimen the navy encouraged other V-5 and V-12 officer candidates to play intramural football. The army allowed only intramural participation for its college officer candidates. Here intramural players at St. Mary's (Calif.) Pre-Flight take the field (*National Collegiate Athletic Association Football Guide 1943*).

## Sampson (N.Y.) Naval Training Station Sailors/ Bluejackets

Primarily a recruit training facility located on the eastern shores of Seneca Lake, Sampson also provided advanced training. Named for a Spanish-American War hero, it cost $50 million to build in 1942, covered 2,500 acres, and closed in 1946. The sailors played four NFL teams and three semi-pro squads.

The 1943 team, coached by legendary Jim Crowley, numbered 60 players. Only 11 players in 1944 had college experience, others only high school or sandlot. The Cornell game program noted: "The burley [sic], big-named professional and collegiate veterans who studded the starry 1943 lineup have scattered to the four winds and the seven seas." Sampson's "sporting sons ... are not pampered and shielded. They are first, last and always navy men, available on a moment's notice for action with our far-flung fleets; and that's why this year's football team is comprised of fresh, young, new faces."[18]

| 1943 SAMPSON NTS (8–3–0) | | 1944 SAMPSON NTS (2–7–0) | |
|---|---|---|---|
| Phila. Yel. Jackets | 47–7 | Syracuse | 6–13 |
| Villanova | 17–7 | Boston Yanks | 0–14 |
| Rome AAB | 47–0 | Green Bay Packers | 14–25 |
| Rensselaer Polytechnic | 7–0 | New York Giants | 0–13 |
| Rome AAB | 48–7 | Cleveland Rams | 12–26 |
| York Vikings | 55–0 | Villanova | 6–7 |
| Army | 7–16 | Rochester Shipbldg Oldenbacks | 60–0 |
| Muhlenberg | 28–7 | Cornell | 6–7 |
| New York Giants | 0–19 | Scranton | 39–0 |
| Unknown | 42–19 | | |

## San Diego (Calif.) Navy, a.k.a. U.S. Naval Training Center Bluejackets

San Diego Navy gained national recognition in 1943 as the first team to defeat Southern California's Rose Bowl team after the Trojans blanked their first six opponents. The score was 10–7. Coached by John J. "Bo" Molenda (Michigan, Giants, Packers, New York Yankees), the Bluejackets stymied every club except for the Fourth Air Force who defeated them in two close games. In 1944 Coach Lieutenant Skip Stahley's (Delaware, coach Brown) team played in three of the season's outstanding battles, all one-touchdown losses. They ranked thirteenth among Williamson's 1944 service teams.

1942 SAN DIEGO NTC (6–1–0)
 4th AF       9–6
 Loyola Fr-JV     20–0
 Stanford Fr      20–13
 California Fr     20–0
 San Diego St Fr-JV   21–13
 College of Pacific    14–0
 4th AF       0–26

1943 SAN DIEGO NTC (7–2–0)
 Redlands      20–0
 Fort Ord       59–0
 Pomona Ord Base   48–2
 4th AF        0–7
 Compton College    35–0
 UCLA        28–0
 USC        10–7
 San Pedro All-Stars   53–7
 4th AF        2–13

1944 SAN DIEGO NTC (4–3–1)
 1005th Army Eng   65–0
 Compton College   85–0
 UCLA       14–12
 El Toro MCAS    0–6
 Fort MacArthur    69–0
 Amphib Trng Base   0–0
 USC        21–28
 4th AF       0–7

1945 SAN DIEGO NTC (4–2–0)
 UCLA         14–20
 USC          33–6
 Compton College    61–0
 El Toro MCAS     0–20
 Santa Barbara Marines   34–7
 San Diego Bombers   19–0

CHAPTER 7

# "Every General Liked to Have His Own Base Football Team": Ramblers, Fighting AA's, Flyers, and Cadets

*"TOUCHDOWN—With the U.S. 7th Army in Sicily, July 22 (delayed) (AP)—An American Force commander yesterday sent this message to Lt. Gen. Patton: 'Can we make a touchdown on our own initiative. Rush reply.' Thirty minutes later the answer came back. 'You have the ball. Call a touchdown play.' With this go ahead the U.S. armored column swung north to Palermo, capital of Sicily."*[1]

A general's base team could be wherever he determined he needed one, whether stateside or overseas in a combat zone.

In this case it was nine days after the Allies invaded Sicily to commence the long, arduous Italian Campaign, and the instigator was Seventh Army Commander and West Point graduate Lieutenant General George S. Patton, Jr. On July 19, 1943, to break out of sluggish beachhead alignments, Patton assembled a provisional corps of his 2nd Armored and 3rd Infantry Divisions under Major General Geoffrey Keyes and boldly dispatched them northwestward posthaste toward the capital of Palermo.

Acting as the coach, Keyes and his mobile machine proceeded with lightning speed and advanced 100 miles in four days through rugged hills, heat, and dust. Greeted mostly by surrendering Italian solders, his men took the city on July 22. This was Patton's "TOUCHDOWN," and a turning point in the U.S. Army's ability and reputation as a fighting force in Europe.

Entering World War II, football and the U.S. Army had enjoyed a long, competitive tradition in units, camps, and at the Military Academy. Although not allowing those officer candidate students ordered to college campuses to participate on varsity teams, unlike the navy and Marine Corps, army officials still encouraged football as a combat conditioner. Prewar teams vied for championships by corps geographic areas and branches (e.g., infantry, cavalry). Football defensive formations, from a four- to eight-man line, were spaced to protect opposition thrusts similar to how the infantry organized strong points along the main line of resistance to an enemy's likely approach path. The secondary deployed as a deep mobile reserve behind the line. Tactics of both the football offense and infantry were designed to attack.[2]

Thus the scene was set for masses of soldiers in a hundred or more army camps and air force bases to play collegiate and inter-military schedules, but soldiers could not play for college varsities. But, most important, "every general liked to have his own base football team of such strength that he could outdo other generals," a postwar recap stated.[3] Except for a handful of air force elevens, the luster and contribution of active-duty army wartime football paled in contrast to that of the sister services. Year in, year out, an army camp might produce a stellar record against varying degrees of quality opposition. Then just as quickly its fortunes could reverse, curtailing a season or disestablishing the team.

Three army air force programs vaulted toward the top of military football, and any could easily qualify for the war's most exciting and productive service eleven. They included the sensational Randolph Field Ramblers and the Second and Fourth Air Force. Each scheduled a collegiate-military mix. In 1945 air force teams played only service counterparts, and seven major commands formed a morale-building 84-game league (with a "man-killer" schedule) to entertain the troops.[4] Wounded veterans nearby received transportation to games. Profits went to army charities. The league became the first football organization to travel exclusively by air and span the continent. Personnel with more than two years of air force participation were ineligible. The results:

| | |
|---|---|
| Third Air Force (Drew Field, Fla.) | 4–1–1 |
| Army Air Forces Training Command (Randolph Field, Tex.) | 4–1–1 |
| Fourth Air Force (March Field, Calif.) | 3–2–1 |
| First Air Force (Mitchell Field, N. Y.) | 2–2–3 |
| Air Transport Command (Berry Field, Tenn.) | 2–3–2 |
| Personnel Distribution Command (Louisville, Ky.) | 2–4–0 |
| Second Air Force (Colorado Springs, Colo.) | 1–5–0 |

Perhaps the best army team was the collection of undergraduate athletes at the Military Academy who dominated college football for three successive seasons beginning in 1944. Playing almost entirely a collegiate schedule and only one fellow army eleven, the Cadets captured sports page headlines with a galaxy of big-name All-Americas and ferocious victories.

West Point led the way among army teams.

## Army — a.k.a. the Military Academy or West Point (West Point, N. Y.) Cadets

Undefeated, "Army rolled through the 1944 season like Patton through France,"[5] slaughtering defending champion Notre Dame, whipping No. 2 Navy in the finale, and winning by an average score of 56-4. The team garnered the Williams Trophy (national championship) and Lambert Trophy (best eastern eleven). "Never before had a college football team authored such astonishing credentials," dominance unduplicated since and the prelude to coach Colonel Earl "Red" Blaik's T-formation dynasty. Some college football historians contend it was the finest ever.[6]

The "Touchdown Twins," FB Felix "Doc" Blanchard and HB Glenn Davis, are perhaps history's most famous college backfield teammates. They finished second and third for the Heisman Trophy before each won it, in 1945 and 1946 respectively. Davis (the "California Comet" with "dazzling speed"), received the 1944 Maxwell Trophy, Walter Camp Trophy (outstanding halfback), and Helms Foundation Award (outstanding college player of the year), and finished runner-up behind Heisman Trophy recipient Les Horvath (Ohio State).

Army's backfield of halfback Glenn Davis, shown here, and fullback Felix "Doc" Blanchard, "the Touchdown Twins," ignited the Cadets' powerful 1944-45 runs through military and college football. Behind these brilliant backs, perhaps college football's most illustrious combo ever, Army "rolled through the 1944 season like Patton through France," compiling a 9-0-0 record and outscoring opponents 504 to 35 (Street & Smith's *Football Pictorial Yearbook 1946*).

The army allowed Blaik to recruit active-duty personnel with football experience and offer them three additional years of eligibility. The service needed officers. This arrangement obligated players to complete the four-year education in those three years. Blaik had so much talent that Blanchard—"Mr. Inside"—and Davis—"Mr. Outside"—did not start as plebes (freshmen).

Blanchard (6'0"/208) began football at North Carolina in 1942 before being drafted in 1943 and appointed to West Point in 1944. Davis (5'9"/170) arrived as a true freshman and played on the 1943 team. The pair blended easily into Army's T-formation arsenal of two separate 1944 squads which averaged 20 years of age: the primarily plebe "Lombardo Team," quarterbacked by Tom Lombardo with Blanchard and Davis, and the "Kenna Team," quarterbacked by senior Doug Kenna, which started every game. Heavy academics and military training limited practices to about 75 minutes daily.

Members earning All-America honors included: Blanchard, Davis, guards Joe Stanowicz and Jack Green, ends Barney Poole (6'3"/215) and Ed Rafalko, tackle DeWitt 'Tex' Coulter (6'4"/220), center Bob St. Onge, and backs Kenna and Max Minor.

Fullback Felix "Doc" Blanchard, "Mr. Inside" to halfback Glenn Davis as "Mr. Outside," won the 1945 Heisman Trophy, Maxwell Award, and Washington (D.C.) Touchdown Club award, as Army went 9–0–0 again and ranked No. 1 in the Associated Press poll for the second straight season (Street & Smith's *Football Pictorial Yearbook 1946*).

Dick Walterhouse kicked 47 straight extra points. Blanchard kicked off 45 times.

"Blaik's blitzboys" returned eight regulars in 1945 including "those twin atomizers" who scored 37 times (222 of the team's 412 points). En route to taking the Sullivan Award as the year's outstanding athlete, Blanchard rushed for 19 touchdowns on 718 yards. Blanchard, a sportswriter observed, "blasts up the middle and when the opposition is massed and maimed ... Davis ... takes to the ends like poetry in motion and you-know-what on wheels." Seldom did either play more than half a game. Blanchard also raked in the Heisman, Maxwell, and Touchdown Club (outstanding college player) awards.

Besides Poole and Coulter, the Cadets featured QB Arnold Tucker, HB Tom McWilliams, and linemen E Hank Foldberg, C Herschel "Ug" Fuson, guards Joe Steffy, Jack "Johnny" Green, and Art Gerometta, and T Al Nemetz, part of "Army's seven Sherman tanks." Blaik later said this was his greatest team.[7]

The 1944-45 Army elevens raised to new heights the cliché equating football and combat. "Mighty armies blend power, speed and a healthy dose of opportunism in battering their opponent in a willful process across the battlefield. What teams better fit that description than the West Point gang of late wartime?" asked *The Sporting News* book naming college's all-time best. Army earned consecutive national titles and a combined 18-0-0 record, played no close games, outscored opponents, 916–81, and fielded one of the greatest legendary backfields in college history.[8]

Some observers rated them superior to any service or professional team. "Once asked to select the best game he saw these teams play, Blaik responded, 'That's easy. It was a Wednesday afternoon in October when they scrimmaged each other. Each scored two touchdowns, but the intensity and execution were the best I have ever seen on any gridiron, any place.'"[9]

| 1942 Army (6–3–0) | | 1943 Army (7–2–1) | |
| --- | --- | --- | --- |
| Lafayette | 14–0 | Villanova | 27–0 |
| Cornell | 28–8 | Colgate | 42–0 |
| Columbia | 34–6 | Temple | 51–0 |
| Harvard | 14–0 | Columbia | 52–0 |
| Pennsylvania | 0–19 | Yale | 39–7 |
| Notre Dame | 0–13 | Pennsylvania | 13–13 |
| Virginia Poly (VPI) | 19–7 | Notre Dame | 0–26 |
| Princeton | 40–7 | Sampson NTS | 16–7 |
| Navy | 0–14 | Brown | 59–0 |
| | | Navy | 0–13 |

| 1944 Army (9–0–0, 504–35) | | 1945 Army (9–0–0, 412–46) | |
|---|---|---|---|
| North Carolina | 46–0 | Pers Dist Comd | 32–0 |
| Brown | 59–7 | Wake Forest | 54–0 |
| Pittsburgh | 69–7 | Michigan | 28–7 |
| CG Academy | 76–0 | Torpedo Boat Base | 55–13 |
| Duke | 27–7 | Duke | 48–13 |
| Villanova | 83–0 | Villanova | 54–0 |
| Notre Dame | 59–0* | Notre Dame | 48–0† |
| Pennsylvania | 62–7 | Pennsylvania | 61–0 |
| Navy | 23–7 | Navy | 32–13‡ |

Avg. Score: 56.0–3.9
*at Yankee Stadium; 74,430

Avg. Score: 45.8–5.1
†at Yankee Stadium; 75,000
‡at Philadelphia; 102,000

## Camp Davis (Holly Ridge, N.C.) Fighting AA's/ Blue Brigade

Sports fans in Wilmington, my hometown, followed the Camp Davis eleven which played five games there in 1942. Located up U.S. 17 some 35 miles, the anti-aircraft artillery training base provided jobs and a huge economic boost to a Southeastern North Carolina escaping the Depression when the army built the post in 1941. Many officers lived in Wilmington, and every weekend the city's restaurants, theaters, bars, USO's, whorehouses, and churches teemed with khaki uniforms on passes.

Only two officers dotted coach Captain Henry A. Johnson's (Michigan State) 35-man roster in 1942, and one, Captain Edwin Holloway, a back, also coached. In what would be a familiar ring throughout wartime army football, "The squad [members] have volunteered eagerly to play the game, knowing that they will receive no extra privileges."[10]

The 1943 45-man roster of four officers and eight returning veterans averaged 189 pounds (line 196, backs 178), 5'10.7" in height, and 22.5 years old. The biggest players were tackles Thornton (6'0"/250) and Dan Solomon (6'1"/225). Acting captain, T John Mellus (6'0"/210, All-America Villanova, New York Giants), directed the defense. "High flying" high schooler G Ralph Primavera (5'9"/190) sought out "fast and furious" action. "He's the original holler guy and when you hear that familiar 'Let's knock 'em dead, fellers,' it will be No. 27 egging his AA mates on."[11] This squad earned the unofficial Carolinas army championship. Its leading players were Mellus, first team Associated Press All-Service, and FB Norm Standlee (Stanford, Chicago Bears) who scored 61 points and rushed for 571 yards. The talented, well-rounded

Camp Davis (N.C.) backs Lieutenants Norm Standlee (Stanford) and George Breeding (right) led the Fighting AA's to an 8–2–0 record in 1943, earning the squad the unofficial army Carolinas championship (provided by John Gunn).

"Standlee Steamer" reputedly could play, distribute programs, usher, and deliver an orientation lecture at the same time. The army closed the AA base in late 1944 and canceled that season.

| 1942 Camp Davis (4–3–2) | | 1943 Camp Davis (8–2–0) | |
|---|---|---|---|
| Citadel | 0–32 | Wake Forest | 24–20‡ |
| Appalachian St | 13–13* | Charleston CG | 25–0 |
| Catawba | 14–21* | N.C. State | 27–0 |
| High Point College | 20–0* | North Carolina PF | 18–23 |
| North Carolina Navy B† | 2–0 | Davidson | 27–0 |
| Presbyterian | 6–26* | Camp Lejeune | 0–14 |
| Cherry Point MCAS | 37–0 | Fort Monroe | 31–6 |
| Daniel Field | 21–7* | Presbyterian | 32–0 |
| North Carolina Navy B† | 6–6 | Daniel Field | 41–0 |
| | | Fort Bragg | 42–0§ |

*at Legion Stadium, Wilmington, N.C.
†a.k.a. North Carolina PF B squad

‡at Camp Davis; 20,000
§at Camp Davis; 30,000

## Camp Grant (Rockford, Ill.) Warriors

The army opened Camp Grant during World War I, closed it, and then reopened it in 1940 as a recruit reception center and medical replacement training center. Playing under coach Lieutenant Glen Rose (Arkansas), the Warriors warrant noting because of their heavy Big Ten and collegiate opposition ("perhaps the most pretentious schedule of all") and 1943 wins over Illinois and Wisconsin.[12]

Athletes received no special treatment. "The soldier gridders arise in early morning with their fellow soldiers and perform their regular duties until mid-afternoon." Then came grueling practices "which usually last[ed] until after the other soldiers [were] through for the day ... the training equivalent of the usual marching, classroom work, etc., for the gridders."[13] The camp fielded no varsity teams in 1944-45.

| 1942 CAMP GRANT (6–6–0) | | 1943 CAMP GRANT (2–6–2) | |
|---|---|---|---|
| Chicago Bears | 6–32 | Illinois | 23–0 |
| Milwaukee Falks | 22–0 | Michigan | 0–26 |
| Wisconsin | 0–7 | Wisconsin | 10–7 |
| Milwaukee Falks | 20–0 | Marquette | 7–7 |
| DeKalb Teachers | 43–0 | Purdue | 0–19 |
| Iowa | 16–33 | Minnesota | 7–13 |
| Bradley Tech | 26–7 | Fort Riley | 13–13 |
| Fort Knox | 20–0 | Great Lakes NTS | 0–12 |
| Great Lakes NTS | 0–33 | Iowa PF | 13–28 |
| St Norbert's | 40–0 | Fort Riley | 6–10 |
| Marquette | 0–34 | | |
| Illinois | 0–20 | | |

## Fort Francis E. Warren (Cheyenne, Wyo.) Broncos/ Fighting Quartermasters

Fort Warren trained almost 20,000 Quartermaster Corps personnel in 280 wooden, temporary buildings constructed without insulation and interior walls to house the onrush of troops. The harsh Wyoming winters jolted them. Just waking up often meant shaking snow from one's blanket before heading for the freezing communal showers. The fort also contained a prisoner-of-war camp.

The 1943 coach, Captain Willis M. Smith (All-America Idaho), gave the ball to QB Earl Meneweather (160, Humboldt State, San Francisco Packers), who excited fans and publicists alike. "A rangy, fleet footed Negro boy [with] lightning fast runs," Meneweather reputedly was "a veritable ebony eel in his ability to writhe through the arms of tacklers in open field," and "the shiftiness and change of pace that goes with it makes him Fort Warren's most formidable threat as a broken field runner." He "combines uncanny broken field running with sufficient power to crack the line when the distance is short."[14]

Facing tough military and collegiate schedules in 1944-45, Fort Warren gained respect as one of the most steadfast non-flying army elevens.

| 1943 FORT WARREN (4–3–0) | | 1944 FORT WARREN (5–4–1) | |
|---|---|---|---|
| Lowry Field | 0–7 | Brooklyn Tigers | 21–20 |
| Colorado | 0–38 | Colorado | 7–6 |
| Utah | 60–0 | Lincoln AAB | 5–14 |
| Kearney AB | 26–6 | Colorado College | 33–13 |
| Kearney AB | 33–6 | Southern Idaho | 66–0 |
| Salt Lake AB | 10–0 | Iowa PF | 0–30 |
| Fort Riley | 7–14 | Lincoln AAB | 19–6 |
| | | 2nd AF | 0–20 |
| | | Great Lakes NTC | 7–28 |
| | | San Francisco Clippers | 21–21 |

| 1945 FORT WARREN (4–6–0) | |
|---|---|
| Colorado | 6–0 |
| 4th AF | 0–25 |
| 2nd AF | 0–19 |
| Colorado St | 61–6 |
| Minnesota | 0–14 |
| Hondo AAF | 28–26 |
| Fleet City | 9–21 |
| Farragut Navy | 27–0 |
| Great Lakes NTC | 14–47 |
| El Toro MCAS | 7–40 |

## Fort Riley (Kans.) Replacement Training Center Centaurs

After two solid seasons, Fort Riley's program lapsed into futility, the 1945 squad ranking 71st among service elevens. Their two best performances were a 1943 one-point road loss to Great Lakes Naval Training Station before

Fullback Ken Roskie (35) surges for a first down for Great Lakes (Ill.) Naval Training Center against Fort Riley (Kans.) in 1943, aided by blocking from Dick Stealy (59) and George Perpich (95). The powerful Bluejackets edged the 6–2–1 Centaurs, 20–19 (*Great Lakes Bulletin*, September 17, 1943).

15,000, and a crushing defeat of Denver when they outrushed the Pioneers, 345 to minus 51 yards. Denver "tried and tried and tried again," but failed to withstand the "mighty, heavy, massive, immovable, fleet-footed" Centaurs.[15]

| 1942 FORT RILEY (7–3–0) | | 1943 FORT RILEY (6–2–1) | |
|---|---|---|---|
| Missouri | 0–31 | Great Lakes | 19–20 |
| Emporia Teachers | 39–14 | Lowry Field | 60–20 |
| Kansas St | 21–7 | Norman NAS | 39–0 |
| Creighton | 7–34 | Denver | 47–0 |
| Missouri "B" | 13–6 | Camp Grant | 13–13 |
| Wichita | 6–0 | Iowa PF | 2–19 |
| Washburn | 13–0 | Fort Warren | 14–7 |
| 2nd AF | 6–54 | Camp Grant | 10–6 |
| Kansas Wesleyan | 39–6 | Kansas | 22–7 |
| Wichita Pros | 10–0 | | |

| 1944 FORT RILEY (0–3–1) | | 1945 FORT RILEY (1–6–0) | |
|---|---|---|---|
| Kearney AFB | 7–19 | Kearney AFB | 0–20 |
| Kearney AFB | 0–16 | Washburn | 0–19 |
| Olathe NAS | 0–20 | Kansas "B" | 0–12 |
| Olathe NAS | 6–6 | Wichita | 13–38 |
| | | Hutchinson NAS | 0–39 |
| | | Kearney AFB | 18–13 |
| | | St Louis | 7–14 |

## Fourth Air Force, a.k.a. 4th AF and March Field (Riverside, Calif.) Flyers

March Field trained many bombardment and fighter groups before they deployed to the Pacific, and at its peak strength trained some 75,000 troops in the Fourth AF's 25 main air bases in five Pacific Coast states. Called "the Buck Rogers Outfit" for its vast new developments in air warfare, the command "built up one of the most intricate aerial defensive systems ever devised," dispensing fighters along the entire coast, ringing targets with antiaircraft weapons, and utilizing thousands of civilian volunteers in aircraft-detecting radar stations, filter centers, and observation posts.[16]

Major Paul Schissler (coach Oregon State) magnificently coached this "G.I. Juggernaut" collection in 1943-44. Schissler picked not one first team but two, "and turn[ed] them loose [one at a] time," alternating periods of play. The "A" team ran the ball, the "B" team passed it. They played home games in the Los Angeles Coliseum. The 1943 team, loaded with "fast, experienced behemoths who don't like to get beat,"[17] recorded five shutouts, including a rout of Rose Bowl–bound Southern California, then the Trojans' worst defeat in history. The star of stars, HB "Indian" Jack Jacobs (All-America Oklahoma), a "pass master, rated one of the three top passers in football," tossed three touchdown passes against the Trojans.[18] The AP ranked the Flyers No. 10

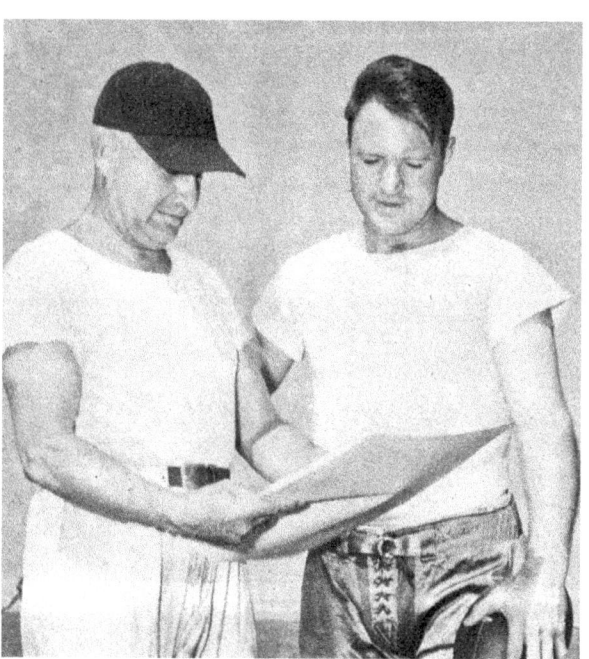

The Fourth Air Force "G.I. Juggernaut" from March Field, Calif., recorded a composite wartime 32-7-3 mark playing home games in the Los Angeles Coliseum. Major Paul Schissler (coach, Oregon State), shown here with back Bob Defruiter (Nebraska), coached the 1943-44 squads. He alternated "A" (run) and "B" (pass) teams and in 1943 routed Rose Bowl–bound Southern California, 35-0 (Street & Smith's *Football Pictorial Yearbook 1944*).

each season, and a premiere sports organization charted them No. 2 nationally behind Notre Dame in 1943.

Professionals did not play on the 1944 team, but Jacobs repeated, joined by All-Americas HB Jimmy Nelson (Alabama) and FB Leo Cantor (UCLA). For the season showdown finale against powerhouse Randolph Field, before 50,000 in the Coliseum, March Field offered no excuses for losing but had limited service from the injured Jacobs and Nelson. For 1945, almost all the 1943-44 Flyers were overseas or assigned outside the Fourth AF area. Coach Lieutenant John Baker (Southern California) replaced the Notre Dame box with the T formation, requiring adjustments by many new players previously out of football on other duties.

| 1942 FOURTH AF (11–2–0) | |
|---|---|
| Bombers | 18–0 |
| Redlands U | 25–14 |
| Fresno St | 0–20 |
| San Diego St | 39–6 |
| Los Alamitos Navy | 47–0 |
| Mather Field | 21–3 |
| San Diego Bombers | 33–12 |
| San Diego NTS | 26–0 |
| Santa Ana AB | 16–7 |
| Hollywood Bears | 19–7 |
| 2nd AF | 13–26 |
| Pro All-Stars | 14–12 |
| San Diego Bombers | 28–14 |

| 1943 FOURTH AF (9–1–0) | |
|---|---|
| Pacific All-Stars | 45–13 |
| Redlands | 40–0 |
| UCLA | 47–7 |
| San Diego NTS | 7–0 |
| Washington | 7–27 |
| St Mary's PF | 7–6 |
| Pomona Ord Base | 72–0 |
| Southern California | 35–0 |
| San Diego NTS | 13–2 |
| College of Pacific | 19–0 |

| 1944 FOURTH AF (7–1–2) | |
|---|---|
| Washington Redskins | 3–7* |
| San Diego Bombers | 56–7 |
| Fleet City | 39–0 |
| Alameda CG | 20–20 |
| El Toro MCAS | 21–14 |
| St Mary's PF | 7–0 |
| UCLA | 35–13 |
| Washington | 28–0 |
| San Diego NTS | 7–0 |
| 2nd AF | 0–0 |
| Randolph Field | 7–20 |
| *exhibition | |

| 1945 FOURTH AF (5–3–1) | |
|---|---|
| Fort Warren | 25–0 |
| 2nd AF | 17–14 |
| Air Transp Comd | 21–14 |
| St Mary's PF | 20–7 |
| AAFTC | 7–19 |
| 1st AF | 6–6 |
| Pers Dist Comd | 7–9 |
| Fleet City | 10–20 |
| 3rd AF | 10–7 |

## Keesler Field/Air Force Base (Biloxi, Miss.) Commandos/Fliers

First Lieutenant George B. Huffman coached both the 1943 and 1944 Keesler Field teams, both led by B Herman Rohrig (All-America Nebraska, Green Bay Packers), "Hurryin' Herman," a "chunky little man with the buggy-whip passing arm and swift-movement hips and legs." In demolishing Camp Gordon, Rohrig played only six minutes and the Keesler defense held Gordon to one first down, one yard net rushing, and 11 passing.[19]

Keesler dominated the Gulf Coast in 1944 while blanking eight of eleven opponents. Gulfport Army Air Field officials offered a war bond to their first player who scored, but Keesler prevailed 39–0 in "the Gulf Coast Classic." Gulfport didn't invade Keesler territory until the final minute. The Commandos' most valuable player was end Robert E. "Bob" Witt (6'0"/200, Mississippi Southern).

| 1943 KEESLER FIELD (3–1–0) | | 1944 KEESLER FIELD (8–1–2) | |
|---|---|---|---|
| Camp Gordon | 56–0 | Algiers Navy | 40–0 |
| Gulfport Seabees | 51–0 | SW Louisiana Inst | 13–0 |
| Arkansas A&M | 7–19 | Selman Field | 20–20 |
| Houma AB | 47–0 | Gulfport AAF | 20–0 |
| | | Fourth Infantry | 7–7 |
| | | Selman Field | 20–0 |
| | | 3rd Infantry | 19–0 |
| | | Mississippi Ordnance | 67–0 |
| | | Gulfport Navy | 39–0 |
| | | Gulfport AAF | 41–0 |
| | | Fort Pierce | 7–34 |

| 1945 KEESLER FIELD (4–6–1) | |
|---|---|
| AAF TC | 0–29 |
| Alabama | 0–21 |
| 2nd AF | 13–2 |
| Missouri | 7–41 |
| Fort Benning | 7–26 |
| Fort Benning | 0–0 |
| Gulfport Field | 14–0 |
| 3rd AF | 0–42 |
| Maxwell Field | 14–7 |
| Fort Pierce | 7–21 |
| Cherry Point MCAS | 41–0 |

# Randolph Field (San Antonio, Tex.) Ramblers, and Army Air Forces Training Command (Fort Worth, Tex.) Skymasters

Opened in 1930 and known as the "West Point of the Air," Randolph Field mowed through a mix of high- and low-caliber opponents en route to a 21–1–1 mark in 1943-44. Fourteen victories came on shutouts, and only three teams scored against them — just 19 points — in 1944. Randolph used officer-players in contrast to the navy's general, but not exclusive, policy of suiting up officers only against military teams. In 1945 the center's name changed to the Army Air Forces Training Command Skymasters in Fort Worth, but the successor perpetuated the football prosperity.

The whiplash arm of QB Glenn Dobbs (6'3"/200, All-America Tulsa) headlined the 1943 aggregation whose lone defeat was by the one-season Cinderella phenomenon Southwest Louisiana Institute. Dobbs's statistics: 105 passes completed for 1,402 yards; seven touchdowns in one game and 20 overall; 29 pass completions in one game; and total yards 2,157. He played in three bowl games, two with Tulsa and with the Ramblers in the cold, rain-drenched Cotton Bowl when he saved the day with peerless kicking and expert passing of the soaked ball. Army aviation thrived from the attention. Airmen worldwide championed their own team, "the Notre Dame of service football."[20]

Lieutenant Frank M. Tritico's (Southwest Louisiana Institute) "sheer power," three-deep squad was the obvious army champion in 1944, led by TB William "Bullet Bill" Dudley (5'10"/175, Walter Camp Award Virginia, Pittsburgh Steelers), recipient of the Washington (D.C.) Touchdown Club's Robert B. Smith Trophy as the

Pitching Flyer at Randolph Field

GLENN DOBBS, FORMER ALL-AMERICAN HALFBACK AT TULSA, MAKING PASSING RECORDS FOR THE RANDOLPH FIELD FLYERS

Quarterback Glenn Dobbs (All-America Tulsa) sparked mighty Randolph Field (Tex.) in 1943 (9–1–1). The Ramblers, who battled Texas to a 7–7 tie in the 1944 Cotton Bowl, lost only to Southwest Louisiana Institute, one of the "Cinderella teams" comprised of V-12 trainees. Airmen everywhere proclaimed Randolph as "the Notre Dame of service football" (*The Football News,* November 27, 1943).

top service player. Dudley, who later saw action in the Pacific, and end Jack Russell (Baylor) made service All-America. Randolph ranked No. 1 in the Williamson military team ratings and was ranked No. 3 overall by the AP. Tritico previously coached only in high school.

Rambler fans boasted that the "star-spangled roster" was the nation's finest and more than capable of holding their own against professionals. Players included backs Frederick "Dippy" Evans (Notre Dame) and Pete Layden (Texas), and E Martin Ruby (Texas A&M). Guard "Burly" Lou Yank came home from 30 bomber missions over Nazi-held Europe, including the first daylight raid and six altogether on Berlin, while earning the Distinguished Flying Cross and Air Medal with four Oak Leaf Clusters.[21]

The Ramblers demolished preseason Southwest Conference favorites Rice, Texas, and Southern Methodist. "It just didn't fit the dignity of those schools to lose by such scores," *Football Prevues 1945* said, causing Randolph unfair and unjust criticism. "Never in the South has such a glittering assortment of big name football talent been corralled on one squad." Authorities wondered if the team was "too good" for its own good.[22]

Keeping the players interested with sufficient playing time was Tritico's only problem. Twenty-two scored. The Ramblers wasted little yardage and charted only 111 first downs (touchdowns did not count as first downs then). Touchdown plays averaged almost 30 yards and only 21 developed inside the opponents' 10-yard line. In NCAA rankings, Randolph earned No. 3 in total offense (377 yards per game), No. 2 in total defense (110.8), No. 8 in rushing (257.4), No. 1 in rushing defense (29.6), and No. 9 in passing offense (121.3).

Major Doug Fessenden (Illinois) coached the 44-man, 1945 AAFTC eleven to a military ranking of No. 4. By then, the AAFTC operated a nationwide network of flying and technical schools, including Randolph. Through V-J Day it produced more than 200,000 pilots, 100,000 bombardiers and navigators, and 300,000 aerial gunners.

| 1942 RANDOLPH FIELD (2–8–0) | | 1943 RANDOLPH FIELD (9–1–1) | |
|---|---|---|---|
| North Texas Aggies | 0–20 | Bryan AFB | 30–0 |
| Texas Fr | 0–66 | Rice | 6–0 |
| San Marcos St | 0–25 | Bryan AFB | 47–0 |
| Tulsa | 0–68 | Ward Island | 39–9 |
| Corpus Christi Navy | 0–52 | Blackland Field | 7–0 |
| Allen Academy | 7–21 | Mexico City | 34–0 |
| Ellington Field | 8–0 | Blackland Field | 26–7 |
| Southwest Teachers | 0–21 | Ward Island | 53–14 |
| Wichita Aero Commandos | 0–55 | North Texas Aggies | 20–13 |
| | | SW Louisiana Inst | 0–6 |
| Stinson Field | 12–6 | Texas | 7–7* |
| | | *Cotton Bowl at Dallas, Tex. | |

| 1944 Randolph Field (12–0–0, 508–19) | | 1945 AAFTC (8–3–1) | |
|---|---|---|---|
| Abilene AAF | 67–0 | Keesler Field | 29–0 |
| Rice | 59–0 | Fort Benning | 27–0 |
| Texas | 42–6 | Fort Pierce | 19–7 |
| Southern Methodist | 41–0 | Air Trans Comd | 14–0 |
| Camp Polk | 67–0 | 4th AF | 19–7 |
| 3rd AF | 19–0 | El Toro MCAS | 0–7 |
| North Texas Aggies | 68–0 | 1st AF | 6–24 |
| SW Louisiana Inst | 25–0 | 3rd AF | 7–7 |
| Southwestern (Tex) | 54–0 | Maxwell Field | 45–7 |
| Amarillo AAF | 33–0 | 2nd AF | 37–7 |
| 4th AF | 20–7 | Pers Dist Comd | 14–0 |
| 2nd AF | 13–6* | 4th AF | 0–27† |
| *Treasury (Bond) Bowl, New York | | †Legion Bowl, Memphis, Tenn. | |

## Second Air Force, a.k.a. 2nd AF (Spokane, Wash., and Colorado Springs, Colo.) Superbombers

Wearing uniforms of the official air force colors — red, blue, gold — the 1942 squad topped Far West military squads, ranked No. 1 nationally among army teams, and defeated Hardin-Simmons in the Sun Bowl. "A real titan in army football circles" and "mythical" army champion, the Superbombers suited up Tony Calvelli (Stanford), Hal Van Every (Minnesota), Vic Spadaccinni (Minnesota), Don Williams (Texas), Bob Townsend (Northwestern), and Billy Sewell and Bill Holmes (Washington State).[23] The command played no games in 1943.

Georgia All-America and 1942 Heisman Trophy recipient quarterback Fran "Flatfoot Frankie" Sinkwich suffered a career-ending knee injury in 1945 playing for the Second Air Force against the El Toro (Calif.) Flying Marines. Ironically, his high school teammate, end Bob Dove, made the injury-causing tackle on the former Detroit Lion (Street & Smith's *Football Pictorial Yearbook 1943*).

In 1944 the team renamed itself Superbombers to coincide with its mission to train B-29 Superfortress crews for the Pacific Theater after sending 14,000 heavy bombardment crews to Europe. It also trained fighter pilots. The team, coached by Major William "Red" Reese, "played on fields carved in salt beds, in a desert and in tiny southwestern and western towns. They ... played from coast to coast, Los Angeles to New York" before 175,000 fans.[24] The "flash and excursion"[25] 35-man roster, composed of players from 40 air bases in 14 states, included "the arm," HB Glenn Dobbs, who played at Randolph Field in 1943, and Washington State All-Americas E Nick Suseoff (6'1"/210) and HB Billy Sewell (6'1"/175). The Superbombers topped the nation in scoring with 513 points (34.2).

Other army commands adopted the Second AF program which culminated in the 1945 air force command league. The Second AF commanding general kept his team around after the war ended, but it produced only a losing record under coach Major Ed Walker (Stanford, coach Mississippi and Princeton) and three straight shutouts to other air force elevens. Having stalwarts such as B Frank Sinkwich (5'11"/200, All-America, Heisman Trophy Georgia, Detroit Lions), C-LB Clyde "Bulldog" Turner (6'2"/250, Hardin-Simmons, Chicago Bears), T Fred Davis (Alabama, Washington Redskins), E Tom Fears (Santa Clara), and B Ray Evans (Kansas) made little difference for this double-wing team. Maybe the thrill was gone, but Sinkwich injured his knee against El Toro and Turner took leave to play for the Bears.

| 1942 Second AF (11–0–1, 359–65) | | 1944 Second AF (10–4–1, 513–76) | |
|---|---|---|---|
| St Martin's | 21–0 | Peru Navy | 38–0 |
| Eastern Washington | 19–7 | Colorado College | 24–0 |
| Idaho | 14–0 | Idaho Southern | 45–0 |
| Fort Douglas | 37–0 | Whitman | 78–0 |
| Portland U | 20–13 | Colorado | 33–6 |
| College of Idaho | 75–0 | Iowa PF | 6–13 |
| Kansas Wesleyan | 37–0 | New Mexico | 89–6 |
| Fort Riley | 54–6 | North Texas Aggies | 68–0 |
| Washington St | 6–6 | Norman NAS | 6–13 |
| Arizona | 27–13 | Amarillo AAF | 46–6 |
| 4th AF | 25–13 | Fort Warren | 20–0 |
| Hardin-Simmons | 13–7* | Washington | 47–6 |
| | | 4th AF | 0–0 |
| | | 3rd AF | 7–14 |
| | | Randolph Field | 6–13 |

*Sun Bowl at El Paso, Tex.

### 1945 Second AF (3–7–0)

| | |
|---|---|
| 4th AF | 14–17 |
| Fleet City | 0–7 |
| Fort Warren | 19–0 |
| Keesler Field | 28–13 |
| El Toro MCAS | 9–20 |
| Pers Dist Comd | 13–0 |
| 3rd AF | 0–33 |
| Air Trans Comd | 0–15 |
| 1st AF | 0–15 |
| AAFTC | 7–37 |

## Third Air Force, a.k.a. 3rd AF and Morris Field (Charlotte, N.C.) and Drew Field (Tampa, Fla.) Gremlins

The Third Air Force headquarters opened at Morris Field and moved to Drew Field in 1945. The command peaked at 180,000 military and civilian personnel with 4,000 planes at bases in 17 states, and trained more than 250,000 pilots and crews for overseas duty in every type of army combat aircraft. Breakaway runner B Charley Trippi (All-America Georgia), selected to the 1944 AP All-Service first team, headlined the Gremlin stars.

### 1944 Third Air Force (8–3–0)

| | |
|---|---|
| Charleston CG | 31–0 |
| Chatham Field | 45–0 |
| Fort Benning 3rd Inf | 32–0 |
| Georgia PF | 19–7 |
| Cherry Point MCAS | 29–7 |
| Randolph Field | 0–19 |
| Georgia PF | 34–12 |
| Great Lakes NTC | 10–12 |
| Maxwell Field | 41–7 |
| Fort Pierce | 6–7 |
| 2nd AF | 14–7 |

### 1945 Third Air Force (7–2–1)

| | |
|---|---|
| Pers Dist Comd | 27–9 |
| Miami NAS | 39–0 |
| 1st AF | 19–0 |
| Cherry Point MCAS | 20–0 |
| Fort Pierce | 12–26 |
| 2nd AF | 33–0 |
| Keesler Field | 42–0 |
| AAFTC | 7–7 |
| Air Transp Cmd | 15–6 |
| 4th AF | 7–10 |

The Third Air Force Gremlins played in 1944 (8–3–0) at Morris Field near Charlotte, N.C., and in 1945 (7–2–1) at Drew Field near Tampa, Fla. Featured players included, top left clockwise: halfback Bob Kennedy, tackle Stan Krall, fullback Ventan Yablonski, tackle Chester Lipka, end John Karmazin, tackle Frank Lopp. Middle: tackle Frank Merritt (game program, Third Air Force vs. Fourth Air Force, December 2, 1945).

## Chapter 8

# "Rollicking, Boisterous, Macho": Flying Marines and Sea Lions

> *The 1945 team "was a rollicking, fun-loving, boisterous, rough, macho group—about half officer, half enlisted." Some had fought in the Pacific. "[Elroy "Crazy Legs"] Hirsch said there was a 'great togetherness among the officers and enlisted. We never wore our bars.'"*[1]

Obviously intent on fielding its finest football team, and one to challenge for service supremacy, seemingly overnight the Marine Corps assembled its aviation football-playing elite at the El Toro Air Station in Southern California in 1944. The gridders came from combat assignments, V-5, and V-12 college programs, and transfers from other commands, most of whom logged significant wartime pigskin experience before checking in to El Toro — by design.

By 1943, a publication noted, football's best players for the most part were "Marine Reserve chattels," wrecking expectations of powers Texas and Rice and giving nova births to Southwestern and North Texas. Marines "supplied the sinews" for Michigan and Notre Dame, the "Muscle-Men of the West. The Leatherneck banners may not fly in the headlines, but their horny-handed scrappers, as usual, are very apt to decide how and where the ride of battle will run."[2]

The aggressive Corps recruited players like they fought, zeroing in on Heisman Trophy winning quarterbacks Frank Sinkwich (Georgia 1942) and Angelo Bertelli (Notre Dame 1943), and each year's runner-up, QB Paul Governali (Columbia 1942) and HB Bob Odell (Pennsylvania 1943). The latter two won the Maxwell Trophy as the East's best player.[3]

With fewer establishments than the other services, the Marine Corps fielded competitive two-year programs at North Carolina's Camp Lejeune

While probably only eight of the football Flying Marines of El Toro (Calif.) Air Station themselves were aviators, during the war's final season the team flew to road games in military transports. Here the 1945 team is shown en route, stuffed into what appears to be a C-54. The Marine Corps, by design, overnight assembled this elite group of highly skilled players into a dynamite two-year program (provided by John Gunn).

Marine Corps Base and Cherry Point Marine Corps Air Station, and with a smattering of temporary teams. These included ones at Quantico, Va.; outlying air fields at Oak Grove, Bogue Field, and Kinston in North Carolina; rehabilitation centers such as Klamath Falls, Ore.; and on Hawaii. There ad hoc all-star squads played other island teams with some success, and in 1945 served as a way station for homecoming Marines suiting up one last time in both uniforms.

The Klamath Falls and Pocatello, Ida., stations recruited interesting prospects. Klamath's players drew from among some 85 wounded or sick men recovering from malaria, filariasis, mumu, elephantiasis, and other tropical ailments. The navy gathered tropical-disease specialists who used sports, hunting, and fishing in the treatment process. The Pocatello Naval Ordnance Plant

Marine Barracks had 50 combat veterans released from a naval hospital on limited duty for afflictions similar to those at Klamath. Two dozen Marines and some sailors agreed to play. The athletic officer "scrounged the Pocatello area for enough helmets, pants, jerseys, pads and shoes to field a team." Idaho State provided cast-off gear and equipment. Residents "got behind the team.... The scores did not tell the real story of 'these brave combat veteran, physically impaired Marines ... against young, physically fit football players."[4] Marines who played V-12 football received two Navy Crosses, seven Silver Stars, three Bronze Stars and numerous other decorations for valor on Iwo Jima and Okinawa.[5]

Each service had its doormat programs, where it took guts and a liking for pain to dress out and play. The Marines' doormat candidate was the 1943 Norfolk, Va., detachment which went 0–9–0 and scored only 25 points against their opponents' 390.

During the war the Coast Guard, the smallest service, technically served in the Department of the Navy and not separately. Because so many of its personnel trained and played with navy and Marine activities, including in the V-5 and V-12 programs, the Coast Guard fielded competitive teams only at Alameda, Calif., and at the Coast Guard Academy. Other establishments fielding temporary teams included the Coast Guard Receiving Station, San Francisco Bay (Berkeley, Calif.), whose 4–2–1 season in 1944 balanced with a 13–0 win over College of Pacific and a 60–0 loss to El Toro; Curtis Bay, Md.; Charleston, S.C.; Manhattan Beach, Brooklyn, N.Y. (6–0–1 in 1942); and Wilmington, N.C.

Some noteworthy teams are described below.

## Alameda Coast Guard (Alameda, Calif.) Sea Lions

As the Coast Guard's strongest station team, the Sea Lions did not shrink from tough opponents. They loaded up on teams

Coast Guard Lieutenant Joe J. Verducci mentored the Alameda Coast Guard Sea Lions to a combined 8-4-3 record during 1943-44. Alameda, which played three seasons against California-based elevens, was the country's strongest Coast Guard program (provided by John Gunn).

in California, whipping College of Pacific and California twice, and took on pre-flights at St. Mary's twice (one a tie) and Del Monte, UCLA, Fleet City, and the Fourth Air Force (a tie).

The 1943 roster contained enlisted men only, but almost all had some college experience with western schools. Lieutenant Joe J. Verducci, who coached the 1943-44 squads, in 1944 said, "We have one of the strongest teams on the Coast at present, but we never know from day to day which ones will be shipped out."[6]

1942 ALAMEDA COAST GUARD (1–7–1)

| | |
|---|---|
| San Francisco Packers | 0–7 |
| California Ramblers | 0–0 |
| St Mary's PF | 0–40 |
| Loyola | 6–38 |
| Mather Field | 0–27 |
| San Jose St | 0–9 |
| College of Pacific | 13–7 |
| San Francisco U | 6–44 |
| St Mary's College | 0–26 |

1943 ALAMEDA COAST GUARD (4–2–1)

| | |
|---|---|
| College of Pacific | 7–14 |
| Del Monte PF | 7–34 |
| San Francisco U | 26–0 |
| St Mary's College | 21–7 |
| Pleasanton Navy | 46–6 |
| St Mary's PF | 13–13 |
| California | 7–0 |

1944 ALAMEDA COAST GUARD (4–2–2)

| | |
|---|---|
| Fleet City | 7–7 |
| Nevada | 35–0 |
| St Mary's College | 18–0 |
| 4th AF | 20–20 |
| College of Pacific | 19–0 |
| UCLA | 13–26 |
| California | 12–6 |
| St Mary's PF | 13–32 |

## Camp Lejeune Marine Corps Base (Jacksonville, N.C.) Marines

First opened in 1941 as New River Marine Corps Barracks and renamed Camp Lejeune in 1942, the Corps' largest eastern facility provided advanced training for officers and recent graduates of boot camp at Parris Island, S.C. The 1st Marine Division, the Corps' initial division-sized unit, formed here for later Pacific assaults on Guadalcanal, Cape Gloucester, Peleliu, and Okinawa. The station later became home for the 2nd Marine Division which fought on Tulagi, Guadalcanal, Tarawa, Saipan, Tinian, and Okinawa.

Lejeune's inaccessibility (in the "boondocks") created the need for $3 million worth of recreation facilities. By 1944 these included 12 theaters, nine baseball diamonds, 18 tennis courts, three football fields, and 11 softball fields. The base cooperated with character-building agencies in neighboring communities, including physical fitness, and musical and dramatic arts activities.

Marine football historian John Gunn found that authorities wanted a "big-time" team, a "million-dollar club on paper," to entertain the trainees and keep them on post — provided it did not interfere with military duties. Players could practice only in their spare time. In 1943 175 tried out; 48 made it. The Bainbridge game drew 20,000 to the new field.[7] Former professional and collegiate players, including four from Notre Dame's 1942 squad, composed the Devil Dogs eleven.

Commentators considered the 1943 eleven, coached by Lieutenant Colonel William Stickney and Lieutenants Marvin Bell and Jack Chevigny (All-America Notre Dame, coach Chicago Cardinals), as one of the top military teams. Half were officers. The Leathernecks defeated nearby Camp Davis, the Southeast's best army team. Lejeune's standout players were Coast Guard E Bob Fitch (6'3"/215), a member of the Associated Press All-America Service team, who trained there, and Murphy.

Lejeune also served as both a troop staging area

First Lieutenant Jack E. Chevigny (All-America Notre Dame, head coach Chicago Cardinals), USMCR, lost his life on Iwo Jima in 1945. He coached at Camp Lejeune (N.C.) Marine Corps Base in 1943 (provided by John Gunn).

and officer candidate halfway house. Gunn learned that many trainees from the football-oriented 1943 V-12 class finished boot camp at Parris Island in June 1944 and transferred to Lejeune for officer training. At first they were prohibited from playing football. After the 53–7 loss to Bainbridge Naval Training Station, the commanding general allowed prospective officers to play. Coach Private Frank X. Knox (Illinois, Detroit Lions), fielded two teams: one of candidates, the other the old camp team.

Coaching instability caused by officer transfers paralyzed both the 1943 and 1944 squads. Lieutenant Bill Osmanski took over as head mentor in 1944 while playing, followed in mid-season by Knox, nephew of the Secretary of the Navy. End Johnny Yonakor (6'5"/230, All-America Notre Dame, Philadelphia Eagles) was massive for his era. Other notables included C "Black Mike" Kerns (235, Penn State, Eagles) and fullbacks George "Potsy" Graves (5'11"/215, Pennsylvania) and Ken Davis, Georgia Pre-Flight in 1943. Quarterback Bruce Locke, a Marine Raiders player in the South Pacific against army teams, saw action on Guadalcanal, Makin Island, and Bougainville.

The Leathernecks finished 1944 unbeaten except for two blowouts by Bainbridge (outscored 13–86). Injuries plagued an otherwise quality season, although they ranked only thirtieth among military elevens. Women Marine reserves acted as cheerleaders. The banged-up, dazzling Hirsch (6'1½"/188, All-America Wisconsin, Michigan) finally played in early November, but could not keep up with the Commodores' sensational back Charlie Justice in what had to be one of the classic wartime downfield chases. "The high school star ... more than lived up to his pre-game ballyhoo. The kid handled the ball seven times from scrimmage for 145 yards and three touchdowns. His speed was proven beyond all doubt in the third quarter as he outran Elroy 'Crazy Legs' Hirsch during an 80-yard scoring sprint around left end."[8]

These players passed through, including five No. 1 National Football League draft picks: Hirsch, QB Bertelli, FB Osmanski (All-America Holy Cross, Chicago Bears), B Johnny Podesta (All-America College of Pacific), B Tony Butkovich (All-America Purdue), T Pat Preston (All-America Duke), and Yonakor. Ends Behan and Murphy, and guard Aurel Bachiak (Eastern Kentucky) died on Okinawa, where much of the 1943 team ended up. Some men played only one or two games before shipping out, but Bertelli, Butkovich, Preston, and back Alvin Dark (Louisiana State) weren't allowed to play. In 1944 at least 105 Marines — some of them Guadalcanal veterans — participated in games. Lejeune announced an impressive 1945 schedule but demobilization and a probable impending invasion of Japan caused its cancellation.

## 8. "Rollicking, Boisterous, Macho": Flying Marines and Sea Lions

Former Notre Dame players participating at Camp Lejeune (N.C.) Marine Corps Base in 1944. Kneeling, left to right: Joe Signaigo, Jim Sullivan, Mike Hines, Bernie Meter. Standing: Gaspar Urban, Julie Rykovich, Bob David, John Yonakor (provided by John Gunn).

| 1943 Camp Lejeune MCB (6–2–1) | |
|---|---|
| Duke | 0–40 |
| Bainbridge NTS | 0–9 |
| North Carolina B | 26–0 |
| Fort Monroe | 51–0 |
| Jacksonville NAS | 20–7 |
| Camp Davis | 14–0 |
| Norfolk Marines | 55–6 |
| North Carolina PF | 14–14 |
| Jacksonville NAS | 13–6 |

| 1944 Camp Lejeune MCB (6–2–0) | |
|---|---|
| Duke JV | 6–0 |
| Bainbridge NTC | 7–53 |
| Camp Detrick | 38–0 |
| Kinston Marines | 33–0 |
| Bogue Field | 41–0 |
| Fort Monroe | 26–0 |
| Bainbridge NTC | 6–33 |
| Camp MacKall | 52–6 |

## Cherry Point Marine Corps Air Station (Havelock, N.C.) Leathernecks/Marines/Flyers

The 1943-44 Cherry Point teams played representative tough schedules, but never scheduled their companion station Camp Lejeune. Although "generally outweighed and outnumbered [they] did establish character." The 1943 eleven, coached by Lieutenant Bill Hopp, had future professional Hall of Famer tackles Leo Nomellini and Ernie Stautner.[9] Lieutenant Joe Bottalico was killed in action on Iwo Jima.

Master Tech Sergeant James T. McMurdo (All-America Pittsburgh, Philadelphia Eagles) mentored the 1944 Flyers. Injuries decimated his squad, as key linemen and backs dropped off "in the dismal procession. Each fracas has been costly." Newcomer G Ray Vranka (American International) emerged as the star.[10]

The 1945 team scrimmaged the Washington Redskins twice. Bogue Field, a Cherry Point auxiliary, "made more headlines by losing one game than it did in the remainder of its two abbreviated seasons" by losing to Duke (6–2–0) 76–0 in 1945.[11]

| 1943 CHERRY POINT MCAS (4–2–0) | | 1944 CHERRY POINT MCAS (3–7–0) | |
|---|---|---|---|
| Camp Lee | 0–20 | North Carolina PF | 14–27 |
| Wilmington CG | 39–0 | Camp Peary | 0–20 |
| Wake Forest Army | 68–6 | Georgia PF | 0–38 |
| Richmond AAB | 20–0 | North Carolina | 14–20 |
| Camp Butner | 40–0 | 3rd AF | 7–29 |
| Greensboro ORD | 0–19 | Camp Lee | 6–0 |
| | | Jacksonville NAS | 0–33 |
| | | Bainbridge NTC | 7–50 |
| | | Chatham Field | 35–0 |
| | | Camp Lee | 13–0 |

| 1945 CHERRY POINT MCAS (3–7–0) | |
|---|---|
| Jacksonville NAS | 0–26 |
| Oak Grove Marines | 6–0 |
| Camp MacKall | 29–0 |
| 3rd AF | 0–20 |
| Air Trans Cmd | 0–27 |
| Camp Peary | 0–27 |
| Camp Lee | 7–27 |
| Camp Peary | 7–0 |
| Keesler Field | 0–41 |

# El Toro Marine Corps Air Station (Irvine, Calif.) Flying Marines

Established in 1942, El Toro served as the Corps' principal West Coast aviation facility as an expansion of the San Diego Marine Corps Air Station and Marine Fleet Air West Coast. In fact, it also grew into the military's largest tactical wartime airfield on the coast. Its name came from a nearby village of 130 residents. Walt Disney designed its patch, the "Flying Bull," in 1944. It closed in 1999.

The team's immediate football prowess matched the station's great size and mission. Officially Lieutenant Colonel Richard E. "Dick" Hanley (coach Northwestern), who mentored the two seasons, was director of combat conditioning for the Marine Corps. This gave him access to the best officers and enlisted men on the coast, and thus "might have had as much effect on the outcome of the war as anyone in Washington or Hawaii." Considered a Neanderthal, he employed the double-wing in 1944-45 but also employed a two-platoon offense, the other the T. "But he pleased neither side."[12]

The 1944 eleven, led by superb QB Paul Governali (All-America, Maxwell Award Columbia), finished No. 16 nationally. The one-touchdown loss to Fourth Air Force, "a mighty scare," prompted some observers to call it "the roughest, toughest grid-battle in Coast history."[13] Reportedly the 1945 all-

The coaching staff at El Toro (Calif.) Marine Corps Air Station in 1945 included, left to right: tackle Wilbur "Wee Willie" Wilkin (St. Mary's, Washington Redskins), head coach Lieutenant Colonel Dick Hanley, USMCR (coach Northwestern), end Bob Dove (All-America Notre Dame), and back Mickey McCardle (Southern California). All except Hanley also played (provided by John Gunn).

The El Toro Flying Marines' starting lineup in 1945. Kneeling, left to right: Vern Gagne, Chuck Huneke, Tony Sumpter, Sam Brazinski, Bill Kennedy, Wee Willie Wilkin, Bob Dove. Back row: Walt Clay, Ernie Lewis, Mickey McCardle, Elroy Hirsch (provided by John Gunn).

star eleven included only eight actual flying Marines, but instead 36 past and future pros (26 in 1944), and both squads produced three NFL Hall of Famers and five College Hall of Famers. "This was the era of two-way players and small rosters." Los Angeles radio station KMPC broadcast the games. Fame spread nationwide. For example, the *Chicago Tribune* extensively covered the games, partly because of Hirsch and the many Midwesterners.[14] El Toro likely would have won more than eight games in 1945 if nine teams had not canceled for various reasons.

Some men played every game in 1945 and several joined the team after action on Iwo Jima, including G Jim Pearcy (Marshall), who received two Bronze Stars, C Don Johnson (Northwestern), and B Bill Kellagher (Fordham). The gyrenes presented a gigantic lineup, including ends Frank Quillen (225, Pennsylvania), Verne Gagne (210, Minnesota), and Bob Dove (205, Notre Dame); tackles Wee Willie Wilkin (6'6"/270 or 290 — recorded as both and huge for those days — St. Mary's, Washington Redskins), Harley McCollum (240, All-America Tulane), John Wickham (245, Tulsa), and Bob Tulis (238); and backs Frank Balasz (225, Iowa) and Kellagher (212).

The 1945 "star-of-stars" was Elroy "Crazy Legs" Hirsch. A wartime pigskin-playing vagabond, Hirsch enjoyed his 1942 sophomore season at No. 3-ranked Wisconsin where he acquired the famous nickname. Following a 13–7 win over Great Lakes, the *Chicago Daily News* reported, "'Hirsch ran like a demented duck. His crazy legs were gyrating in six different directions all at the same time." In 1943 he played at Michigan as a Marine Corps trainee and paced the No. 2 team with 68 points and also lettered in track, baseball, and basketball. He participated at Camp Lejeune in 1944 as duties allowed. El Toro officials pulled strings to have his orders changed from nearby Camp Pendleton in September 1945. "'What the hell, the war was over," said the El Toro business manager.[15] Hirsch repaid with 15 touchdowns.

| 1944 EL TORO MCAS (8–1–0, 307–34) | |
|---|---|
| Fleet City | 13–7 |
| Fairfield | 56–0 |
| Beaumont | 51–0 |
| San Diego NTC | 6–0 |
| 4th AF | 14–20 |
| Fleet City | 14–0 |
| San Diego ATB | 51–7 |
| Fort Bliss | 42–0 |
| San Francisco CG | 60–0 |

| 1945 EL TORO MCAS (8–2–0) | |
|---|---|
| Hollywood Rangers | 13–12 |
| Los Angeles Bulldogs | 68–0 |
| Fleet City | 7–21 |
| Camp Pendleton | 61–0 |
| 2nd AF | 20–9 |
| AAFTC | 7–0 |
| San Diego NTC | 20–0 |
| St Mary's PF | 7–0 |
| Fort Warren | 40–7 |
| Fleet City | 25–48 |

## Coast Guard Academy, a.k.a. Coast Guard (New London, Conn.) Bears

The 1942 Coast Guard team paced New England independents. The 1943 squad, considered the equal of any predecessor in talent, played their most ambitious schedule in history but could not match the strong Ivy League competition. The Academy reigned supreme among New England colleges in 1944, playing five "big boys," defeating Brown and Dartmouth after a shellacking by Army. Brown transfer B Tommy Dorsey, "one of the East's most able climax runners," sparked the Bears.[16] Lieutenant Commander J. S. Merriman coached both 1943-44 elevens.

| 1942 COAST GUARD (6–2–0) | |
|---|---|
| Wesleyan | 14–6 |
| Worcester Tech | 40–0 |
| Colby | 14–12 |
| Norwich | 0–13 |
| Trinity | 35–7 |
| Rensselaer Poly Inst | 33–0 |
| Middlebury | 52–0 |
| Connecticut | 0–16 |

| 1943 COAST GUARD (3–6–0) | |
|---|---|
| Bates | 25–6 |
| Yale | 12–20 |
| Dartmouth | 0–47 |
| Holy Cross | 0–32 |
| Rensselaer Poly Inst | 7–0 |
| Bates | 27–6 |
| Tufts | 7–20 |
| Worcester Tech | 12–19 |
| Brown | 31–34 |

| 1944 COAST GUARD (6–3–0) | |
|---|---|
| Bates | 33–0 |
| Tufts | 40–7 |
| Yale | 3–7 |
| Worcester Tech | 39–0 |
| Rensselaer Poly Inst | 38–6 |
| Army | 0–76 |
| Holy Cross | 14–26 |
| Brown | 20–0 |
| Dartmouth | 19–0 |

| 1945 COAST GUARD (0–7–1) | |
|---|---|
| Tufts | 6–14 |
| Virginia | 0–39 |
| Scranton | 0–0 |
| Rensselaer Poly Inst | 7–18 |
| Harvard | 0–25 |
| Brown | 6–33 |
| Holy Cross | 6–39 |
| Yale | 6–41 |

## CHAPTER 9

# "Around the Globe the Message Winged": The 1942–45 Seasons

*"Battling Mars, the blue-whiskered barbarian now swaggering the globe, has muddled the maps of both war prophets and football prognosticators with the same quick thumb. In a gridiron situation so scrambled, only a reckless oracle would venture predictions — but this forecaster was always one to climb out on a limb and saw it off behind him. So, war or no war, here goes!"*[1] — George Trevor

When previewing a "who knows?" season, sportswriters rolled the dice blindfolded, without certainty or pride. George Trevor, in the *Illustrated Football Annual 1943*, stabbed wildly but cleverly, like the rest. The season unraveled more recklessly than forecast into wartime football's low point, a hectic elevator ride of peak nova teams and games and valleys of despair. At least most colleges played, and more military teams formed, if only temporarily.

Topsy-turvy 1943 nevertheless produced the war's most exciting college-military spectacle, the amazing 19-14 last-minute victory by Great Lakes Navy over Notre Dame on December 2. "Bluejacket Eleven Ends Season in Blaze of Glory — Wins Service Title Claim," the station's *Bulletin* proclaimed. "Around the globe the message winged, to navy men, to Notre Dame men, to fighting men everywhere who prize football as a bit of the American way of living they are fighting to preserve."[2] Armed forces radio carried the broadcast to an estimated one million listeners. And the sportswriters anointed Notre Dame No. 1 in the nation regardless.

## 1942

When America entered the war obvious questions arose concerning the continuation of sports and other forms of entertainment. For institutions, players, coaches, programs, systems, and fans, what forms and who would stay, and what and who would go? For those staying, how could they be manipulated to work? Prior to the 1942 season, football commentators began conjecturing wildly on the unclear road ahead. "Overall the wiseacres predicted tackling and blocking would be harder," the National Collegiate Athletic Association wrote in its review, "as the future servicemen of our country would throw off all shackles, prior to entering the 'big fight.' Coaches would inspire men to outdo themselves in their assignments, and the war fever promised a reckless, daring form of play. No one was disappointed. The 1942 brand of football had a noticeable freshman blend." Teams shortcut peacetime comforts and normal conditioning routines "by playing right up to the hilt. Call it pent up energy, call it American resourcefulness, call it wartime fever or what you may, college football asked for no quarter and gave none."[3] Yet somehow 1942 produced more scoring punch than in the previous 12 years.

Navy-base teams and colleges using navy and Marine Corps student-players immediately leaped in front of military football. En route to a No. 1 service ranking, Great Lakes (Ill.) Naval Training Station (8–3–1) played all 12 games away against major opponents, spurring recruiting drives in each city and campus visited. Among military teams, the navy pre-flight schools grabbed headlines. But navy officials prohibited its teams from postseason play for the duration. Navy players filled 100 percent of the all-service squad chosen by *Collier's* magazine. No military elevens made the Associated Press top ten. Sports journalist voters had not experienced their enormous impact.

The newly formed Second Air Force (11–0–1), strongest West Coast military eleven, whipped undefeated Hardin-Simmons in the Sun Bowl. The seasons' best college teams were national champion Ohio State, Wisconsin, and unbeaten Georgia. Wisconsin kept its tentative title hopes alive when Jack Wink intercepted a Great Lakes pass and ran the length of the field to score in a 13–7 victory. He later said "he would never have intercepted the pass had he known he had one foot in the end zone," and admitted "for an instant he was 'lost' on the field and that instinctively he kept the ball instead of batting it down. 'I never knew 101 yards was that long, either.'"[4]

Minnesota, winners of six of the previous eight Big Ten championships, lost to the Iowa Pre-Flight Seahawks coached by its former mentor, Marine Major Bernie Bierman. Georgia beat UCLA in the 1943 Pasadena Rose Bowl. Missouri edged Iowa Pre-Flight 7–0 on a snow-covered field in Kansas City in December on a 58-yard run by B Bob Steuber (All-America), "more than

Quarterback Otto Graham (Northwestern), shown here carrying the ball in a 1942 game, played for North Carolina Pre-Flight as a Coast Guard trainee in 1944 where he learned the T formation under assistant coach Lieutenant Commander Paul "Bear" Bryant. Ranked No. 1 among service teams on November 5, the host Cloudbusters then lost to Bainbridge (Md.) Naval Training Center, 45–20 (Street & Smith's *Football Pictorial Yearbook 1943*).

200 pounds of speed and power," on the game's second play.[5] Steuber also booted the extra point.

Harvard and Pennsylvania lost most of their players, causing Harvard to close its program. Pennsylvania coach George Munger worked in a defense plant each morning and coached in the afternoon. Among the 1,200 V-12 trainees reporting he looked for "a few lads not unacquainted with the bounceful ways of a prolate spheroid."[6] At the Rocky Mountain schools, only a handful of 1942 players remained on campus for the spring semester and most awaited calls to duty.

Four teams toppled the modern total-offense high of 375.4 yards per game. "This unprecedented fierceness of attack left defenses groggy and for the first time in modern history no eleven was able to hold its foemen to an aggregate of less than a thousand yards total net gain for the season," the NCAA stated.[7] Georgia led in total offense: 11 games, 4,725 yards (average 429.5), and 186 first downs. In the top 10, Iowa Pre-Flight (10, 3,356) was the lone military team. Texas led total defense: (10,1173 allowed) and opponents first downs, 63. North Carolina Pre-Flight (10,1428) ranked No. 5, and Great Lakes (12,1917) No. 10. Hardin-Simmons led in rushing (307.4). Military top 10 teams: Iowa Pre-Flight (No. 6, 249.3) and Great Lakes (No. 8, 242.2). Boston College led rushing defense (48.9). The military leaders: pre-flights at North Carolina (No. 8, 84.2) and St. Mary's (No. 10, 85.2).

Star 1942 players included quarterbacks Otto Graham (Northwestern), "Pitchin' Paul" Governali (All-America, Maxwell Trophy Columbia); and Bob Waterfield (UCLA); and backs Glenn Dobbs (All-America Tulsa); Frank Sinkwich (5'10"/185, Heisman Trophy 1942, All-America Georgia), the "Georgia Fireball"; Rudy "Little Doc" Mobley (155, Hardin-Simmons); Ray Evans (Kansas); Bob Steuber (Missouri); and Mike Holovak (Boston College).

The Washington Touchdown Club annual award to the Outstanding Armed Forces player went in 1942 to HB Bruce Smith, Great Lakes; in 1943, to HB Richard Todd, Iowa Pre-Flight; and in 1944, to HB "Bullet Bill" Dudley, Randolph Field. The trophy eventually was named the Lieutenant Robert B. Smith Memorial Trophy, for the club's first member killed in action (Sicily, July 7, 1943, air force).

"What might have been a drab campaign was surcharged with new vigor, new excitement by the competition of these dynamic soldier and sailor arrays," the *Illustrated Football Annual 1943* summarized. Throughout football "these amply manned and admirably coached outfits" won most of their games against big-time college competition.[8]

   1942 COLLIER'S (GRANTLAND RICE) ALL-SERVICE TEAM
  (The Associated Press did not select a 1942 all-service team)

E Jim Poole (Mississippi, New York Giants), Georgia PF; Ed Fruitig (Michigan, Green Bay Packers), Corpus Christi NAS

T Steve Hudacek (Fordham), North Carolina PF; Bill Davis (Texas Tech, Chicago Cardinals), Georgia PF

G Buddy Jungmichel (Texas), San Diego NTS; Joe Huetz (Notre Dame), St. Mary's PF

C   George Svendsen (Minnesota, Packers), Iowa PF
QB  Frankie Albert (Stanford), St. Mary's PF
HB  George McAfee (Duke, Chicago Bears), Jacksonville NAS; Dick Fisher (Ohio State), Iowa PF
FB  Bruce Smith (Minnesota), Great Lakes NTS

A word about polls and rankings: beside the AP, considered the standard, several other national pollsters offered postseason rankings. The AP 1942 poll listed only collegiate teams; for other years it listed mixed collegiate-military. Dr. L. H. Baker, a noted student of the game, issued the most reliable mixed poll. Baker was research director of the Baker Football Information Service in New York City, a well-respected football historian and statistician, and the author of *Football Facts and Figures* (New York: Rinehart & Company, 1945). Paul B. Williamson issued "The Williamson National Football Rating and Prediction System" of military teams. The *Red and Green Sport Star* also published rankings.

### 1942 AP Service Teams Rankings

1 — Great Lakes NTC
2 — Iowa PF
3 — Georgia PF
4 — North Carolina PF
5 — St. Mary's PF
6 — Jacksonville NAS
7 — Camp Grant
8 — Pensacola NAS
9 — Manhattan Beach CG
10 — Corpus Christi NAS
11 — Second Air Force
12 — Fort Knox
13 — Lakehurst NAS
14 — Fort Monmouth
15 — Fort Riley
16 — Camp Davis
17 — Fourth Air Force
18 — Mather Field
19 — Fort Totten
20 — Spence Field

### 1942 Army Teams Standings

|  | W–L–T |
|---|---|
| 2nd Air Force | 10–0–1 |
| 4th Air Force | 11–2–0 |
| Minter Field | 6–2–0 |
| McClellan Field | 5–2–0 |
| Fort Monmouth | 5–2–2 |
| Fort Riley | 6–3–0 |
| Fort Douglas | 5–3–0 |
| Mather Field | 3–2–0 |

|  | W–L–T |
|---|---|
| Albuquerque AB | 4–3–0 |
| Camp Davis | 4–3–2 |
| Santa Ana AB | 5–4–0 |
| Camp Grant | 6–6–0 |
| Will Rogers Field | 4–4–0 |
| Carlisle Barracks | 3–3–1 |
| Daniel Field AB | 4–6–0 |
| Fort Totten | 3–5–1 |
| Patterson Field | 3–6–1 |
| Fort Knox | 2–7–0 |
| Camp Pickett | 1–6–0 |
| Colorado Springs AB | 1–6–0 |
| Indiantown Mil Reservation | 0–5–1 |
| Hill Field | 0–5–0 |
| Fort Benning | 0–5–0 |
| Fort Hamilton | 0–6–0 |

1942 NAVY TEAMS STANDINGS

|  | W–L–T |
|---|---|
| Georgia PF | 7–1–1 |
| North Carolina PF | 8–2–1 |
| Jacksonville NAS | 9–3–0 |
| Great Lakes NTS | 8–3–1 |
| Iowa PF | 7–3–0 |
| California (St. Mary's) PF | 6–3–1 |
| Corpus Christi NAS | 4–3–1 |
| Lakehurst NAS | 4–4–1 |
| Grosse Isle NAS | 4–4–1 |
| Iowa PF "B" | 3–3–0 |
| Pensacola NAS | 3–5–1 |
| Wahpeton NTS | 0–4–1 |

# 1943

"Undoubtedly one of the most difficult years for college football since 1905," stated a national publication about 1943. It cited "marked inequalities in material and competition ... lagging interest at all except those few fortunate schools" with the navy's "lend-lease material," and some criticism "that

Meryl Toepfer (29) and George Martin of Ottumwa (Ia.) Naval Air Station block the punt of Fort Crook's (Neb.) Al Dunagan, in 1943. Ottumwa (5–1–0) prevailed, 29–0 (*National Collegiate Athletic Association Football Guide 1944*).

the spectacle of a football game should be permitted at all in the strenuous times of war." It cited everyone's constant doubting, coaches not knowing what players would be available next week, "the boys themselves who faced the grave uncertainties of war, of the public distracted by the intensity of the fighting and the enormity of operations in the coming invasion of Europe."[9]

The NCAA noted that the 1943 season was the longest to date, from the annual College All-Star game in August in Chicago until the final reported overseas military game in March 1944. And this didn't include June practices. Again the scribes hesitated to venture into preseason minefields. "Not even the gamblingest Forty-Niner would risk an easy-come easy-go fortune on the chances of any one Pacific Coast team in this unpredictable season," sportswriter Bill Leiser said.[10]

As the national emergency war effort shifted into high gear, college football slipped to its lowest ebb. Men left for the service, schools struggled to field teams, and approximately 150 abandoned football. Teams held summer practice of three weeks of light drills and one week with contact, because the season started earlier than ever, by September 11. Traditional spring practices essentially served as conditioners for players about to enter active duty.

As the college quality diminished, military quality blossomed. Service teams dominated the AP poll, with six of the top 12, along with three colleges, Michigan, Purdue, and Duke, dotted with former professional and college players in navy and Marine Corps training programs. Michigan's All-Big Ten backfield featured trainees Bill Daley (Minnesota) and Elroy Hirsch (Wisconsin). Approximately 80 percent of the Cornell varsity came from other schools.

National champion Notre Dame played seven games against top-13 teams. After ascending to No. 1, the Irish held on with victories over the No. 2 squads, Michigan (35–12) and then Iowa Pre-Flight (14–13), and beat both Army and Navy when each ranked third. Fighting Irish QB Angelo Bertelli received the Heisman Trophy for playing only six games before entering the Marines. In his final game, "the Springfield Rifle" Bertelli threw three touchdown passes, ran for a score, and kicked three conversions while leading the Irish over Navy, 33–6. It mattered little to the AP that Notre Dame's season ended with that last-minute loss to Great Lakes.

Michigan (8–1–1, No. 3), with mostly V-12's, and Purdue (9–0–0, No. 5), the only unbeaten-untied school playing a full schedule with Marines and sailors from other league teams on their first two squads, shared the Big Ten crown. Boilermaker Fullback Tony Butkovich (Illinois) transferred into the V-12 program, made All-America, led the nation in rushing, and set a Big Ten scoring record with 78 points. He later lost his life on Okinawa. Marine reservists from Minnesota helped Northwestern (6–2–0, No. 9) to one of its best-ever seasons. Duke's powerful V-12 squad went three or four deep with top-quality college players and ran away with the Southern Conference championship, losing only to Navy by one point.

Marine reservists from Texas helped "Cinderella" Southwestern University to 10–1–1, including a win over their benefactor. The Longhorn "Lend-Lease huskies" used military trainees otherwise to sweep through the

Southwest Conference. "The fortunes of wartime wiped out the fine degree of balance" that the league ordinarily possessed. The navy's decision to let aviation candidate FB James Ross Calahan (185, Texas Tech) play for Texas in November on five-days notice turned "Texas from a fair ball club into a genuinely good one."[11] North Texas Agricultural College, loaded with V-12's, was considered equal to the Southwest elevens. Colorado College, with V-12's, dominated in the Rocky Mountains, whose football "wasn't so much as a shell of normal times."[12]

Big Six teams, playing far below their standards even from 1942, lost 13 of 19 non-conference games. The conference eliminated all scouting because of coaching shortages, and agreed to exchange offensive formations a week before each game. "'Of course, some of the boys may not line up exactly as they're supposed to,' observed Oklahoma's Dewey 'Snorter' Luster. 'They may surprise their own coach as much as the opponents.'"[13]

On the West Coast, observers rated the service teams superior to most collegiate ones, headed by the Fourth Air Force command (March Field) and the pre-flights at St. Mary's and Del Monte. The College of Pacific bolstered "Mr. Amos Alonzo Stagg's Season" (coach of the year) with victories over strong military elevens at Alameda Coast Guard, the two pre-flights, and Yuma Air Base.[14] V-12-manned Southern California (7–2–0) used its great defensive line and pass interceptions (13 in the first four games) to capture its first six games without surrendering a point before San Diego Navy (10–7) and Fourth Air Force (35–0) brought them to earth.

Marine Corps Tony Butkovich (Illinois) made All-America while a V-12 program trainee playing varsity football at Purdue in 1943. The bruising fullback is shown checking into Parris Island, S.C., for boot camp in 1944. He lost his life on Okinawa in 1945 (provided by John Gunn).

Fourth Air Force, a.k.a. March Field, headed West Coast military teams in 1943 (9–1–0). In its 35–0 victory over Southern California, back "Indian" Jack Jacobs (All-America Oklahoma) goes high to catch an air force aerial (Street & Smith's *Football Pictorial Yearbook 1944*).

"In what [was] perhaps the recruiting coup of the century," some 175 two-year starters converged on Southwestern Louisiana Institute in 1943 for V-12 training. The state banned SLI from intercollegiate football, but players formed all-star teams which went 5–0–1, including a win over Randolph Field. Back Alvin Dark (Louisiana State) and lineman Weldon Humble (All-America Rice) starred.[15]

Camp Davis posted one solid season in three, 1943, before dropping football. The AA's edged unbeaten Wake Forest 24–20 before 20,000 on base when T Johnny Mellus (All-America Villanova, New York Giants), an all-service selection, recovered a last-minute Wake Forest fumble. In whipping Fort Monroe 31–6, "There was nothing the Virginians could do about it," the Davis newspaper declared. "To begin with, they had no manpower. Only six substitutions attest to that. But they did have plenty of guts." Monroe's

48-man squad contained only four college players, nine semi-pros, and the rest had high school experience only. All 41 Davis players saw action.[16]

Having V-12 students guaranteed no success. Redlands, with many Marines, gave up the most points, blaming it on the "coach's unique 'Y' formation. The quarterback often got sacked before he could get rid of the ball."[17] Some schools, like Temple, without military trainees, pulled together a squad of 17-year-olds, but paid a financial price as attendance dropped two-thirds from 1942. Ohio State's athletic director, with only civilians, announced, "'We'll play football just so long as there are eleven boys who want to put on shoulder pads.'"[18] So they did, finishing 3–6–0 and hanging tough against Iowa Pre-Flight and Great Lakes. Buckeyes coach Paul Brown prohibited water buckets on the field, or a player from lying down unless hurt. "When Paul Brown sends a team on the field it is as tough mentally and physically as any commando unit."[19]

Whereas the 1942 Great Lakes roster contained almost all players with expired collegiate eligibility and several National Football League veterans, the average 1943 player equaled a freshman-sophomore, and no officers could play. Never mind. The Bluejackets soared as armed forces champions. When the sailors traveled a short distance to Evanston to meet Northwestern, the station's welfare and athletic fund paid for transporting 6,000 recruits.

Fielding informal teams, Boston College and Harvard tied 6–6 in front of 30,000 paying 50 cents per head at Harvard. Record keeping among "unofficial" team slipped a bit. Another account reported 40,000. Big Ten games drew 1,639,249 spectators (average 29,194) for 58 games, despite travel and transportation difficulties. The Columbia Lions (0–8–0) of coach Lou Little, an outspoken proponent of football as a combat conditioner, were outscored 33–313. Pennsylvania's back Bob Odell took the Maxwell Trophy as the best collegiate player.

Great Lakes 19, Notre Dame 14, December 2, 1943, Great Lakes, Illinois. This monster game originally was scheduled for Chicago's Comiskey Park in Chicago as a Fighting Irish Thanksgiving Day home game. University president Reverend J. Hugh O'Donnell generously offered to play the game at Ross Field on the station to entertain the sailors. Stadium seats were borrowed in part from the University of Chicago or constructed right there. Three times as many fans would have seen the game in Comiskey. Consequently, the Notre Dame athletic department lost some $50,000.

Lieutenant Paul Hinkle's inspired Bluejackets in every department outshone the Irish team hailed as one of the best in its history. "While millions listened in or awaited the news, nearly 22,000 officers and men of the station watched the making of a champion and the end of Notre Dame's dream of its first perfect season since [coach Knute] Rockne's last team in 1930."[20]

Rivalry between the two teams began in 1918 during World War I when Great Lakes opened.

Quarterback Steve Lach (6'1"/200, All-America Duke, Chicago Cardinals) played sparingly until the Irish went 80 yards in 20 plays to take a 14–12 lead with 66 seconds remaining. Told to pass, within 33 seconds Lach threw to Cecil Pirkey for 15 yards and to Paul Anderson for 55 for the winning touchdown. The Bluejackets snuffed the Notre Dame hopes when B Emil Sitko, recently a Notre Dame player, intercepted QB Johnny Lujack's desperation pass to end the game. Sitko and B Dewey Proctor scored the other touchdowns for Great Lakes.

Statistically speaking, the service teams performed well in the 1943 NCAA mix. "The freshmen war babies of college football's most difficult modern season ... completely upset expert predictions that they would rush to the air lanes because of inability to [master] of the ground attack." To the contrary: teams combined for less passing than any other recent season.[21] Notre Dame led the nation in total offense (10 games, 734 plays, 4,180 yards, 418.0 average). Iowa Pre-Flight was second (10, 583, 3,929, 392.9) and Army sixth (354.5). In rushing offense, Iowa Pre-Flight led with 324.4, followed by Army sixth (256.8) and Navy ninth (240.6).

In total defense, Duke led (9 games, 121.7), with Army seventh (152.5) and Navy eighth (161.2). In rushing defense, Navy (74.1) and Army (76.5) ranked seventh and eighth. No service teams placed in the top 10 for passing offense, passing defense, or punting. Army intercepted 29 passes (second) for 515 return yards. Navy was first in kickoff returns (14 for 28.8). Depauw's V-12 student Bob Steuber topped individual scoring (19 touchdowns, 15 conversions, 129 points). Among service teams, Len Eshmont of Del Monte Pre-Flight scored 73, Harvey Johnson of Bainbridge 68, and Tex Aulds of Randolph Field, Norm Standlee of Camp Davis, and Smith of Lubbock Field, 61.

### 1943 ASSOCIATED PRESS TOP 20*

| | Team | Record | Coach | After Bowls |
|---|---|---|---|---|
| 1 | Notre Dame | 9–1–0 | Frank Leahy | — |
| 2 | Iowa PF† | 9–1–0 | Don Faurot | — |
| 3 | Michigan | 8–1–0 | Fritz Crisler | — |
| 4 | Navy† | 8–1–0 | Billick Whelchel | — |
| 5 | Purdue | 9–0–0 | Elmer Burnham | — |
| 6 | Great Lakes NTS† | 10–2–0 | Tony Hinkle | — |
| 7 | Duke | 8–1–0 | Eddie Cameron | — |
| 8 | Del Monte PF† | 7–1–0 | Bill Kern | — |
| 9 | Northwestern | 6–2–0 | Pappy Waldorf | — |

### 9. "Around the Globe the Message Winged": The 1942–45 Seasons

In what observers generally considered the most exciting big-name wartime game, Great Lakes (Ill.) Naval Training Center defeated mighty Notre Dame, 19–14, on December 3, 1943, on a last-minute touchdown pass from quarterback Steve Lach to back Paul Anderson. The Fighting Irish had gone up 14–12 with 66 seconds remaining. Here former Irish back Emil Sitko (17) gains ground against his old team. Originally scheduled for Chicago's Comiskey Park, the game was moved to Great Lakes, with extra bleachers installed. Despite its loss, the Associated Press named Notre Dame No. 1 in its final poll (*National Collegiate Athletic Association Football Guide 1944*).

|    | Team              | Record | Coach             | After Bowls |
|----|-------------------|--------|-------------------|-------------|
| 10 | 4th Air Force*    | 9–1–0  | Paul Schissler    | —           |
| 11 | Army†             | 7–2–1  | Red Blaik         | —           |
| 12 | Washington        | 4–0–0  | Ralph Welch       | 4–1–0       |
| 13 | Georgia Tech      | 7–3–0  | Bill Alexander    | 8–3–0       |
| 14 | Texas             | 7–1–0  | Dana X. Bible     | 7–1–1‡      |
| 15 | Tulsa             | 6–0–1  | Henry Frnka       | 6–1–1       |
| 16 | Dartmouth         | 6–1–0  | Earl Brown        | —           |
| 17 | Bainbridge NTS†   | 7–0–0  | Joe Maniaci       | —           |
| 18 | Colorado College  | 7–0–0  | Hal White         | —           |
| 19 | College of Pacific* | 7–2–0 | Amos Alonzo Stagg | —           |
| 20 | Pennsylvania      | 6–2–1  | George Munger     | —           |

*Fourth Air Force defeated College of Pacific 19–0 after final poll released
†Military team
‡Texas tied Randolph Field 7–7 in Cotton Bowl

Ten organizations and publications selected All-America squads in 1943: Associated Press; *Colliers* (Grantland Rice); *The Sporting News*; *The Football News*; United Press; *Look* Magazine (Bill Stern), *Stars and Stripes*; International News Service; *New York Sun*; and Carlson's 3-Deep.

### 1943 CONSENSUS ALL-AMERICA

E   Ralph Heywood, Southern California; John Yonakor, Notre Dame
T   Donald B. Whitmire, Navy; James J. White, Notre Dame
G   Alex Agase, Purdue; John W. Weber, Georgia Tech; Pat Filley, Notre Dame
C   Casimir Myslinski, Army
B   Creighton Miller, Notre Dame; Angelo Bertelli, Notre Dame; Otto Graham, Northwestern; William Daly, Michigan; Bob Odell, Pennsylvania

### 1943 AP ALL-SERVICE TEAM
(AP ALSO SELECTED REGIONAL TEAMS)

E   Robert Finch, Camp Lejeune; Jack Russell, Blackland AAB
T   John Mellus, Camp Davis; Raymond Bray, Del Monte PF
G   Marion Rogers, South Plains AAB; Garrard Ramsey, Bainbridge NTS
C   Vince Banonis, Iowa PF
QB   Glenn Dobbs, Randolph Field
HB   Richard Todd, Iowa PF; Leonard Eshmont, Del Monte PF
FB   Bruce Smith, St. Mary's PF

### 1943 ALL-NAVY ALL-AMERICA *(COLLIER'S* /GRANTLAND RICE)

E   Jim Poole, Georgia PF; Ed Frutig, Corpus Christi NAS
T   Steve Hudacek, North Carolina PF; Bill Davis, Georgia PF
G   B. Jungmichel, San Diego NTS; Joe Ruetz, St. Mary's PF
C   George Svendsen, Iowa PF
QB   Frank Albert, St. Mary's PF
HB   George McAfee, Jacksonville NAS; Dick Fisher, Iowa PF
FB   Bruce Smith, Great Lakes NTS

# 1944

After characterizing 1943 as "wallowing in this mire," the same national magazine saw an entirely different 1944. Football "knew at last where it stood, what it could expect, and it started forward," mostly expunging inequalities. Even schools with navy students lacked "the good, veteran, carry-over material.... Crowds were bigger. Criticism of the game died down." Freshmen proved they could compete on the varsities, and coaches better understood the landscape.[22]

Forty-four schools returned to football: Princeton, Alabama, Mississippi State, Kentucky, Auburn, Tennessee (undefeated till losing the Rose Bowl to Southern California), Florida, Michigan State, Southern Illinois, Syracuse, New York University, and Boston College among others. As traditional, the season opened with the College All-Stars versus the NFL champion, that year the Chicago Bears. Gate receipts of $78,000 went to the Army Air Forces Aid Society and the Chicago Service Men's Center. Hundreds of war veterans starred upon returning to gridiron action, including Joe Saia (Mississippi State), Buzzy Gher (Yale), George Savitsky (Pennsylvania), and Bon Turner (Rice). The Second Air Force suited up 19 combat veterans.

Military football, and consequently the college game, zoomed to its finest season in 1944. Clever coaches donning service uniforms mentored sparkling professional and collegiate talent on bases and in the officer trainee programs. Called "gladiator giants," the service personnel "set a standard of play that bristled with cleated brilliance from warm autumnal openings through frigid New Year's Day." Saddled with curtailed practices

Quarterback Frankie Albert (All-America Stanford) made the Colliers/Grantland Rice first team, all-navy squad in 1943, at St. Mary's Pre-Flight. He learned the T formation under coach Clark Shaughnessy, considered the offense's father (Street & Smith's *Football Pictorial Yearbook 1942*).

because of duty and study obligations, service elevens sometimes lacked a competitive preparation for Saturday's games, tending to offset their edge in material.[23] For many colleges, sea duty and the draft beckoned "Lend-Lease" talent and recent high-school graduates respectively, leaving green players and substandard football to complete ambitious schedules.

Randolph Field (Tex.) and Bainbridge (Md.) Naval Training Center topped the military elevens. "Never in the South has such a glittering assortment of big name football talent been corralled on one squad as the West Point of the Air [Randolph] boasted in 1944."[24] Some observers felt the sailors earned No. 1 for their consecutive unbeaten campaigns. But aside from Bainbridge and Fleet City (Calif) Navy, the numbered air force commands took front and center, and within the military mix, beat up on each other. Randolph (11–0–0) outscored the opposition 508–19. The Third Air Force, around HB Charlie Trippi, lost to Great Lakes and Randolph. The Fourth Air Force, leaning on triple-threat "Indian" Jack Jacobs, tied Alameda Coast Guard and Second Air Force (which led the nation with 513 points), and lost only to Randolph. Second Air Force did not hesitate to schedule the best. Its 15 games, enormous for the time, saw losses to Iowa Pre-Flight, Norman Naval Air Station (6–0–0), Third Air Force, and Randolph.

Army stockpiled young players as Navy collected a number of outstanding college players. Neither lost a player to the draft. West Point climaxed a season of total domination which still invokes notoriety as the greatest college team of all time. They administered

Back Linus Parker "Bullet" Hall (Mississippi, Cleveland Rams) starred at Del Monte (Calif.) Pre-Flight in its only season, 1943, and at St. Mary's (Calif.) Pre-Flight in 1944 (Street & Smith's *Football Pictorial Yearbook 1945*).

each opponent's worst defeat of the season while earning the Williams Trophy as national champions and the Lambert Trophy for eastern "gridiron supremacy." Coach Earl "Red" Blaik remarked: "'Seldom in a lifetime's experience is one permitted the complete satisfaction of being part of a perfect performance.... To the squad members, by hard work and sacrifice, you superbly combined ability, ambition, and the desire to win, thereby leaving a rich heritage for future Academy squads. From her sons West Point expects the best—you were the best. In truth, you were a storybook team.'"[25]

Both North Carolina Pre-Flight, behind QB Otto Graham (Northwestern), and Georgia Tech, beat Navy early. The Midshipmen whipped Notre Dame before losing 23–7 to Army's gridiron machine before 70,000 in Baltimore for the national championship, the Cadets' first ever. Going in, the academies ranked No. 1 (Army) and 2, with Navy favored against Army's untried line. The Cadets celebrated the Point's 150th anniversary by breaking a five-game skid to the Midshipmen. Army had "speed and power to burn ... equipped with the greatest array of talent in contemporary football," but Navy was "the riddle of 1944."[26]

Two all-time greats scored touchdowns in the 7–6 win by Fourth Air Force over St. Mary's Pre-Flight. The naval Air Devils' B Bruce Smith (All-America Minnesota, previously Great Lakes) scooped up a bouncing punt and ran 58 yards for a first half score. Then followed a sensational kickoff return and lateral play characteristic of that era's style. Back "Indian" Jack Jacobs (Oklahoma, Cleveland Rams) grabbed the kick at his three, cakewalked up the middle and fought hard to get to midfield before being cornered. "With a deft flip," he lateraled to Morris Buckingham (San Jose State, Washington Redskins), who "careened to the sideline where he lateraled in turn to Ollie Day (Southern California). Day zipped around Buckingham's neat block to the end zone." Hank Norberg (Stanford) booted the winning point after.[27]

Creative scribes piled on the South. Its 4-F players were the "Loose Ear Drum and Tight Ulcer Society," the Southern Conference region "the cigarette factory section" that "loves its football regardless of quality." Duke, coached by Eddie Cameron, dominated again, "a veritable rhapsody in blue ... supplied by those swashbuckling, navy-subsidized Blue Devils from the Grand Duchy of Durham." Stars like Tom Davis, a Marine dischargee, Jim LaRue, Cliff Lewis, Gordon Carver, and George Clark led Duke over Alabama in the Sugar Bowl, 29–26. Other quality coaches included Tom Young (North Carolina), Doc Newton (South Carolina), Frank Murray (Virginia), Beattie Feathers (N.C. State), and Peahead Walker (Wake Forest), who fielded perhaps the country's strongest all-civilian team (8–1–0), losing only to Duke.[28]

Saddled with army trainees prohibited from playing, eight Southeastern Conference ("the Hot Biscuit Belt") members had dropped football. Seven returned for 1944 with civilians, but Vanderbilt again played junior colleges. Georgia Tech doubled its season ticket sales and defeated Navy 17–15 in what might have been the year's best game, tabbed by Grantland Rice and others as a "sizzeroo ... the all-time tingler" at the top of pigskin thrillers. Navy's B Bobby Tom "Bob" Jenkins carried the opening kickoff 85 yards for a score, and Tech intercepted a goal-line pass in the last second. A late 18-yard field goal by Dinky Bowen provided the margin. Navy had just jumped ahead 15–14 on a safety.[29]

Perhaps the most exciting New England game saw the Melville Patrol

Always a classic matchup, the 1944 game between Great Lakes (Ill.) Naval Training Center and Notre Dame failed to produce an encore nail-biter as the Irish romped, 29–7 (game program, Great Lakes vs. Notre Dame, December 2, 1944).

Torpedo Boat team edge Holy Cross, otherwise unbeaten, 13–12. Man for man, the PT Boaters possibly fielded the most powerful players in the East. Their decorated veterans of fighting against the Japanese, former college stars, physically towered over smaller foes. Coach Leo "Dutch" Meyer's Texas Christian eleven (7–3–1), "a small, rugged band of opportunists," took the Southwest crown.[30] In the Rockies, 1943 doormats Denver and Utah pieced together entertaining squads of returning combat veterans, freshmen, and 4-F's.

The Big Ten staged perhaps the year's finest gridiron classics before large crowds, typical of the prewar environment. League champion Ohio State (9–0–0) set an attendance record using civilians. Playing mostly freshmen, Notre Dame (8–2–0) attracted half a million fans and lost only to Army and Navy. Iowa Pre-Flight rebounded from an opening loss to Michigan, 12–7, with ten straight wins.

Only four of the Pacific Coast Conference teams — Washington, UCLA, Southern California, and California — played, and depreciated material meant deteriorated quality. Coach Jeff Cravath built a Trojan team of navy and Marine trainees paced by HB Gordon Gray to capture their eighth consecutive Rose Bowl. San Diego Naval Training Center gave the Trojans their toughest game before losing 28–21. The hardest-fought military games matched Fourth Air Force over El Toro Marine Corps Air Station, 20–14, and the 0–0 air force deadlock between the Fourth and Second commands. Future Supreme Court justice B Byron "Whizzer" White (All-America Colorado, Pittsburgh Steelers, Detroit Lions), a navy man, played for Fort MacArthur.

Field goals won games for North Carolina Pre-Flight over Georgia Tech 3-0, and Atlantic City Naval Air Station over Swarthmore 3-0. Atlantic City, behind "All-around Tony Veteri," also beat Princeton, 31–6. Appropriately named FB Randall Rushing rushed the ball for Iowa Pre-Flight. But John Sailers played with the Third Air Force. Fullback Mark Major and HB Alex Minor played for Tennessee and Army. William Penn played at Yale, and Sgt. Harvard Yale Princeton was a paratrooper player at Fort Benning. Game attendance jumped to 5,555,000, for 333 home games played by 67 colleges covered in the AP's annual canvass, an increase of about 1.5 million (273 by 57) in 1943.

## 1944 ASSOCIATED PRESS TOP 20

|   | Team | Record | Coach | After Bowls |
|---|---|---|---|---|
| 1 | Army | 9–0–1 | Earl Blaik | — |
| 2 | Ohio State | 9–0–0 | Carroll Widdoes | — |
| 3 | Randolph Field | 11–0–0 | Frank Tritico | — |
| 4 | Navy | 6–3–0 | Oscar Hagberg | — |

| Team | Record | Coach | After Bowls |
|---|---|---|---|
| 5 Bainbridge NTC | 9–0–0 | Joe Maniaci | — |
| 6 Iowa Pre-Flight | 10–1–0 | Jack Meagher | — |
| 7 Southern California | 7–0–2 | Jeff Cravath | 8–0–2 |
| 8 Michigan | 8–2–0 | Fritz Crisler | — |
| 9 Notre Dame | 8–2–0 | Ed McKeever | — |
| 10 4th Air Force | 7–1–2 | Paul Schissler | — |
| 11 Duke | 5–4–0 | Eddie Cameron | 6–4–0 |
| 12 Tennessee | 8–0–1 | John Barnhill | 8–1–1 |
| 13 Georgia Tech | 8–2–0 | Bill Alexander | 8–3–0 |
| 14 Norman NAS | 6–0–0 | John Gregg | — |
| 15 Illinois | 5–4–1 | Ray Eliot | — |
| 16 El Toro MCAS | 8–1–0 | Dick Hanley | — |
| 17 Great Lakes NTC | 9–2–1 | Paul Brown | — |
| 18 Fort Pierce | 9–0–0 | Hampton Pool | — |
| 19 St. Mary's Pre-Flight | 4–4–0 | Jules Sikes | — |
| 20 2nd Air Force | 7–2–1 | Bill Reese | — |

### 1944 TEAM RATINGS & RANKINGS, COMPILED BY DR. L. H. BAKER

| | Natl. Rank | Coll. Rk. | Svc. Rk. | Coach | |
|---|---|---|---|---|---|
| 1 | Randolph Field | | 1 | Frank Tritico | 11–0–0 |
| 2 | Army | 1 | | | |
| 3 | Iowa Pre-Flight | | 2 | Jack Meagher | 10–1–0 |
| 4 | Bainbridge NTC | | 3 | Joe Maniaci | 9–0–0 |
| 5 | Ohio State | 2 | | | |
| 6 | 4th Air Force | | 4 | Paul Schissler | 7–1–2 |
| 7 | Southern California | 3 | | | |
| 8 | Norman NAS | | 5 | John Gregg | 6–0–0 |
| 9 | Navy | 4 | | | |
| 10 | Michigan | 5 | | | |
| 11 | St. Mary's Pre-Flight | | 6 | Jules Sikes | 4–4–0 |
| 12 | Notre Dame | 6 | | | |
| 13 | Camp Peary | | 7 | | |
| 14 | El Toro MCAS | | 8 | Dick Hanley | 8–1–0 |
| 15 | Georgia Tech | 7 | | | |
| 16 | Indiana | 8 | | | |
| 17 | Duke | 9 | | | |
| 18 | Tulsa | 9 | | | |

|  | Natl. Rank | Coll. Rk. | Svc. Rk. | Coach |
|---|---|---|---|---|
| 19 | Fleet City | | 9 | |
| 20 | 3rd Air Force | | 10 | |
| 21 | North Carolina Pre-Flight | | 11 | |
| (25) | Great Lakes NTC | | 12 | Paul Brown 9-2-1 |
| 27 | Georgia Pre-Flight | | 13 | |
| 27 | San Diego NTC | | 14 | |
| 30 | Alameda CG | | 15 | |

### 1944 WILLIAMSON RANKINGS — SERVICE TEAMS
(By 1944, the only ranked army teams of consequence were air force commands or airfield teams.)

1 — Randolph Field
2 — Iowa PF
3 — Bainbridge NTC
4 — Camp Peary
5 — Norman NAS
6 — North Carolina PF
7 — 4th Air Force
8 — Great Lakes NTC
9 — Fort Pierce
10 — 3rd Air Force
11 — El Toro MCAS
12 — 2nd Air Force
13 — San Diego NTC
14 — Shoemaker Field
15 — St. Mary's PF
16 — Amarillo AAF
17 — Alameda CG
18 — Georgia PF
19 — Melville PTB
20 — Maxwell Field
21 — Lincoln AAF
22 — Jackson AAB
23 — Daniel Field
24 — Fort Warren
25 — Lubbock AAF

### 1944 CONSENSUS ALL-AMERICA TEAM

E   Philip Tinsley, Georgia Tech; John Dugger, Ohio State; Paul Walker, Yale
T   Don Whitmire, Navy; John Ferraro, Southern California
G   William C. Hackett, Ohio State; Benjamin S. Chase, Navy
C   Caleb Warrington, Auburn; John Tavener, Indiana
B   Leslie Horvath, Ohio State; Robert T. Jenkins, Navy; Glenn Davis, Army; Felix Blanchard, Army

### 1944 AP ALL-SERVICE TEAM
(AP ALSO SELECTED REGIONAL TEAMS)

E   Jack Russell, Randolph Field; Nick Suseoff, 2nd AF
T   Joe Stydahar, Fleet City; John Woudenberg, St. Mary's PF
G   Garrard Ramsey, Bainbridge NTC; Russell Letlow, Camp Peary
C   George Strohmyer, Iowa PF
QB  Otto Graham, North Carolina PF
B   Charley Trippi, 3rd Air Force; Leonard Eshmont, Norman NAS; William Dudley, Randolph Field

## 1944 Conference Champions

| | |
|---|---|
| Big 10 | Ohio State 6–0–0 |
| Big 6 | Oklahoma 4–0–1 |
| Ivy League | Army 3–0–0 |
| Missouri Valley | Oklahoma A&M (now State) 1–0–0 |
| Pacific Coast | Southern California 3–0–2 |
| Skyline | Vacant (World War II) |
| Southeastern | Georgia Tech 4–0–0 |
| Southern | Duke 4–0–0 |
| Southwestern | Texas Christian 3–1–1 |

## 1944 Official NCAA Records (Selected)
### (Yards per Game)

*Total Offense*

| | | |
|---|---|---|
| 1 | Tulsa | 434.7 |
| 2 | Army | 430.8 |
| 3 | Randolph Field | 377.0 |
| 4 | Auburn | 365.2 |
| 5 | Ohio State | 362.7 |
| 9 | Navy | 351.0 |
| 12 | Great Lakes NTC | 328.0 |

*Total Defense*

| | | |
|---|---|---|
| | Virginia | 96.8 |
| | Randolph Field | 110.8 |
| | Michigan State | 115.3 |
| | Army | 129.1 |
| | Wake Forest | 129.6 |
| | Navy | 136.3 |

*Rushing Offense*

| | | |
|---|---|---|
| 1 | Army | 298.6 |
| 2 | Tulane | 296.3 |
| 3 | Illinois | 294.0 |
| 4 | Auburn | 292.0 |
| 5 | Ohio St | 278.4 |
| 8 | Randolph Field | 257.4 |
| 10 | Navy | 240.7 |
| 14 | Great Lakes NTC | 230.8 |

*Rushing Defense*

| | | |
|---|---|---|
| | Randolph Field | 29.6 |
| | Navy | 53.8 |
| | Virginia | 55.4 |
| | Army | 57.6 |

*Passing Offense*

| | | |
|---|---|---|
| 1 | Tulsa | 206.3 |
| 2 | Georgia Tech | 142.0 |
| 3 | Georgia | 138.2 |
| 4 | Army | 132.2 |
| 5 | Oklahoma A&M | 126.0 |
| 9 | Randolph Field | 121.3 |
| 13 | Navy | 110.3 |

## 1945

Because the season swung into motion before August 14, 1945, the war's end failed to raise the level of college football. The armed forces did not rush to release players, nor did many colleges with suspended programs immediately restart them. Servicemen counted their discharge points and anxiously awaited civilian life. Lifting gasoline rationing helped attendance to soar. But what about the talent? "Mistakes, due to inexperience, will mark every game — and the people, they love it. There's nothing duller than perfection."[31]

Some players enjoyed a fifth year of competition versus three allowed prewar. Texas Christian's roster carried 17 dischargees. Many navy–Marine trainees hailed from combat fleets and the "hell-blasted atolls of the Pacific. Few of them have high-test football experience, and none are superstars.... Most of the better yearlings are bordering 18, and service needs will thin them with every call-up."[32] Those coaches and players back on campus were "mature and relaxed, relieved to get on with football after their experiences in uniform ... a release from the emotions of war, a chance to show off some of that know-how they had picked up playing with old pros and old collegians." These effects sustained through the 1950 College All-Star game when the last of the "war veteran" players upset the NFL champion Philadelphia Eagles.[33]

Before 102,000 in Philadelphia, Army sank Navy, 32–15 to maintain its second straight undefeated season as No. 1. Scalpers sold tickets for many times their face value. Five games earlier, a woefully underdog Melville (R.I.) Motor Torpedo Boat squad, loaded with Pacific veterans but short of bodies, shocked the gridiron world by leaping ahead of Army 13–0 before succumbing to the cadets' depth, 55–13.

Two of the sport's fastest backs dueled for a "stirring play." Navy's Clyde "Smackover" Scott scored on a 62-yard reception, but only after Army's Glenn Davis missed the interception. "Davis started from seven yards behind and the chase was on. Who can say which player was faster? ... There was a split second before Scott could reach full speed.... Davis caught Scott at the goal line and they both tumbled into the endzone. It's safe to say no other back in America at the time, over 40 yards, could have survived pursuit by Davis to paydirt."[34]

Three weeks prior, the Midshipmen, "stumbling like an awkward giant through most of the season," tied Notre Dame 6–6 in the final quarter as Scott blazed in with a long interception return.[35] However, a third-string halfback, Anthony "Skippy" Minisi (Pennsylvania), saved Navy's day in the last minute by tackling Irish HB Phil Colella at the goal line in the season's most controversial call. Was he over? Navy then stopped bucks by QB Frank Dancewicz and HB Terry Brennan on the final plays. The NCAA opined that "many seasons will pass before the grandstand quarterbacks cease debating whether or not the Irish pushed over the last period touchdown which the camera proved was shy a hair or two."[36]

Scott, who was on the field, remembered the controversial play and believes the ball carrier was stopped short. "Tony Minisi came across at the right angle and hit the guy. In those days there was nothing like reaching the ball across the goal line. He tucked the ball under him and fell. The play was legitimate. If I'd have been on the Notre Dame side, I would have hollered touchdown! Touchdown!"[37] Notre Dame was suffering: HB Elmer Angsman lost 11 teeth, FB Frank Ruggerio entered the university infirmary with 13 stitches in his chin, FB John Panelli went out for the season with a separated shoulder, and G Vince Scott had a concussion.[38]

Fleet City 48, El Toro 25, Dec. 9, Los Angeles (Calif.) Coliseum, before 55,000 spectators — this decided the national military championship. *Los Angeles Times* writer Al Wolf called it "the wildest scoring duel the Coliseum ever witnessed," the College Football Historical Society notes. Wolf added: "Touchdowns piled up so rapidly for a while that the scoreboard smoked." One account stated as many as 60,000 attended, and another that more than 90,000 attended when servicemen were admitted free at halftime. Undoubtedly it was the biggest West Coast game of 1945.[39]

After El Toro QB Paul Governali tossed a scoring pass to HB Elroy Hirsch, sailor B Buddy Young retali-

El Toro (Calif.) Marine Corps Air Station quarterback Paul Governali (All-America, Maxwell Trophy Columbia) passed the Flying Marines to a 16-3-0 mark in 1944-45 (Street & Smith's *Football Pictorial Yearbook 1945*).

ated with a 94-yard kickoff return and 88-yard punt return for two lightning strikes. Governali's pass put the Flying Marines ahead at halftime, 18–14. Fleet City's 78-yard drive made it 21–18, but the gyrenes forged ahead with another Hirsch scoring catch, 25–21, their final points. Young ran 20 yards as the third quarter ended, 28–25. Then the sailors poured it on with three fourth-quarter touchdowns. "'Never have I seen an individual [Young] totally humiliate 11 top-flight performers so woefully,'" stated the *Los Angeles Herald Examiner*. "He ran away from them. Made them look like novices."[40] Governali completed 29 of 45 for 228 and three scores.

Before the game Flying Marine coach Lieutenant Colonel Dick Hanley said, "There had been charges the week before that Fleet City was loading up by importing the nucleus of the Pearl Harbor navy team. I want it known that we are not complaining about the addition of these men. More power to the sailors." Afterward: "We just ran out of gas. They had too much reserve strength for us and wore us down. Do you realize they employed 16 backs?" The war was over, of course, but reportedly in a fit of pique, Marine commander Lieutenant General Roy Geiger shipped a number of key El Toro players to Japan or China for occupation duty.[41]

"The last hurrah for the training center teams" came on the final Saturday. Starless Great Lakes, playing mostly high schoolers, enlisted men, former college reserves, and small college stars, stunned football by lashing Notre Dame, 39–7, with 26 fourth-quarter points. Some Great Lakes players were long overdue for a discharge. The Bluejackets completed their World War II gridiron record "'with a blaze of triumph.'"[42]

Numerous bases canceled schedules. The Second Air Force claimed QB Frank Sinkwich (5'11"/200, Heisman Trophy 1942, All-America Georgia, Detroit Lions), T Fred Davis (Alabama, Redskins), and lineman Clyde "Bulldog" Turner (6'1"/250, Hardin-Simmons, Bears). However, Sinkwich injured a knee against El Toro and went out for season. Turner took five days leave to play for the Chicago Bears. The *Denver Post* reported team dissension because the Superbomber coaches would not use the T formation.[43]

Attendance rose considerably, with 7,927,000 in 1945, an increase of 2.4 million over 1944. St. Mary's College, led by All-America QB Herman Wedemeyer, achieved the No. 7 ranking using 22 17-year olds. No gridiron deaths occurred in college games.

Sportscaster Bill Brandt selected an "All-Purple Heart Collegiate All-America" team, then perhaps the most noteworthy all-star eleven ever. The selectees, who had recovered from combat wounds to star for their colleges, included ends Bill Hearn (Texas Christian) and Bob Korte (Nebraska); tackles Bill Schuler (Yale) and Chan Caldwell (Tennessee); C Jack Miller (Georgia); backs Bob Cain (Virginia), Ernie Case (UCLA), Bob Ravera (Nevada),

Playing mostly high schoolers, previous military power Great Lakes (Ill.) Naval Training Center immediately skidded into unaccustomed mediocrity (6–4–1) in the final wartime season, yet crunched Notre Dame 39-7. Here Ohio State's back Dick Flanagan scores a one-yard touchdown against the Bluejackets (9–2–1) in 1944. The No. 2-ranked Buckeyes (9–0–0) won, 26-6, before 73,477 in Columbus (*National Collegiate Athletic Association Football Guide 1945*).

and Merrill Frost (Dartmouth). Hearn lost an eye in the South Pacific. Korte was severely wounded twice in Germany. Combat pilot Schuler was badly burned in an air crash. Caldwell was shot in the stomach invading Italy. Miller was shot down over St. Lo, France. Cain was wounded at Tinian and Iwo Jima. Case was shot down in a B-26, severely wounded, and captured by the Germans. Ravera lost his left hand and wrist in France. Frost was shot down over Italy, almost burned to death, was in a hospital 18 months, and had new face grafted, including ears. The most courageous college player was Army's "Blondie" Saunders, who lost his left leg after being shot down in Burma on his 241st combat mission.[44]

### 1945 AP POLL (NO SERVICE TEAMS EXCEPT ARMY/NAVY)

1 Army
2 Alabama
3 Navy
4 Indiana
5 Oklahoma A&M
6 Michigan
7 St. Mary's College (Calif.)
8 Pennsylvania
9 Notre Dame
10 Texas
11 Southern California
12 Ohio State
13 Duke
14 Tennessee
15 Louisiana State
16 Holy Cross
17 Tulsa
18 Georgia
19 Wake Forest
20 Columbia

## 1945 Consensus All-America

E   Max Morris, Northwestern; H. Richard Duden, Jr., Navy; Hubert Bechtol, Texas; Bob Ravensberg, Indiana

T   Dewitt "Tex" Coulter, Army; George Savitsky, Pennsylvania

G   John F. Green, Army; Warren Amling, Ohio State

C   Richard Scott, Navy; Vaughn Mancha, Alabama

B   Herman Wedemeyer, St. Mary's (Calif.); Bob Fenimore, Oklahoma A&M; Glenn Davis, Army; Felix Blanchard, Army

## 1945 AP All-Service Team

E   Hampton Pool, Fort Pierce; Nick Susoeff, 4th AF

T   Bruiser Kinard, Fleet City; Fran Merritt, 3rd AF

G   Rocco Canale, 1st AF; Jack Freeman, AAF Training Command

C   Bulldog Turner, 2nd AF

B   Paul Governali, El Toro MCAS; Claude "Buddy" Young, Fleet City; Bill Paschal, 1st AF; John Stryzkalski, 4th AF

## 1945 Williamson Service Rankings

1. Fleet City (Shoemaker Field)
2. El Toro MCAS
3. 3rd AF
4. AAF Training Command
5. Jacksonville NAS
6. 4th AF
7. San Diego NTC
8. Corpus Christi NAS
9. Great Lakes NTC
10. Little Creek Navy
11. Air Transport Command
12. Hutchinson NAS
13. Personnel Distribution Center
14. 1st AF
15. 2nd AF
16. EFTC
17. Fort Pierce
18. Fort Benning
19. St. Mary's PF
20. Camp Cooke

As the final wartime season kicked off, a national magazine cast doubts on military football on the West Coast, which could be interpreted as having national application. Many coaches had "failed to get the most out of their men," it stated, "some of whom haven't been particularly interested in playing football anyway." Of course. Understandably. What mattered most to the boys in uniform was discharge, home, family, and future. The war was over. Time to get on with life. The magazine sarcastically made one final prediction: Service football "will pass with little regret among the dyed in the wool ... football filberts who have displayed a strange apathy to their big name stars all along." Those stars "will be only a war memory by this time next year."[45]

Maybe so, but many of those stars played on and gathered fame for self and team. What has been easily forgotten or simply ignored is how the sport itself played on, overcoming or coping with innumerable obstacles, and its vital role in helping to win the war.

CHAPTER 10

# "All America Will Cheer a Champion, Whether He Is Black, Brown, Yellow or White": Black Players and Professional Football

*"Fourth Air Force had a black player named Woody Strode. Ernie Nevers — the only game he played — was supposed to block Strode but he hadn't blocked him yet. Our colonel [coach Dick Hanley] was yelling at me. Walter Clay said 'put me in, I'll get him.' Clay threw him an uppercut and he went down. We didn't know why everyone was booing us. We were the only players on that side of the field. We thought we were going to need an armed guard to get off the field."*[1] — Julian Pressly

For Woodrow Wilson Woodwine Strode, former UCLA lineman and future Los Angeles Ram and long-time movie character actor, surely it would not be his last time on the deck.

For Pressly, El Toro (Calif.) Flying Marines guard and white, this 1944 experience with a superb opponent never faded. Besides, Fourth Air Force (7-1-2) administered the powerful Marines' only loss in an 8-1-0 season, 20-14.

Strode was among a number of military wartime or postwar standout black football players. Determining the extent of black player participation in World War II military football, however, is difficult. I found scant records, and the annual National Collegiate Athletic Association guides among publications provided limited details about black players in the military or at black schools. Even then the reviews or previews focused on collegiate programs.

For certain, though, by 1945 black college football was institutionally secure. "Athletics exemplify America's democracy and have done more to break down racial barriers and discrimination than any other organization in the world," a commentator claimed. "All America will cheer a champion, whether he is black, brown, yellow or white."[2]

Racial segregation in the South necessitated separate teams on any base fielding a white team, although military officials formed far fewer black teams. Those segregated elevens played limited "black schedules" primarily among other southern bases, and only a handful sponsored multiple seasons. Racially mixed teams were confined to northern, Midwestern, and western bases. Identifying a black player on such a roster is possible if a sportswriter or observer noted it, particularly if that player excelled. Yet overwhelmingly whites dominated military rosters, either 100 percent or close to it. And blacks did not play at southern white schools participating in the navy and Marine Corps V-5 and V-12 officer training programs.

Besides Strode, HB Claude "Buddy" Young (5'5"/160, Illinois) of Fleet City (Calif.) Navy ran rings around the opposition, as Pressly also recalled. "I spent the whole [1945] game chasing him all over the field. We never caught him. We were aware Fleet City was bringing another team from Pearl Harbor. They outsmarted us. They brought 10–12 players from the All-Stars. We were literally just worn out. We were aware of QB Charlie O'Rourke [All-America Boston College], but not Buddy Young."[3] The sailors defeated El Toro (8–2–0) twice that year, including 48–25 in the game considered to be the greatest all-military matchup of the war. After Illinois tied perennial wartime power Great Lakes at 26 in 1944, the Bluejackets agreed that the sprint champion Young and black HB Paul Patterson (5'9"/185) "were two of the fastest men they ever faced."[4] Patterson also suited up for a navy team the next season.

We don't know how many blacks played on white service teams outside the South. Roster, game program, and football publication photographs I examined rarely showed black players. For instance, the great Bainbridge (Md.) Naval Training Center 1943-44 elevens apparently had none. In 1942 four blacks played for Fort Knox in Kentucky, including HB John Foston (6'1"/190, Alabama State) and FB Ed Perkins. Quarterback Earl Meneweather (Humboldt State) created a journalistic buzz with his lightning runs for Fort Warren (Wyo.) in 1943. End Sam Baker was shown in the *Great Lakes Bulletin* playing against Michigan in 1945.

Those blacks who starred burst on the national scene in 1944-45 and included a number who achieved postwar collegiate or professional recognition. They included Strode, Young, and FB Marion Motley (6'1"/210, South Carolina State, Nevada) at the Great Lakes (Ill.) Naval Training Center.

The 1943 *NCAA Guide* reported on the first wartime black collegiate season. "The Great War boosted football morale and fighting spirit. The slogan for all teams was VICTORY. Believing their team could win awakened 'the do or die' spirit in players and kept them fighting determinedly throughout games. The military draft claimed many star players, broke up several schedules, and caused the disbandment of a few teams."[5] Thus small schools such as St. Paul's, St. Augustine's, and Shaw could not execute their schedules. In 1943 rosters were smaller than usual and schedules shorter. Army elevens at Camp Butner (N.C.), Camp Pickett (Va.), Bryan Air Field (Tex.), Camp Holabird (Md.), and Camp Swift (Tex.) played one-and-done seasons. For instance, opponents outscored Butner (0–4–0) 155–6.

The number one collegiate team, Morgan State College (5–0–0 and unscored-on), beat Florida A&M in the Capitol Classic in Washington, D.C., 50–0. Hampton scared Morgan, before losing on a safety, 2–0. Clarence Gaines, later the Hall of Fame basketball coach at Winston-Salem State, was a Morgan All-America tackle. Attempting to sustain football interest and morale and continue traditional rivalries, several teams played each other twice. Winston-Salem and Allen University of Columbia, S.C., met three times. Allen prevailed 33–0 and 12–6; the other game ended 6–6. Wilberforce, the only black Midwestern school playing, defeated West Virginia State twice. Only the Colored Intercollegiate Athletic Association, which operated with only six of its 14 members, and the Southwestern Association played as conferences.

In 1944 more black colleges fielded clubs than in 1943. Rail and motor transportation restrictions did not hurt attendance.

The 1943 Fort Francis E. Warren (Wyo.) Quartermasters featured black quarterback Earl Meneweather (Humboldt State), who created a journalistic buzz for his lightning runs. He was "a veritable ebony eel in his ability to writhe through the arms of tacklers in open field" and "the shiftiness and change of pace that goes with it makes him Fort Warren's most formidable threat as a broken field runner" (provided by John Gunn).

Eight CIAA schools fielded teams in 1944. The league took "pride in the belief that it [was] doing a small part on the home front in bolstering morale and in giving at least some mental diversion for those who [were] carrying the ball in that all-important game on foreign fields." Again fielding teams, Howard and Lincoln resumed their traditional Thanksgiving classic which highlighted the season.[6]

Black football that year surpassed 1943 but failed to reach prewar levels. Teams resuming the sport generated more interest and better schedules, and attendance surpassed any in history for two reasons: "(1) higher incomes; (2) the Negro colleges carried their games to the public rather than waiting for the public to come to their games." Most of the black schools were located in small, remote towns. Transportation difficulties and gasoline rationing restricted their drawing power. Tuskegee and Wilberforce played in bigger cities twice, including their annual game in Chicago. Wiley and Prairie View played their annual state-fair match in Dallas, Tex., before 16,000. Tuskegee (6–3–1) and Florida A&M (7–3–0) switched their game to heavily black-populated Jacksonville, the Aggies prevailing, 14–13.[7]

"Negro football," a national publication stated, "is no longer a tug-of-war or a push-and-shove, but is played scientifically, and with much skill and color. Each year brings about an increase in white patronage, one of

One of the multitude of future great professionals donning the military uniform was fullback Marion Motley (South Carolina State, Nevada) of Great Lakes (Ill.) Naval Training Center. The bruising runner later entered the National Football League Hall of Fame after a stellar Cleveland Browns career (*Great Lakes Bulletin*, November 9, 1945).

the signs that the game has improved."[8] Black coaches remained longer at their institutions than white coaches at theirs, perhaps because of relatively equal salaries at black schools among both faculty and coaches.[9]

A description of some representative military black teams appears below.

## Camp Lejeune (Jacksonville, N.C.), a.k.a. Montford Point Panthers

For 1944, a late-fall, seven-game schedule was arranged, but war requirements limited the team to a 2–1–0 record. The coach was William Porter (South Carolina State). Ben Whaley is believed to have been the first black Marine in pro football.

1945 MONTFORD POINT (5–3–1)

| | |
|---|---|
| Tuskegee AAF | 0–27 |
| Tuskegee AAF | 0–26 |
| Godman Field | 0–12 |
| Benedict College | 46–0 |
| Fayetteville State | 20–0 |
| Charlotte Bees | 21–0 |
| Charlotte Bees | 13–6 |
| Atlanta All-Stars | 7–7 |
| Atlanta All-Stars | 33–6 |

## Camp MacKall (Hoffman, N.C.) Chutists

Camp MacKall, located near the Fort Bragg complex, served as the black airborne training station. Although without a victory in two seasons, the 1945 club still ranked 63rd among Williamson's service rankings.

| 1944 CAMP MACKALL (0–3–0) | | 1945 CAMP MACKALL (0–5–0) | |
|---|---|---|---|
| Johnson C Smith | 0–20 | Kinston Marines | 0–6 |
| Morgan State | 0–39 | Presbyterian | 20–34 |
| Camp Lejeune | 6–52 | Cherry Point MCAS | 0–29 |
| | | Oak Grove Marines | 6–20 |
| | | Fort Bragg | 0–20 |

## Tuskegee (Ala.) Army Airfield Warhawks

The Warhawks, representing the future legendary Tuskegee Airmen on the gridiron, trained at Tuskegee Institute and Moton Field. In 1943 the team posted a 9–1–1 mark, losing to Clark 7–0 and tying Morris Brown 0–0, but avenged those games later by beating Morris Brown 32–13, and Clark in the postseason, 12–7.

The 1944-45 coach was Lieutenant William N. Bell (Ohio State). The NCAA called the 1944 team the year's top black military eleven. Tuskegee's 2–0 victory in Washington, D.C., over powerful Morgan State, their only loss, was reported as "one of the best games ever played by colored football teams." Thousands of fans from Virginia and Maryland joined Washingtonians in a crowd of 22,000. Some 20,000 attended the 13-all deadlock with Wilberforce in Chicago. On Thanksgiving Day in 1945, Tuskegee edged the white New London (Conn.) Submarine Base 14–7, before 20,000 in New York's Polo Grounds.

Ed Perkins (43) and F.E. Magar (61) shared fullback duties at Fort Knox (Ky.) in 1942. Four blacks played on that squad. How many blacks played on white military teams outside the South is impossible to determine. None played on white teams in a segregated South. Roster, game program, and football publication photographs rarely showed black players (provided by John Gunn).

| 1944 TUSKEGEE AAF (5–0–2) | | 1945 TUSKEGEE AAF (6–2–0) | |
|---|---|---|---|
| Algiers Navy | 32–12 | Camp Lejeune | 27–0 |
| Wilberforce | 13–13 | Camp Lejeune | 26–0 |
| Fort Benning (4th Inf) | 0–0 | Fort Benning | 0–26 |
| Fort Benning (4th Inf) | 7–6 | Fort Benning | 18–7 |
| Daniel Field | 34–0 | McDill Field | 0–6 |
| Montgomery Teachers | 21–0 | Fort McClellan | 33–0 |
| Morgan State | 2–0 | N.C. College | 14–0 |
| | | New London Sub Base | 14–7 |

Other bases fielding black teams in 1944 included Columbus AAF (Ga.), Bryan AAF (Tex.), Fort Benning (Ga.), Fort Riley (Kans.), Norfolk NTS (Va.), Aberdeen Proving Ground (Md.), Selman Field (La.), Randolph Field (Tex.), MacDill AAF (Ala.), Daniel Field (Ala.), and the 56th Engineers Training Battalion (Wash.).

In 1945 they also included Godman AAF (Ky.), MacDill, Fort Benning, Randolph Field, Fort Leonard Wood (Mo.), Jacksonville NAS (Fla.), Norfolk NTS, Galveston Naval Station (Tex.), Robins AAF (Ga.), Aberdeen Proving Ground, Fort McClellan (Ala.), and Camp Plauche (La.).

## Professional Football

Professional football reached its watershed in 1940, according to historian Robert W. Peterson, with the first game radio broadcast. Popular Red Barber announced the Chicago Bears' 73–0 trouncing of the Washington Redskins for the National Football League championship. Among the 36,034 spectators were 150 sportswriters. The year "heralded a revolution in offenses"— the T — which trickled down to colleges and high schools. In 1941 the league owners named as commissioner Elmer Layden, of the famed Notre Dame "Four Horsemen," and "sought to change pro football's image from a working stiff's sport to high-class entertainment."[10]

After December 7, Layden stuck with the regular schedule, but stated "everything we decide today may have to be abandoned tomorrow." "While we believe professional football has a definite place in the recreational program of a nation at war, nothing connected with it should or will be permitted to hinder the war effort.'"[11]

Preseason scrimmages and exhibition games formed the wartime relationship between the NFL and military football. A number of East Coast service elevens scrimmaged area NFL teams, such as the New York Giants and Redskins, often giving a worthy accounting. Veteran NFL players in uniform sometimes battled their former employers. In Hawaii and on the West Coast, without NFL teams, military and minor-league pro or semi-pro teams and service elevens played regularly scheduled games. A handful of eastern pro clubs dotted military schedules.

Several minor leagues folded or suspended operations, including the American Football League (the 1940-41 incarnation), the American Association, and the Dixie League. The Pacific Coast Professional Football League, founded in 1940 and one of the top minor leagues, continued operating and reached its zenith. Like other pro leagues, it suffered from a dearth of players. In 1944 a rival area league opened play, considered probably the only pro football league organized from scratch during wartime. The PCPFL faded after 1946 when the NFL expanded to California, but for a while it was probably second only to the NFL.[12]

Some teams, such as the San Diego Bombers, hired military players in their off-duty hours under assumed names. One of these was Marine Bob Dove (El Toro). "The Marines didn't want us playing outside ball. They didn't care if we got killed or got our leg broken playing football in the Marine Corps, but they didn't want us doing it on Sunday.'"[13]

As war siphoned the NFL ranks, by 1943 clubs desperately attempted to field adequate rosters. Several all-star players long-ago retired laced up the cleats again, including FB Bronco Nagurski, QB Arnie Hebner, and HB Ken Strong. The Brooklyn Dodgers greeted only seven returnees at training camp. The Cleveland Rams canceled the season. The Pittsburgh Steelers and Philadelphia Eagles became the "Steagles" and split the home schedule between cities.

In 1944 the NFL experienced severe problems recruiting players and bottomed out. College players facing military duty no longer could look ahead to entering the pros after graduation. Philadelphia regained its identity, but Pittsburgh merged with the Chicago Cardinals and were known as Card-Pitt Combine (0–10–0), jokingly called the "Carpets." The next year both Pittsburgh and Chicago operated separately, but the Boston Yanks and the Brooklyn Tigers (nee Dodgers) merged and played the 1945 season as the Boston Yanks, or just the Yanks.[14]

By 1944, "[f]ortified by the experience of two seasons of wartime operations, major league owners no longer wince at mention of the manpower problem. Selective Service had leveled the quality of material to a point where there are more favorites in the championship divisional than liberated towns in a Russian communiqué."[15] The season opened with 445 players on its ten clubs. Rosters contained only men "who actually participated in championship contests and who were active in the league at the time of their induction." Despite losing proven material to the services, the league believed "sufficient first class" could sustain compeititon.[16]

The NFL regrouped in 1945 with these franchises: the Yanks, Bears, Cardinals, Cleveland Rams (would move to Los Angeles in 1946), Detroit Lions, Green Bay Packers, Giants, Eagles, Steelers, and Redskins.

The following tables show the 1942–45 standings and champions.

### 1942 Regular Season

| *Eastern Division* | | *Western Division* | |
|---|---|---|---|
| Washington | 10–1–0 | Chicago Bears | 11–0–0 |
| Pittsburgh | 7–4–0 | Green Bay | 8–2–1 |
| New York | 5–5–1 | Cleveland | 5–6–0 |
| Brooklyn | 3–8–0 | Chicago Cardinals | 3–8–0 |
| Philadelphia | 2–9–0 | Detroit | 0–11–0 |

CHAMPION: Washington 14, Chicago Bears 6

### 1943 Regular Season

| *Eastern Division* | | *Western Division* | |
|---|---|---|---|
| Washington | 6–3–1 | Chicago Bears | 8–1–1 |
| New York | 6–3–1 | Green Bay | 7–2–1 |
| Phil-Pitt Combine | 5–4–1 | Detroit | 3–6–1 |
| Brooklyn | 2–8–0 | Chicago Cardinals | 0–10–0 |

CHAMPION: Chicago Bears 41, Washington 21

### 1944 Regular Season

| *Eastern Division* | | *Western Division* | |
|---|---|---|---|
| New York | 8–1–1 | Green Bay | 8–2–0 |
| Philadelphia | 7–1–2 | Detroit | 6–3–1 |
| Washington | 6–3–1 | Chicago Bears | 6–3–1 |
| Boston Yanks | 2–8–0 | Cleveland | 4–6–0 |
| Brooklyn | 0–10–0 | Card-Pitt Combine | 0–10–0 |

CHAMPION: Green Bay 14, New York Giants 7

### 1945 Regular Season

| *Eastern Division* | | *Western Division* | |
|---|---|---|---|
| Washington | 8–2–0 | Cleveland | 9–1–0 |
| Philadelphia | 7–3–0 | Detroit | 7–3–0 |
| Boston Yanks | 3–6–1 | Green Bay | 6–4–0 |
| New York | 3–6–1 | Chicago Bears | 3–7–0 |
| Pittsburgh | 2–8–0 | Chicago Cardinals | 1–9–0 |

CHAMPION: Cleveland 15, Washington 14

Six hundred thirty-eight active players served in the armed forces, and 69 were decorated. Twenty-one lost their lives: 19 active or former players, an ex-head coach, and a team executive. Of these, perhaps the best known player was Giants T Al Blozis (6'6"/250, all-league) killed in action in the Vosges Mountains, France, just six weeks after playing in the 1944 NFL championship game. The NFL donated the $680,383 in revenues from 15 exhibition games to military charities, the USO, and the Red Cross, and also raised $4 million in war bond sales in 1942.

That the NFL continued through the duration likely is due to the most famous players in the country, QB Sammy Baugh (Washington), QB Sid Luckman (Bears), and E Don Hutson (Green Bay), who remained with their clubs.

## CHAPTER 11

# "Not Satisfied to Listen to Short-Wave Broadcasts": Overseas Football, Postseason Games, and the Postwar

*"The American fighting man was not satisfied to listen to short wave broadcasts from bowl games played in the States. He wanted to play in a game or else be an actual spectator. Thousands of soldiers, sailors and Marines in Europe and the Pacific war areas put on their own football bowls with uniformed teams, cheering sections, regulation officials, bands and parades modeled after real American college football games."*[1]

During World War II, American armed forces transported freedom and football around the globe. Whenever space, time, and conditions allowed, the sport helped war-weary GI's maintain touch with home. From the desert to jungles to the ruins of the atomic bomb, officials organized pickup games for morale and entertainment and did their best to provide stateside gridiron news. After the war, some American occupying forces in Europe, particularly army units led by the 3rd Infantry Division, in 1945 traveled to play each other before the soldiers mustered out of service.

## Overseas Football

The U.S. Office of War Information (OWI), tasked with supplying news for troops overseas, soon found itself swamped with requests for football facts. Before the 1942 season ended, the OWI sent by cable and wireless about 7,500 words daily plus scores of hundreds of games, photographs, weekly roundups of college and professional leagues, and feature material for publication in military newspapers such as the *Stars and Stripes*.

The material circulated worldwide via hand, newspapers, mimeographed copies, headquarters directives, and short- and long-wave radio. Distribution showered without letup on troops stationed in or passing through New Guinea, North Africa, the Mediterranean, England, the Central Pacific, and Japan and in foxholes, barracks, and crew mess decks. The boys and girls in uniform wanted more, especially about the military teams. The official prevailing feeling: if they were home in peacetime, they would probably spend Saturdays or Sundays attending games.

On November 14, 1942, in what may have been the first overseas game played by U.S. forces, 8,000 in Belfast, Ireland, watched Hale defeat Yarvard, 9–7. That's right, Hale and Yarvard.

By 1943, the army organized a Special Services Division within the Army Service Forces to facilitate getting both the news and football equipment abroad. The troops introduced global football informally without fanfare. For one, the army formed teams which played in London's White City Stadium on May 8, 1943, with proceeds to a British charity.

Except for Hawaii, Australia, and New Zealand, Marines lacked rear-echelon areas in the Pacific suitable for football. To keep in shape for football, the gyrenes once took on an Australian club in a half-football, half-rugby match. "You never saw such a donnybrook and melee in your life, and it continued after the game followed by a few Australian beers." In February 1943 the artillery 11th Marines defeated the 5th Marine Raiders 6–0 for the First Marine Division championship at the Melbourne Cricket Ground. A packed house of 35,000 experienced American football for the first time, complete with a band and cheerleaders.[2]

Southwest Pacific Marines in 1944 invented "Ocean Football" around a 40-yard "field" of water. A team had to advance the distance under water in four downs. When a ball carrier surfaced, it was a down. Nevada traveled 1,650 miles by air to play the Alaska Clippers of the Army Air Transport Command.[3]

## Hawaii Teams

During the war, the U.S. Territory of Hawaii was considered overseas duty. Fourth Marine Division teams training on Maui could not use the division name for security reasons until after the Iwo Jima campaign in 1945, where at least four members died and eight were wounded. Thus, as Marine football historian John Gunn pointed out, its Central Pacific Armed Forces League (Hawaii teams) champions called themselves the "Maui Marines."[4]

## 11. "Not Satisfied to Listen to Short-Wave Broadcasts"

Before 25,000 on Oahu, Hawaii, a navy all-star eleven beat the army stars 14–0 for the Pacific Ocean championship on January 7, 1945. Sailor Jack Fields (Texas) carries. Sixteen All-Americas and 16 ex-professionals played in that game. Football after the war ended included sterling groups of military all-stars playing on Oahu. In 1945 military officials assembled ad hoc all-star teams of available personnel with snazzy new uniforms to entertain the troops and civilians (*Pacific Fleet at Play*, U.S. Navy postwar publication).

Football after the war ended included sterling groups of military all-stars playing on Oahu. In 1945 military officials assembled ad hoc all-star teams of available personnel, outfitting them with snazzy new uniforms to entertain the troops and civilians. Nearly every fall weekend saw a glamor game in Furlong Field at Pearl Harbor. Sailors played Marines, Marines played soldiers, soldiers played sailors, and sailors played airmen. Many stateside facilities had been shut down or curtailed as victory neared. So the services transferred many pigskin-playing servicemen to the West Coast and Hawaii in preparations for the planned invasion of Japan. Football welcomed them.

Navy all-stars included a number who had played for Bainbridge — B Charlie Justice (5'10"/175), B Dewey Proctor (5'11"/200, Furman), G Buster Ramsey (6'1"/200, William & Mary), C Lou Sossaman (6'1"/200, South Carolina), B Lloyd Cheatham (6'1"/200, Auburn) — plus B George McAfee (5'11½"/175, Duke), B Steve Lach (6'1½"/195, Duke, Chicago Cardinals), T Frank Hrabatin (6'4½"/215), T Bill Young (Washington Redskins), C Al

Matusa (Chicago Bears), B Bob Sweiger (6'0"/195, Missouri, Chicago Bears), and FB Bob Morrow (Chicago Cardinals). Lieutenant Jack White (Manhattan, Philadelphia Eagles, Providence pros) coached the group.

Marine stars included backs Alvin Dark (5'11"/175, Louisiana State), Bill Gray (Southern California), Bob Perkins (Rice), Rajah Rodgers (Alabama), John Podesto (5'11"/175, College of Pacific), Don Kasprzak (5'11"/165, Dartmouth), Chalmers Elliott (5'11"/175, Purdue), Hosea Rodgers (6'1"/192, North Carolina), and E John Yonakor (6'5"/215, Notre Dame).

An October clash between sailors and Marines prompted this message: "The battle is over. Victory is ours. But the spirit of the valiant Leathernecks and of courageous Bluejackets carries on. The scene of the never-to-be-forgotten sneak attack of nearly four years ago has been transformed into a field of friendly strife."[5]

Several representative pro and semi-pro teams formed to play military elevens and among themselves, notably the Honolulu or Hawaii Bears. The Bears signed former college and club players including B Edgar "Special Delivery" Jones (5'11"/200, All-America Pittsburgh) for $100 per game. But Jones performed only once, received his paycheck, and was dismissed along with B Harold Stratton. "Bear management told them it did not like their attitude," a newspaper revealed.[6] The Hawaii Senior Football League later validated the dismissals.

The Seventh Air Force fielded the most stable island military program against mostly pro and semi-pro teams. Established in 1940 and decimated by the attack on December 7, 1941, the command later played key roles in the aerial bombardments during the Battles of Midway and Wake Island, the assault on the Marshall, Gilbert, and Mariana Islands, and against Iwo Jima.

An interesting sidelight: Coach Captain Charles Erb, Jr., cared less for the huddle and instructed his 1943 team to call plays from their formations, and sought an old-fashioned quarterback/field general. His 36-man team had few college stars but some with collegiate or pro experience. Others played for the first time. Three hundred showed up for first practice. Lieutenant Mun Charn Wong of the Seventh Air Force, born and educated in Honolulu, had never played football but made the squad. Lacking the size and experience of his teammates, "this slender, unimposing chap has been coming along fast under Coach Erb's tutelage. His specialty is the rifling of a forward pass. Wong is one of those gridiron technicians who can add airmail to special delivery, to the great delight of the fans who like their football out in the open."[7] The non-conventional Erb was not shy. He wanted a ditty composed in Hollywood and recorded by his friend Bing Crosby. He phoned Crosby long distance and asked him for it, and immediately the crooner responded.[8]

The Seventh Air Force motto: "Attack and attack again ... paramount in the minds of every officer and man, from the commanding general to the newest yard bird. No exceptions."[9] For a January 1944 benefit game against the defending league champion Rainbows, Erb recruited Edgar Jones and several other military stars.

| 1943 SEVENTH AIR FORCE (2–3–0) | | 1944 SEVENTH AIR FORCE (7–1–0) | |
|---|---|---|---|
| Honolulu Bears | 13–10 | Hawaiian Pine | 18–6 |
| Hawaii U | 14–13 | Boulevard AC | 41–0 |
| Kaalas | 6–19 | Lanakilas | 56–0 |
| Hawaii U | 6–28 | Healani | 19–6 |
| Healani | 13–47 | Hawaii U | 27–10 |
| | | Kaalas | 37–0 |
| | | Sr League All-Stars | 13–6 |
| | | All-Navy | 0–14 |

**End Robert Witt (Mississippi Southern), who previously played for Keesler Field (Miss.) and was one of many service veterans playing for teams in Hawaii, suited up one last time for the Hawaiian Flyers air force eleven in 1945 (provided by John Witt).**

## Postseason and Bowl Games

The armed forces staged at least 27 bowl and all-star games following the 1944 season, 11 within the United States and 16 known games around the world. Combat action dictated when those games took place, with dates running from November 4 through January 21, 1945. Some of the postseason and bowl games included:

### 1943 Games

- Sun Bowl, El Paso, Tex., January 1— Second Air Force 13, Hardin-Simmons 7 (before 14,000)
- Lily Bowl, Hamilton, Bermuda, January 3 — Army 19, Navy 18
- London game, London, England, White City Stadium, May 8 — Crimson Tide Artillerymen vs. Fighting Irish Engineers

### 1944 Games

- Cotton Bowl, Dallas, Tex., January 1— Randolph Field 7, Texas 7
- Potato Bowl, Belfast, Ireland, January 1— Navy 0, Army 0
- Arab Bowl, Oran, Algeria, January 1— Army 10, Navy 7; second game, Oran Refrigeration Termites vs. Casablanca Ordnance Rabchasers. The Arab Bowl was described, "Here, in San Phillipe Stadium beside the sparkling waters of the Mediterranean, some 15,000 grid-hungry generals, admirals, nurses, WACs, soldiers and sailors — and a fair-sized sprinkling of high French and Arab dignitaries — witnessed the first doubleheader football bowl game ever

Major General William S. Key, the acting U.S. commander, European Theater of Operations, meets players prior to the game between the Crimson Tide (artillerymen) and Fighting Irish (engineers) in White City Stadium, London, England, May 8, 1943 (*National Collegiate Athletic Association Football Guide 1943*).

played." Actress Rosalind Russell and four army enlisted women were queens. The day included camel and burro racing with WACs as jockeys, WAC drills and reviews, martial music and a camera field day.[10]

- G.I. Bowl, London, November 12 — Army G.I.s 20, Navy Bluejackets 0 (60,000)
- Parc des Princes Bowl, Paris — Ninth Air Force vs. First General Hospital (20,000)
- Tea Bowl, London — Air Service Command vs. Eighth Air Force (12,000)
- Tea Bowl, London — Canada 16, USA 6 (30,000)
- Coffee Bowl, London — USA 18, Canada 0
- Bambino Bowl, Bari, Italy, November 23 — Technical School 13, Playboys 0
- Iranian Bowl, Tehran, December 12 — Camp Amirabad 20, Camp Khorramshahr 0 (9,000)
- Treasury Bowl, New York City, December 16 — Randolph Field 13, Second Air Force 6 (8,356)
- Lily Bowl, Hamilton, Bermuda, January 2 — Navy 19, Army 0
- Chigger Bowl, Dutch Guiana — two army air forces teams
- Poi Bowl, Honolulu, Hawaii, Pacific Ocean Area Service Championship — Navy 14, Army Air Forces 0 (29,000). The game program trumpeted, "King Football graciously bows his head today amid pageantry and color.... Even while the war rages ... the leaders of our fighting forces also realize this fact because they have cooperated to their utmost in seeing that all the color and splendor of a bowl gridiron contests are made available."

Oran, Algeria, was the scene of one of the most exotic military football bowl and postseason games. On January 1, 1944, the Arab Bowl doubleheader between army and navy elevens attracted 15,000 to San Phillipe Stadium. On a day of camel and burro races, famed actress Rosalind Russell and four army enlisted women were crowned queens (*Illustrated Football Annual 1944*).

Both teams came loaded. Navy posted nine All-Americas: Backs Lach, Edgar Jones, Charles Timmons (5'11"/215, Clemson), Andy Uram (5'11"/185, Minnesota); G Garrard Ramsey (6'1"/200, William & Mary), C Ki Aldrich (6'0"/210, Texas Christian); and tackles D. F. Palmer (6'2"/230, Texas Christian), Bob Suffridge (210, Tennessee), and C. W. Schultz (6'2"/225, Minnesota). Ten others had professional experience. The losers sported seven All-Americas, including backs John Kimbrough (6'2"/210, Texas A&M), Joe Williams (5'6"/175, Ohio), Jimmy Nelson (5'11"/180, Alabama), "Indian" Jack Jacobs (6'1"/190, Oklahoma), and Glenn Dobbs (6'4"/200, Tulsa); G Dick Barwegan (6'0"/200, Purdue); and E Harold Newman (6'1"/210, Alabama), plus five others with professional experience. Lieutenant Commander Tex Oliver (Oregon coach) coached the winners. Authorities prohibited civilians from attending but admitted service personnel free.[11]

The *Honolulu Advertiser* reported the navy dominated practically the entire distance and outplayed the air force everywhere. "Vicious line play turned the game into a battle of forward walls for most of the way." The Tars' ground attack generated 155 yards against the Bombers' 11, and "Special Delivery" Jones threw two touchdown passes.[12]

- Jungle Bowl — All-Stars 49, Marines 0
- Coconut Bowl, New Guinea
- Mosquito Bowl, Guadalcanal, Solomons, December 24 — 4th Marines 0, 29th Marines 0 (more about this game below).

## 1945 GAMES

- Spaghetti Bowl, Florence, Italy, January 1 — Fifth Army 20, 12th Air Force 0 (25,000). "When the victorious U.S. troops successfully invaded Sicily and then Italy, football went along with the boys. The name of the [bowl] game had to coincide with the presiding atmosphere."[13]
- Riviera Bowl, Marseille, France, January 1 — R. R. Shop Battalion 37, Army All-Stars 0 (18,000)
- Lily Bowl, Hamilton, Bermuda, January 7 — Navy 39, Army 6
- Manila Bowl, Manila, Philippines, July 4 — Army vs. Navy
- Rice Bowl, Tsingtao, China, November 10 — 3rd Battalion/29th Marines 7, 3rd Battalion/22nd Marines 7 (5,000; a semi-touch game)
- Brooklyn Bond Bowl Game, Brooklyn, N. Y., November 11 — First Air Force 24, Army Air Force Training Command 6
- Legion Bowl, Memphis, Tenn. — Fourth Air Force 27, AAFTC 0

## 1946 Games

(The services organized only a handful of post–1945 bowl games because too many personnel were transferring from former combat zones back to the States.)

- Tokyo Bowl, Tokyo, January 1—11th Airborne Division 26, 41st Division 12 (15,000)
- Army Pacific Olympics championship, Tokyo, January 27—11th Airborne Angeles 18, Honolulu All-Stars 0
- Bamboo Bowl, Manila, Philippines, Philippine Olympic title, January 1— Clark Field Acpacs 14, Leyte Base 12 (40,000)
- China Bowl, Shanghai, January 27—Navy 12, Army 0
- Atom Bowl, Nagasaki, Japan, January 1—Isahaya Tigers 14, Nagasaki Bears 13. Attention focused on the game site relative to where the second atomic bomb detonated. Snow covered the field and flurries fell. "The command [Second Marine Division] had no trouble finding a level surface to use as the playing field, which is how devastating 'The Bomb' actually was." Bill Osmanski and Angelo Bertelli captained the squads. Osmanski scored both touchdowns and booted the winning extra point.

Perhaps the most unusual bowl or overseas game was the Mosquito Bowl, played on the island of Guadalcanal, site of the first major American Pacific land victory, which by 1944 operated as a major Marine Corps depot and rear-echelon training base. On December 24, two infantry-regiment pickup teams from the 4th Marines and 29th Marines of the Sixth Marine Division met on a coral-base, dirt and gravel field, with temperature in the eighties and horrible humidity, and without helmets or shoulder pads. But tackling was disallowed so as "to preserve the men for more important things ahead." In other words, they could just be Marines.[15]

To the participants, it might as well have been the Rose Bowl, discarding the fact that the slugfest produced only a scoreless deadlock before 10,000 standing-room-only service personnel and island natives with nowhere else to go. "The outcome mercifully made academic the payoff of many thousands of dollars bet by the Marines on a game held on a Sunday, the day before Christmas," noted John Gunn in his meticulous research of this game.[16]

The "Mosquito Network" of the armed forces radio service broadcast the game throughout the South Pacific. Regimental bands played and a public address system blurted the action. Division commander Major General Lemuel Shepherd, Jr., attended, and, along with the regimental colonels, occupied the only folding chairs. Shepherd changed sides of the field at halftime. The 4th wore green T-shirts with a stenciled number on the back, and the

29th wore white similarly. Cut-off dungarees at the knees and field boots resembled football pants and cleated shoes.

The idea started as members of the 4th Marines enjoyed a few beers and boasted to the 29th about their great players. "Pretty soon, we each had bet $100 on the game. By game time, I'd bet $200," one Marine recalled. Then $100 was two months pay for some Marines.[17] Lacking sufficient practice time, both sides squandered opportunities to score within the 5-yard line. Players later remembered the games as one of the roughest they had ever played, as hard blocking and physical contact produced serious bruises and scraped knees and elbows.

Gunn determined for these players the game "had a life-or-death aspect. Within three and a half months, they would be fighting on Okinawa and twelve would die on the war-ravaged island." Almost all survivors received wounds and Purple Hearts or injuries. Two posthumously received the Navy Cross, two the Silver Star, and three the Bronze Star. Rosters shone with former professionals or NFL draftees, All-Americas, college players, and decorated combat veterans.

Those who died in Okinawa included:

> 4th Marines: E Jim Quinn (Amherst); E David Nathan Schreiner (All-America Wisconsin); T Bob Bauman (Wisconsin); and T Hubbard Hinde (Southern Methodist).
> 29th Marines: E Chuck Behan (DeKalb Teachers, Detroit Lions, Camp Lejeune 1943, Navy Cross); E George Edward Murphy (Notre Dame, Lejeune 1943); T Ed Van Order (Cornell); T John Hebrank (Lehigh); C Red DeGreve (Michigan); B Tony Butkovich (Illinois, All-America Purdue); B Wayne "Rusty" Johnston (Marquette); and B Johnny Perry (Wake Forest, Duke, Navy Cross).[18]

Two must be singled out. First Lieutenant Schreiner died of mortal wounds leading an assault on the last Japanese stronghold near the Kiyuma Gusuku castle just 12 hours before Americans secured the island on June 20, 1945. The former rifle platoon leader, elevated to company commander because of casualties, had gone forward of his unit to observe the terrain, and fell to grenades and small-arms fire.

First Lieutenant Murphy's rifle platoon was one of the first ordered against the heavily fortified Sugar Loaf Hill near Naha. Repelled, he helped evacuate wounded to an aid station. There a mortar shell killed him.

## Postwar

From August 1945 through 1949, "pent-up consumer demands" rejuvenated all sports.[19] As football charted a new era, thousands of young men entering colleges in 1946 after being discharged immediately turned to competitive athletics by nature, training, and instinct. Football boomed. "What you had after the war was about four classes' worth of teams all backed up and released at once," stated the College Football Hall of Fame historian.[20] Veterans came in all sizes and ages. "It was the strangest thing," future Kansas coach Don Fambrough said. "We had two types of players on the [Kansas] team. You had us 24- and 25-year guys who were married with kids and your 17- and 18-year-old freshmen who were calling us 'sir.' You never saw a happier bunch of guys than we were on those teams. We were so happy to be out of the service, back in school, and getting back with normal lives."[21]

Service football experience immediately impacted collegiate programs as dynasties continued at Notre Dame or were built at Oklahoma. The 1946 Fighting Irish national champs would include at least 11 military players, including HB Emil Sitko, FB Gerry Cowhig, T Luke Higgins, QB Johnny Lujack, and T Ziggy Czarboski. Taking nothing for granted, veterans everywhere fought for starting positions along with the youth who had recently finished high school.

One widely read 1946 preview magazine predicted the veterans would be "bigger, stronger, more experienced.... Whether they will have the zip and dash of the teenagers may be strictly up to the coaches," but competition for varsity jobs would be keen.[22] On campuses, officials thanked those who served and who came back ready to resume an interrupted career, or launch a new one. Optimism and enthusiasm prevailed and ticket sales zoomed. Coaches no longer worried about suiting up enough practice players, only having adequate equipment for them.

CHAPTER 12

# Clyde "Smackover" Scott and Bob Steuber: Personalities, Vignettes, and Anecdotes

*"Only a world war could have created a situation where Steuber was allowed to play again in college and nobody made a fuss."*[1]

Bob Steuber's odyssey was a trip and a half. An ace halfback (6'2"/190) for Missouri from 1940 to 1942, All-Big Six, All-America in 1942, he then played one game for the Chicago Bears in September 1943 before being drafted. The navy sent the future Hall of Famer to DePauw University in 1944 in the V-12 officer-candidate program, where he and his team exploded. With one collegiate season of eligibility left, he returned to play at Missouri in the late 1940s and is probably the only known man in the game's history to play collegiately after playing professionally.

In whipping the National Football League champion Washington Redskins 27–7, the 1943 College All-Star team fielded perhaps the finest backfield in the history of the series: QB Otto Graham, FB Pat Harder, halfbacks Bob Kennedy, Glenn Dobbs, Charlie Trippi, Steve Filipowicz, and Steuber. All later played service ball.

Once Steuber reported to DePauw, the team outscored opponents 206–6 over the final five games. "Apparently nobody questioned Steuber's right to play with the team, and none of DePauw's five remaining opponents, only one a service club (Fort Knox, 40–0), voiced an objection," wrote historian Bernie McCarty. He "literally ran wild and compiled a record so incredible that he may rank as the greatest 'small college' player of all time," with 19 touchdowns and 15 points-after for 129 points, and he led the nation in both scoring and rushing. "Imagine what Steuber's figures would have been if he had played a full season's schedule."[2] Only a world war....

An attempt to introduce American football at a German prisoner of war camp in Breckinridge, Ky., failed. "Both teams made after the ball-carrier and almost killed him."[3]

Touch football became popular at redistribution and rehabilitation centers. Two such stations in 1944 organized unusual rosters. They were the Klamath Falls (Ore.) Marine Corps Rehabilitation Center team (2–2–1, see Chapter 8), and the Pocatello (Idaho) Naval Ordnance Plant (1–5–0) Marine barracks team. The latter scrounged the Pocatello area for jerseys and equipment to suit up two dozen combat-hospitalized Marines and sailors. The game scores didn't matter.

"This souvenir program was designed especially for your entertainment and information," read the program for the game between Bainbridge (Md.) Naval Training Center and Camp Peary (Va.) in 1944. "Mail it home to the folks with your next letter, they'll enjoy it too."[4]

The NCAA rated the best civilian teams of 1944 as Ohio State, Tulsa, and Wake Forest. Many schools without military trainees were hard hit in mid-season. Northwestern lost 14 men, including two to Minnesota. Notre Dame lost six players.

In 1944 Aberdeen (Md.) Ordnance School tied Lincoln University, 2–2.

Back Bob Steuber (All-America Missouri, Chicago Bears) was drafted after one professional game in 1943. The navy sent him to V-12 training at DePauw University where he and his team exploded offensively, outscoring opponents 206–6 over the final five games. With one year of eligibility remaining, he returned to Missouri after the war, thus being perhaps the only man ever to play collegiately after playing professionally (Street & Smith's *Football Pictorial Yearbook 1942*).

Cornell beat Sampson (N. Y.) Naval Training Station in a 7–6 "story-book finish," on a touchdown pass with three seconds left. Tulsa beat Arkansas 33–2 with 33 points immediately after starting the second half. It then refused to take the offense, punting on first down each series.

Apparently soldiers were more sports-minded and more in favor of the continuation of sports in wartime than civilians, according to an *Esquire* magazine poll for its December 1943 issue. Voting yes to the continuation of sports were 96.5 percent. When put to civilians in the recent regular *Esquire* poll, numbers ran 10–15 percent lower. Football led with 45.77 percent polled saying it was the best combat-conditioning sport.[5]

## Dave Rankin

Dave Rankin offered a different perspective on playing wartime football. The Chicago Bears drafted the 6'0"/175, Purdue All-America end (1939-40) on graduation, but he never played pro ball. He was captain of the college all-star team in 1941. Rankin received his naval aviator wings at Corpus Christi (Fla.) Naval Air Station and a Marine Corps commission in 1942, but played no football. He recalled that Sonny Franck and others asked him "why don't you come play with us?" on the NAS team, but his commanding officer told him, "We are training people to fight the war, not to play football." In the Pacific, "I didn't have a chance to follow football and lost track of it."[6]

Rankin flew F4F *Wildcat* and

Guard Alex Agase, one of the era's most dominating linemen, earned an unprecedented All-America honors at two Big Ten schools during the war: Illinois in 1942 and Purdue in 1943 after entering Marine Corps V-12 training. He received the Bronze Star and Purple Heart in Pacific action. In 1946 he made All-America again at Illinois (Street & Smith's *Football Pictorial Yearbook 1944*).

"I wish the colonel would stop making these bets" (Bo Brown in game program, First Air Force vs. Army Air Forces Training Command, November 11, 1945).

F4U *Corsair* fighters (VMF-214 and VMF-221) in two tours in the Solomon Islands. His was the first squadron to land at Yokohoma, Japan, when the war ended. After the war he returned to Purdue and coached track and field for 30 years. The Purdue track stadium is named for him.

When Fort Knox visited Ohio State in 1942, spectators were advised: "Drinking in the Stadium ... of intoxicating liquor will not be tolerated.... Drinking or drunkenness will cause your ejection from the game. Patrons disturbed will assist in solving this problem if they will call an officer at the first annoyance."[7]

A 1943 Parris Island (S. C.) boot camp photo pictured former college players Tom Davis and Pat Preston (Duke), Mike Micka (Colgate), Johnny Podesta and Bart Gianelli (College of Pacific), Buck Jones (Franklin & Marshall), Alex Agase (5'10"/210, All-America Illinois, All-America Purdue), Ralph Heywood (Southern California), Angelo Bertelli (Notre Dame), Tony Butkovich (Purdue), and Mickey McCardle (Southern California). Not a team; just a photo.

The National Football League drafted at least 160 Marine V-12 trainees, 16 from Duke and North Carolina, 12 from Michigan and 10 from Southwestern Louisiana Institute. Future All-Americas who played as Marines included G Agase, T Tom Hughes (Missouri, Purdue), and B Bump Elliott (Purdue, Michigan).

The Great Lakes (Ill.) Naval Training Center's 62–0 win in September 1944 was Fort Sheridan's (Ill.) second and last game of the season. After losing 67–6 to Western Michigan the week before, officials cancelled remaining games "because of numerous injuries and lack of manpower." Against the Bluejackets Sheridan suited only 28 players, half with only high school experience and one former Chicago Bear (T Ed Watkins).[8]

V-12 trainees joked that V-12 stood for "victory in twelve years or we fight" and said "Join the V-12: release a WAVE for active duty." They sang to the tune of "My Bonnie Lies Over the Ocean": "Take down your service flag, Mother; your boy is safe in V-12; he'll never get hurt by a slide rule; he'll always stay happy and well."[9]

## Julian Pressly

El Toro G Julian Pressly, involved in the Woody Strode incident described in chapter 10, remembered that his 1944 El Toro (Calif.) Marine Corps Air Station eleven was "getting a reputation in Washington, D.C. about playing dirty. They sent two generals down to watch us. They were sitting on the bench. My job was to hit the punter. I knocked him into the bench right into the two generals. The colonel [Coach Dick Hanley] made a point of telling me to get my seabag packed — he was going to send me to the Pacific islands. 'You damn stupid Texans — that was a great block.' We had orders not to get a 15-yard penalty under my conditions. Our group was real close, even with the officers. Forty percent of our team was officers."[10]

Pressly scored 12 points against Fort Bliss (Tex.) in 1944 (42–0). "Tony Canadeo (Gonzaga, Green Bay Packers) threw two interceptions which I ran back for touchdowns." El Toro used two different platoons. QB Paul Governali (All-America Columbia) ran the single wing, and QB Mickey McCardle (Southern California) the T. Pressly played 75 percent of the time although he didn't start. "I never even thought about being an aviator." After the 1944 season, the colonel wanted eight players to return for 1945. Pressly was among those who enrolled at Santa Barbara Junior College. He had no previous college education.

Pressly recalled the 20–9, 1945 win over the Second Air Force. "They had [Frankie] Sinkwich, [Bulldog] Turner, [Don] Fambrough, [Jay] Berwanger. They had beaten Fleet City and had a good ball club. Sinkwich and Dove were high school teammates. Wilkin hit Sinkwich, who was then hit by Dove. I don't believe [Sinkwich] ever played again. Our planes almost hit a mountain going out of there, and also when trying to land at Long Beach." Later, when traveling to Denver, they went by train. Wilkin wore no pads. "I played behind him. He was so big anybody could play behind him. He had to be the biggest guy who ever played in our games, so strong." Pressly called HB Elroy "Crazy Legs" Hirsch (Wisconsin, Michigan) El Toro's best ever. Pressly was right: Sinkwich never played again.

Pressly turned down an opportunity in 1946 to play with the Chicago Rockets of the All-America Conference because of an injured knee. Hanley coached the Rockets. Ninety percent of the roster were former El Toro players. Pressly graduated from Texas A&M and later coached high school football and baseball at Odessa, Tex., the subject of the book and TV series *Friday Night Lights*.

## Commander William R. "Killer" Kane

"He is there for the full sixty minutes."[11] Reporting in 1945 on combat courage and leadership among naval aviators in the Pacific, Commander William R. "Killer" Kane, USN, head of naval aviation physical and military training, wrote:

> Being a football player is by no means a prerequisite for leadership, but I shall wager that more leaders will be produced from a group of football players than from any other kind of group.
> 
> Aggressiveness? There are so many tales to illustrate that characteristic—the boy who being out of ammunition, flew the Jap into the ocean ... the pilots who carried out a beautiful attack against the Jap fleet in the Philippine Sea, knowing full well that a water landing after dark would be the result because of the extreme range.
> 
> Flying tight formation, fighters weaving over the bombers, strafing dives by fighters coordinated with the attacks of dive bombers and torpedo planes all call for timing and coordination that is duplicated on the football field by the offensive play of the linemen, the interference of the backs ahead of the ball carrier, the open field running of the ball carrier, himself.
> 
> We cannot all be ball carriers. Some of us must block. As it is in football, so it is in combat flying. Orders must be followed strictly. There is no room here for an individualist, a non-conformist, for he becomes a menace to his own mates. Teamwork in the air is as necessary (perhaps more so) as it is on the gridiron. The lad who wanders off to do a little hunting on his own usually enjoys a short career. But far worse he weakens the team....
> 
> Toughness? Well, if the pilot is not tough he will not last. There are to substitutions to be made in the air over Tokyo. He is there for the full "sixty minutes." ... Quick reaction, physical condition, esprit [d] corps, a sense of humor when the going is rough (one of the greatest characteristics of our American boys) eagerness to get into the game, these and many more characteristics are to be seen every day in the combat zone. All of these characteristics are to be seen every day on the gridiron.... Football in naval aviation as a training device to develop the characteristics desired in our combat pilots *has paid off.*

Kane, a 1933 Naval Academy graduate and football right-tackle letterman (1931-32), flew fighters in VF-10 (the "Grim Reapers") in the Pacific from the USS *Enterprise* (CV-6) from 1942 to 1944, serving as squadron commander in 1943-44. His eight kills earned him the designator "ace," the Navy Cross, two Distinguished Flying Crosses, and a Presidential Unit Citation. In 1942 he was shot down in the Battle of Santa Cruz. A rising naval star, he died in a jet aircraft accident in 1957.

Camp Grant (Ill.) took on the Big Ten to record its only two wins of 1943. In the opener, "a courageous, determined little group of 17- and 18-year olds, constituting a sort of impromptu lineup, went up against veteran ex-college stars and professionals Sep. 11 to open the Illinois season.... A few hours before, four of the best men in the Illini camp ... were declared ineligible. Three hadn't taken entrance exams, the fourth's credits hadn't arrived. So coach Ray Eliot switched a right end to left end, found Eddie Nemeth back from the army on a furlough and rushed him into uniform." Grant scored on three interceptions and a safety to win, 23–0.[12]

Camp Grant (Ill.) unabashedly took on the Big Ten big boys in 1942-43, its lone seasons, defeating Illinois 23-0 and Wisconsin 10-7 for its only two 1943 wins. Here the home-field soldiers stop a Wisconsin back in that game (Street & Smith's *Football Pictorial Yearbook 1944*).

"Rockford, Ill., Sep. 26, 1943 — Wisconsin's football team, a lamb supposedly being led to slaughter here Saturday afternoon, roared and kicked like a lion instead and held Camp Grant's heavy, hard-running soldiers to a skimpy 10–7 victory. It was a disheartening licking of the worst kind.... [Wisconsin] hurled back most of Camp Grant's heaviest charges, at least in the danger zones, and lashed out itself with a touchdown drive of 70 yards.... It was the toughest kind of break that it had to lose."[13]

Camp Davis (N.C.) opened the 1943 season by hosting Wake Forest (24–20) "in a typical World Series football atmosphere." An overflow crowd of 10,000 at the new field featured the 3rd Army Ground Forces band, an officer candidate school review, Women's Army Corps cheerleaders, and female civilian workers — plus lineman Ralph Primavera, "aggressive almost to a fault, [who was] nevertheless a spirited and inspirational factor up front."[14]

North Carolina, my alma mater, began V-12 with 796 sailors and 298 Marines. The navy version ended in October 1945, the Marine Corps program in June 1946. Trainees occupied 12 fraternity houses and seven older dormitories — 2,000 V-5 cadets already occupied the newer and better-equipped dorms. In 1944 authorities tightened discipline, with duty watches, compulsory study hours, and bed checks. V-12's comprised most of the Tar Heel athletic teams; 37 Marines manned the 1943 football squad. Both civilians and V-12's operated on a trimester schedule. Profits from the canteen, called the "Scuttlebutt," supported social activities. British Ambassador Lord Halifax reviewed trainees in February 1944. Carolina V-12's included three admirals and one general, U. S. Sen. Robert Morgan, and Tom Wicker of the *New York Times*. Numerous signs of the navy presence on campus remain, including Navy Field where I played lacrosse for four seasons, the swimming pool, and the building containing the navy and air force ROTC programs.

## George "Sonny" Franck

For the Corpus Christi (Fla.) Naval Air Station Comets in 1942, B George "Sonny" Franck (All-America Minnesota, New York Giants) was rated the outstanding back in Texas and made Service All-America. "If the Texas sportswriters said you were the outstanding back in Texas, you were an automatic," he recalled. "I played in the prehistoric days. You stayed on the field all the time. I was a wingback but also played safety. I ran the 100-yard dash in 9.6 and 9.7. I was the fastest guy who ever played college or pro football at that time."[15]

"We played against the Texas teams. At the Texas A&M game, most of our guys were out partying the night before." (Corpus won 18–7.) The day of the Texas game was hot. "We just ran out of gas [and lost 40–0]. If you were a football player the base commander grabbed you and put you on the football team. Some of the Randolph Field players stayed around a long time like that." Phil Ragazzo, a New York Giants teammate and earlier a teammate of Bainbridge Navy phenom Charlie Justice, told Franck: "'He's [Justice] the best halfback I've ever seen in my life.' I knew of him at the time."

The most valuable player in the 1941 College All-Star game, Franck played a few games with the Giants in 1941 before entering naval aviation that fall with Dave Rankin, and reporting to Corpus Christi for flight training. Halfway through he had to select either the navy or Marines. His coach at Minnesota, Bernie Bierman, was a Marine and that influenced him. Franck flew F4U *Corsair* fighters in the Pacific, and was shot down once. "After I crashed seven of them they decided I was a lousy pilot," he said, and was placed in an aviation support position on the carrier USS *Hornet* (CV-12).

Franck saw action with El Toro in three 1945 games, then rejoined the Giants after being discharged. On his 87th birthday on September 2, 2005, he said: "I wanted to give back to kids. Football got me into college, the service, and the pros; so I went into teaching." Franck taught high school math and biology in Illinois, and is in the College Football Hall of Fame.

Ticket prices for the Alameda Coast Guard–California game at Berkeley in 1944 ranged from 55 cents to $2.40, servicemen admitted for half price.

Tony Veteri of Atlantic City (N. J.) Naval Air Station punted 100 yards in a 31–6 win over Princeton (1-2-0) in 1944.

Northern Illinois State Teachers, unbeaten and untied in 1943, had a normal enrollment of 450. It dropped to 90 the next year. Georgia coach Wallace Butts dressed only rookies in 1943. No varsity or freshman player from 1942 returned because of regulations and the draft.

"Teen-aged, peach-fuzzed lads found themselves playing beside and against their heroes, All-Americas and All-Pros they had read about in the newspapers," Furman Bisher wrote. Players moved around like free-agent baseball players. The former Clemson captain, a center, later donned the uniform of hated rival South Carolina, and became the Gamecocks captain. The star Wake Forest tackle moved 15 miles away to arch enemy Duke.[16]

Coach Frank Murray of Virginia on 1943 wartime football: "'Frankly, I am not greatly alarmed about this year. If football is in the way of all-out effort, suppress it for the duration. But the letters I receive from my former players on every front say that the sport is too valuable to be side-tracked. I am not afraid of Hitler spiking the guns in our sports set-up. The biggest danger to college football is not planning for the future.'"[17]

Duke's 1943 team was "set back about two months by the clean-sweeping Marine detachment orders which sent 23 of their top varsity players off to more advanced training centers.... Where the Dukes once had three excellent fullbacks ... [coach Eddie] Cameron will now have to rely upon a couple of boys from the Jayvees."[18] In 1943 the campus hosted a 1,600-man navy/Marine Corps unit and only a handful of regular student players.

Think of what might have been. Fullback Felix "Doc" Blanchard "ran riot in Kenan Stadium" at North Carolina as a freshman before going into the army after failing to qualify for the Naval Reserve. "Service calls have watered down what might have been a really great team."[19]

"Hogan, you go in at right tackle, and you, Simpson, go along and explain the signals to Hogan" (Bo Brown in game program, Texas Tech at Lubbock Army Air Field, September 13, 1943).

The *Bainbridge* (Md.) *Mainsheet* wove poetry into football.

"Football Hero"[20]
*An end who's fast
And plenty tricky
Is that Arkansas guy
We call Red Hickey.*

"He's Top Man"[21]
*A player who carries
His share of the burden
is that Oregon flash
Who's known as Don Durdan.*

## Clyde "Smackover" Scott

Clyde Luther "Smackover" Scott (6'0"/175) played five years of varsity football, 1944-45 at Navy and 1946–48 at Arkansas. He of the colorful, indelible nickname overnight became "one of the premier college performers of the Fabulous Forties. Extraordinary speed and a fearless attitude resulting in

flaming headlines one week, and confinement to the bench with injuries the next week. Few football players ever ran faster or performed more heroically on defense with complete disregard for personal safety." He made All-America mention each season and consensus first team in 1948. Scott started as a Navy plebe because the team "needed a dependable operative at fullback who was also mean on defense." During his Annapolis service, the Middies equaled arch rival West Point in talent but lost both times.[22]

Halfback Clyde Luther "Smackover" Scott of Navy picked up the most colorful, indelible wartime football nickname based on his Arkansas home town, just edging out Charlie "Choo Choo" Justice of Bainbridge (Md.) Naval Training Center. Maybe that was a reason the author took to Scott as his football hero in 1945, the reward coming in their 2006 long telephone interview (Street & Smith's *Football Pictorial Yearbook, 1946*).

Accolades fit Scott naturally, and attention riveted on his extemporaneous nickname. Following Navy's 26–0 victory over Pennsylvania in Philadelphia in 1944, Harold Classes of the Associated Press said, "Navy put the foot back into football Saturday and with little Clyde Scott of Smackover, Ark., doing the key work.... It was a tremendous 73-yard quick kick by the 175 pounder that set up the first touchdown and it was his consistent long-range punting that set up the second." Scott recalled when the Middies quick-kicked, a common offensive ploy then but extremely rare today. "I'm not a punter but I kicked the ball. It got into the air and kept going, a long one, probably the only thing I did. A great play for Navy. After the game I was interviewed. 'Where are you from, mister?' the reporter asked. All midshipmen were called mister. I said 'Smackover.' There was silence. They were waiting for the punch line. 'No, no, I am from Smackover, Ark.' Check the *Philadelphia Inquirer*. That's when they hung the handle on me. From then on I was 'Smackover' Scott."[23]

The following week the Mids blanked Notre Dame, 32–0, behind Scott's two first-quarter scores. Added Whitney Martin of the AP, "If there was one outstanding Navy man, it was the kid from Smackover, Clyde Scott, who was a demon on defense as well as offense."[24]

Bernie McCarty wrote that by running the T formation, the 1945 team enabled Scott, "a terrifically fast starter, to bust loose off tackle and leave grasping, gasping tacklers in his wake.... Not a fancy-Dan broken-field runner, he relied on pure acceleration, pure speed, and strength.... He changed direction in an open field to make the use of blockers, but no sideline scrambles. Defenders had only one shot at him."[25]

How did Smackover itself get its name? "The Naval Academy tracked it down, sent someone there to check it out," Scott said. "The most practical name was based on the sumac plant which covers the whole country around Smackover. They got the name from sumac that covered the ground." His parents are buried there (population about 2,500) and he visits occasionally. In the middle of Main Street the town erected a metal monument to him.[26]

On the 1945 Army game: "They were a better team than we were, no doubt. The best running backs then, a great line. I honestly think it [difference between teams] was the coaching. After a play you would see all the Midshipmen on the turf." He tried tackling Doc Blanchard once and bounced off him. "We had some good football players on those Navy teams. The Army leaders, the coaches, they did a much better job." The team always traveled by train. On coach Commander Oscar E. Hagberg, who coached Navy in 1944-45 after commanding the submarine USS *Albacore* (SS-218) in Pacific combat: "He was a nice guy but limited in coaching ability." On E Dick Duden: "He was a gentleman type, a nice guy to be around."[27]

Scott married Leslie Hampton of Lake Village, Ark., the 1944 Miss Arkansas. She and Scott fondly reconstructed their story. En route to Atlantic City for the Miss America pageant, the state queens alternated stopping between West Point and Annapolis. As a plebe he was picked to escort her around campus, but the day she arrived found him practicing football. His roommate met her at the gate and brought her over to sit in the stands to watch. On meeting her, Scott remembered saying, "'Gee whiz, oh my gosh!' I dressed rather hurriedly. We visited and talked and corresponded. She was so faithful, writing a letter every day." She came to the Army game. He

A sketch of Smackover Scott drawn by the author at the age eleven, following the Navy win over Duke in Durham, N.C., on October 6, 1945.

visited her in Lake Village later that year, and soon they decided to get married.[28]

"I immediately turned in my resignation but it was denied. I moved in with coach Captain [Tom] Hamilton. Football was over. The war was over. And I wanted to get married. Maybe my letter wasn't written properly." He wrote a second letter. The commandant of midshipmen helped him. Her father called a congressman "and we got some action." In August 2006 they celebrated their sixtieth wedding anniversary. They have two children and three grandchildren.

Scott left the Academy in early 1946. "There were coaches literally standing outside the gate when I got out. I didn't have time to spend with them, and said they'd have to do it in Arkansas. All the returning veterans were sought after. I was not thinking about any school, but yeah, I really wanted to go to Arkansas. I was only thinking about getting married. Some of the coaches were very convincing." Arkansas coach John H. Barnhill recruited him, and from there he enjoyed a storybook college career.

His other achievements included the 1948 Olympics silver medal in high hurdles, and tying the 100-yard dash world record at 9.4. "I'm within three pounds of my Olympic weight," he boasted 58 years later. He played four years with the Philadelphia Eagles and Detroit Lions before embarking on a career with the Stevens, Inc., insurance firm in Little Rock.

Postscript: Smackover Scott was my wartime, boyhood football idol. It must have been the name and uniform. After watching Smackover Scott's Navy team defeat Duke 21–0 in Durham on October 6, 1945, at age eleven, I made a sketch of the Middies' star halfback. The drawing was stashed away for years with my boyhood wartime memorabilia. In 2006 I sent him a copy.

JOHN GUNN'S GREATEST WORLD WAR II MILITARY TEAMS[29]

1 — 1945 Fleet City
2 — 1945 El Toro
3 — 1944 Randolph Field
4 — 1944 Bainbridge
5 — 1943 Iowa PF
6 — 1942 Georgia PF
7 — 1944 Iowa PF
8 — 1943 Great Lakes
9 — 1944 4th AF
10 — 1943 4th AF
11 — 1943 Del Monte PF
12 — 1942 2nd AF
13 — 1944 2nd AF
14 — 1944 Fort Pierce
15 — 1944 Great Lakes
16 — 1943 Randolph Field
17 — 1943 Bainbridge
18 — 1944 Camp Peary
19 — 1942 Great Lakes
20 — 1942 North Carolina PF
21 — 1942 Iowa PF
22 — 1944 El Toro
23 — 1942 St Mary's PF
24 — 1943 Greensboro AAB
25 — 1943 San Diego NTS

"A Switch in Lullabies"
An Ode to Navy Flyers
by Grantland Rice[30]

*Somewhere beyond the Southern Cross above the Seven Seas,*
*Along the bitter far-off roads, their pinions catch the breeze.*
*Their wings are black against the sky, by desert, surf and dune,*
*An ancient lullaby is lost against a rougher tune —*

*Some flew east — some flew west —*
*And some will fly no more,*
*Far, far out from the eagle's nests*
*Their mighty motors roar.*
*And wing by wing their rule will grow*
*Above all sea and sod,*
*Until they strike the final blow*
*For Country and for God.*

*Faintly, I hear the old, old song when golden dreams were young.*
*But louder still I hear the wings where sudden death is flung.*
*Bravely the eagle rides the air, but in my fading dreams,*
*The dim, lost lullaby returns — how far away it seems —*

*Some fly east — and some fly west —*
*They take an endless track.*
*Through flame and steel they face the rest*
*Around the world and back.*
*Their golden youth blots out the sky,*
*They let the comets plod,*
*As each one flies to live or die*
*For Country and for God.*

Amen.

Former Naval Academy superintendent and athletic director Admiral Jonas H. Ingram, who commanded the wartime South Atlantic task force, once laid the foundation for military football participation. "The closest thing to war in time of peace is football," he said.[31] And so it turned out.

# Glossary: Wartime Football Expressions, Abbreviations, and Jargon

## Keys

TEAM RECORDS: Team records are shown parenthetically as won-lost-tied, and occasionally points for-against.

PLAYERS AND COACHES: Players and coaches are identified parenthetically, when known, by their wartime height/weight, pre-military football experience: college, All-America and award honors; and National Football League team or other professional experience.

PLAYER POSITIONS: B — Back; C — Center; E — End; FB — Fullback; G — Guard; HB — Halfback; QB — Quarterback; T — Tackle; TB — Tailback.

## Abbreviations

AAB — Army air base
AAF — Army air field
AAFTC — Army Air Forces Training Command
AB — air base
AF — Air Force
AFB — Air Force base
Amphib — Amphibious base
CG — Coast Guard
Cmd — Command
Coll — College
Ctr — Center
Fr — Freshmen
Inf — Infantry
Inst — Institute
JC — Junior college

JV — Junior varsity
MCAS — Marine Corps air station
MCB — Marine Corps base
NAS — Naval air station
NS — Naval station
NTC/NTS — Naval training center/station
ORD — Overseas replacement depot
Pers Dist Comd/Ctr — Personnel distribution command/center
PF — Pre-flight
St — Saint or State
Trans — Transportation
Trng — Training
U — University
UCLA — University of California at Los Angeles
USC — University of Southern California

## Terminology

**aggregation** Team, squad, eleven, outfit
**All-America(s)** Nation's top-ranked football player(s)
**APO** Army post office; usually assigned to units overseas
**armed forces** The military: army (USA), army air forces (USAAF), navy (USN), Marine Corps (USMC), Coast Guard (USCG) (in wartime)
**army** General reference to army branch of the armed forces
**Army** U.S. Military Academy at West Point, N.Y.
**Army Air Forces** Part of the army; redesignated from Army Air Corps on June 20, 1941; includes Army Air Corps (on paper only), combat command, training commands, and numbered air forces
**array** Lineup, grouping of players (e.g., backfield)
**balanced line** Seven-man line, from left to right: end, tackle, guard, center, guard, tackle, end (see also "unbalanced line")
**Big Six** Missouri Valley Intercollegiate Athletic Association: Kansas, Oklahoma, Nebraska, Iowa State, Kansas State, Missouri; now Big 12 with Texas, Texas A&M, Oklahoma State, Texas Tech, Colorado, Baylor added
**Big Ten** *see* "Western Intercollegiate Conference"
**birdmen** Aviators, namely pilots but also crewmen
**blocking back** Primary blocker in single and double-wing offensive formations
**booters** Placekickers and punters
**boy(s)** Contemporary usage: any male not one's father or grandfather; civilians and military
**cakewalk** An easy victory
**colleges** Includes universities, schools, military academies, other institutions of higher learning

**contest** A football game

**crack** Top-notch, high-quality

**Department of the Navy** Includes office of the Secretary, the navy, the Marine Corps, and Coast Guard (see Navy Department and Marine Corps)

**dope** The "latest facts," "straight scoop" on a story

**double lateral** lateral used twice in one offensive possession

**double wing (wingback)** Similar to single wing with two wingbacks spread in backfield as blockers and receivers (blocking back became wingback), tailback handling the ball as principal runner and passer, and fullback (No. 2 runner)

**dreadnaught** Predecessor to battleships as principal capital warship

**drop kick** Kick made by dropping the ball to ground on end and booting it straight on; occasionally used for field goal attempts

**duration** U.S. period of wartime: December 7, 1941 to August 14, 1945

**eleven** Team, squad, outfit, aggregation (based on playing a total of eleven players on a team at one time in the era before the platoon system, when players tended to play both offense and defense)

**enemy** Opponent, foe, opposition

**flanker** Potential pass receiver or blocker positioned wide of the line

**flash** Fast runner (ball carrier)

**fleet/fleet-footed** Very fast, swift runner

**flip** Short pass from tailback or quarterback to receiver

**forward wall** Seven-man front line from end to end, in era where both ends played on the line rather than split

**4-F** Selective Service (draft) classification for a man physically or mentally disqualified from being inducted; conditions ranged from flat feet, missing teeth, and color blindness to mental instability

**game officials** Usually four: referee, umpire, linesman, field judge; wore bow ties but usually no caps

**GI(s)** American servicemen (not women); primarily used to connote army soldiers; stood for "government issue"

**GI Bill** Passed by Congress and signed by the president, the "Servicemen's Readjustment Act of 1944" law provided veterans with college expenses and favorable home and business ownership conditions; considered one of the nation's most important statutes, it helped propel the United States into a world power, and remains in effect.

**girl(s)** Contemporary usage: any female not one's mother or grandmother; civilian and military

**green/greenies** Inexperienced young players

**gridder/gridster** Football player (played on the gridiron)

**gridiron (grid)** Football playing field

**gyrenes** Marines

**high-flying** Energetic, fast, vocal, robust, ready to roll

**intramurals** Internal college sports activities; no off-campus or outside encounters

**juggernaut** High-powered football team which wins most or all of its games

**KP** Kitchen police; non-cooking duty in the kitchen or mess

**lateral** Offensive team player shoveling ball backward to teammate to continue the play

**leather-lugging** Hearty, rugged back who carried the ball often and well

**line bucker** Hard-running, straight-ahead ball carrier

**line plunge** Basic "T" formation dive play with back carrying into hole in the forward wall

**loop** League or conference

**lulu** Nice play, player, team, or situation

**Marine Corps/Marine(s)** Always capitalized; a Marine was neither a soldier nor associated with the maritime (merchant marine) service or ocean sciences; see Department of the Navy

**military** see armed forces; primarily referred to army and army air forces, but for this book, the generic term for the services and service personnel

**moleskins** Football uniform pants

**navy** Ships, aircraft, craft, and shore establishment of the Navy Department; general reference to the navy

**national emergency** Official term given to U.S. involvement in World War II during the first year or so

**Navy Department** The navy

**Notre Dame box** Most common formation shifted into after lining up in T; similar to single wing with balanced line; relied on deception rather than power

**outfit** Unit, organization, team

**oval** Football, pigskin

**PATs** Points after touchdowns

**Pacific Coast Conference** Southern California, Washington, UCLA, California; inactive: Washington State, Idaho, Stanford, Oregon, Oregon State

**paydirt** Touchdown territory beyond the goal line

**phenom** Phenomenon, a truly gifted and great young player

**pigskin** A football

**plunge** Ball carrier hitting the line, usually for short yardage

**press** newspapers and magazines, and their writers; radio stations and broadcasters

**prognosticator** Sports journalist who dared to predict

**PT boat** Patrol-torpedo boat

**quick-kick** Punt out of running or passing formation on less than fourth down

**ROTC** Reserve Officer Training Corps; army and navy programs instituted at college and high school levels

**scamper** Quick, speedy run with ball

**scatback** Shifty, agile, athletic, swift ball carrier

**scribe** Sportswriter
**scuttlebutt** Navy jargon for rumors or gossip
**sea services** Navy, Marine Corps, Coast Guard
**service(s) (military)** *see* armed forces; generic term referring to all or any one of them
**single wing** Most popular offensive formation entering World War II football: seven linemen; backfield composed of tailback (primary ball handler, runner, and passer), fullback (blocker and No. 2 runner), blocking back (primary blocker), and wingback (receiver and No. 3 runner); similar to modern shotgun formation
**1630 hours** (for example) Military time (4:30 p.m.)
**skivvies** Underwear, usually underpants
**sorties** Rushes or carries with ball
**Southeastern Conference** Georgia Tech, Tennessee, Mississippi, Mississippi State, Georgia, Alabama, Louisiana State University, Tulane, Florida, Kentucky, Auburn
**Southern Conference** Duke, Clemson, North Carolina, Wake Forest, North Carolina State, William & Mary, Maryland, South Carolina, Virginia Military Institute, Richmond
**Southwest Conference** Texas Christian University, Texas, Arkansas, Texas A&M, Rice, Southern Methodist University
**speedster** Very fast player
**squad** Team, aggregation, outfit, eleven
**stanza** Playing quarter or period
**star-studded** Loaded with great players
**stateside** Within the continental United States (48 states)
**stint** Individual's turn or time at something; e.g., a coach's tenure at a college, or player's at tailback
**swivel-hipped** *see* scatback
**tailback** *see* "single wing"
**T-formation** Offensive formation that gained popularity and proved to be dominant by end of war: seven linemen; backfield composed of quarterback (primary ball handler and passer, took snaps under center), two halfbacks (running backs, No. 1 ball carriers and also receivers), fullback (blocker and No. 2 ball carrier)
**T.H.** Territory of Hawaii, prior to statehood
**tilt** A football game
**triple-threat** Tailback who could run, pass, and punt well
**trounced** Defeated, usually badly
**unbalanced line** Seven linemen positioned with four or more to either the left or right of the center (see also "balanced line"); "strong side" was that with four or more
**VMF** Marine Corps fighter squadron

**War Department** The army and army air forces, headed by the Secretary of War (member of president's cabinet); reorganized in 1947 as Department of the Army and separate Department of the Air Force

**WAVES** Women Accepted for Volunteer Emergency Service (navy)

**Western Intercollegiate Conference** Big Ten: Illinois, Indiana, Iowa, Michigan, Michigan State, Minnesota, Northwestern, Ohio State, Purdue, Wisconsin; today: original colleges plus Penn State

**white hats** Enlisted navy male personnel

**wingback** *see* "double wing" and "single wing"

# Chapter Notes

## Preface

1. Harry Wismer in *Football Pictorial Yearbook 1944*, 5.
2. *Ibid.*
3. Frank Knox and A.A. Vandegrift, quoted in *The Football 1943 Review: Yearbook of The Football News*, 1944, 19.
4. Charles Moran in *Football Pictorial Yearbook 1943*, inside front and rear cover.

## Introduction

1. Furman Bisher, "You're in the Army, Mr. Trippi," *Southern Living,* Sep. 1984.
2. *Ibid.*
3. *Football Pictorial Yearbook 1942*, inside front cover.
4. *Ibid.*, 4.
5. Mike Vaccaro, *1941: The Greatest Year in Sports* (New York: Doubleday, 2007), 4.
6. Benjamin G. Rader, *American Sports: From the Age of Folk Games to the Age of Spectators* (Englewood Cliffs, N.J.: Prentice-Hall, 1983), 209.
7. Richard O. Davies, *Sports in American Life: A History* (Malden, Mass.: Blackwell Publishing, 2007), 135, 162.
8. Rader, op. cit., 209–210.
9. *Ibid.*, 267–268.
10. Douglas A. Noverr and Lawrence E. Ziewacz, *The Games They Played: Sports in American History, 1865–1980* (Chicago: Nelson-Hall, 1983), 137–138, 142–144.
11. John A. Gunn, *(Quite) A Few Good Men* (Costa Mesa, Calif.: J&J Publishing, 1992), 140.
12. Thomas Harbrecht and C. Robert Barnett, "College Football During World War II: 1941–1945," *The Physical Educator,* March 1979; Allison Danzig, *The History of American Football: Its Teams, Players, and Coaches* (Englewood Cliffs, N.J.: Prentice-Hall, 1956), 368.
13. Bisher, op. cit.
14. Charles Moran in *Football Pictorial Yearbook 1943*, 4.
15. Walter R. Okeson in *The Official National Collegiate Athletic Association Football Guide 1943*, 9. Hereafter cited as *NCAA Guide [year]*.
16. Charles Moran in *Football Pictorial Yearbook 1945*, 6, 11.
17. Moran in *Football Pictorial Yearbook 1943*, 5.
18. Brown quoted in Bisher, "You're in the Army, Mr. Trippi," op. cit.
19. Jack Byrne in *Illustrated Football Annual 1943*, 16.
20. Theodore P. Bank in *NCAA Guide 1943,* 27.
21. *Ibid.*
22. Moran in *Football Pictorial Yearbook 1943*, inside front and back cover.
23. Joe Hoppel, Mike Nahrstedt, Steve Zesch, eds., *College Football's Twenty-Five Greatest Teams* (St. Louis, Mo.: The Sporting News, 1988), 31.
24. Francis J. Powers in *NCAA Guide 1944*, 108.
25. Danzig, op cit., 371.
26. *Great Lakes* (Naval Training Center) *Bulletin,* Oct. 29, 1943.
27. John A. Gunn, *(Quite) A Few Good Men*, op. cit., 140.
28. "Franka's 4-F's," *Time*, Dec. 13, 1943, quoted in Harbrecht and Barnett, op cit.
29. John "Ox" DaGrosa and Edward H.

Nichterlein in *NCAA Guide 1944*, 25; John L. Griffith in *ibid.*, 30.
30. Ned Cronin in game program, Fourth Air Force vs. Randolph Field, Los Angeles, Calif., Dec. 10, 1944.
31. Don Parker, "The World of Sports," *While You Were Gone* (New York: Simon & Schuster, 1946), 304, quoted in Harbrecht and Barnett, op. cit.
32. Wilton Hazzard in *Illustrated Football Annual 1944*, 4.
33. Dick Saunders in game program, Fourth Air Force vs. Randolph Field, op. cit.
34. Henry W. Clark in *NCAA Guide 1945*, 39.
35. Grantland Rice in *Illustrated Football Annual 1945*, 2.
36. John DaGrosa and Bob Hall in *NCAA Guide 1946*, 17.
37. Noverr and Ziewacz, op. cit., 171.
38. DaGrosa and Hall in *NCAA Guide 1946*, op. cit., 20.
39. Thomas J. Hamilton in *NCAA Guide 1943*, 31.

## Chapter 1

1. *Bainbridge* (Naval Training Station/Center) *Mainsheet*, Jun. 10, 1944. Hereafter cited as *Mainsheet*.
2. *Mainsheet*, Dec. 11, 1943; Associated Press article in *New York Times* quoted in *Mainsheet*, Dec. 11, 1943.
3. A montage of the following material from: *Baltimore & Ohio Railroad Magazine*, Aug. 1946; Bainbridge Naval Training Center Historical Association undated flyer; pocket-sized information booklet, Bainbridge Naval Training Station; *Mainsheet*, Jun. 29, 1973.
4. Bainbridge Naval Training Center Historical Association undated flyer, op. cit.
5. *Our Navy* Magazine, Mid-Nov., 1943.
6. Bainbridge Naval Training Center Historical Association undated flyer, op. cit.
7. Game program, Curtis Bay Coast Guard at Bainbridge Naval Training Station, Oct. 16, 1943; *Mainsheet*, Oct. 9, 1943.
8. Interview with Albert F. Bagley, Jr., Jul. 21, 2004.
9. *Mainsheet*, Oct. 30, 1943.
10. Wartime folding postcard photo booklet, Bainbridge Naval Training Station.
11. *Ibid.*
12. *Mainsheet*, Sep. 25, 1943.
13. *Mainsheet*, Aug. 7, 1943; game program, Curtis Bay Coast Guard at Bainbridge Naval Training Station, op. cit.
14. *Illustrated Football Annual 1944*, 48.
15. *The Football News: The American Collegiate Sports Weekly*, Oct. 9, 1943, 1, 9.
16. *Mainsheet*, Aug. 21, 1943.
17. *Mainsheet*, Sep. 4, 1943, and Oct. 9, 1943.
18. *Mainsheet*, Oct. 16, 1943.
19. *The Football News*, op. cit.
20. Paul Scalera in *Baltimore Sun*, Nov. 14, 1943.
21. *Mainsheet*, Oct. 23, 1943.
22. *Mainsheet*, Nov. 26, 1943.
23. Burton Hawkins in unknown newspaper, Oct. 11, 1943.
24. Unknown newspaper, Nov. 12, 1943.
25. *Mainsheet*, Nov. 20, 1943.
26. Scalera, op. cit.
27. *Ibid.*
28. Unknown football publication, 1943.
29. Attributed to Grantland Rice in *Mainsheet*, Dec. 18, 1943.
30. *Mainsheet*, Nov. 6, 1943.
31. *Mainsheet*, Nov. 27, 1943.
32. *Mainsheet*, Aug. 12, 1944.
33. *Mainsheet*, Aug. 14, 1944.
34. Kenneth Crotty in *Football Prevues 1944*, 34.
35. Game program, Cherry Point Marine Corps Air Station at Bainbridge, Nov. 11, 1944.
36. *Mainsheet*, Sep. 23, 1944.
37. *Mainsheet*, Sep. 30, 1944.
38. *Ibid.*
39. Game program, Cherry Point at Bainbridge, op. cit.
40. *Mainsheet*, Nov. 4, 1944.
41. Ben Kopp in *The Official National Collegiate Athletic Association Football Guide 1945*, 38.
42. Associated Press item from Washington, D.C., in unknown newspaper, Nov. 21, 1944.
43. *Illustrated Football Annual 1945*, 40.
44. *The Football News*, Sep. 29, 1945.
45. *Ibid.*
46. *Ibid.*

## Chapter 2

1. Donald W. Rominger, Jr., "From Playing Field to Battleground: The United States Navy V-5 Preflight Program in World War II," *Journal of Sport History*, Winter 1985.

2. Game program, Great Lakes Naval Training Center at Northwestern, Oct. 16, 1943.
3. Clark Shaughnessy quoted in *The Football News: The American Collegiate Sports Weekly*, 4; Shaughnessy book *Football in Peace and War* reviewed in www.time.com.
4. *Athletic Journal* quoted in Rominger.
5. Lou Little in *NCAA Guide 1942*, 19–21, 23.
6. *Ibid.*, 19.
7. Frank Murray quoted by Dick Williamson and Fred Russell in *Illustrated Football Annual 1943*, 63.
8. University of North Carolina newsletter cited in *Wilmington Morning Star*, December 8, 1945.
9. 1942 Press Guide, Iowa Navy Pre-Flight School, Iowa City.
10. Francis J. Powers in game program, Camp Lejeune at North Carolina Pre-Flight, Nov. 13, 1943.
11. Walter R. Okeson in *NCAA Guide 1942*, iv–v.
12. W. Madison Bell in *NCAA Guide, 1944*, 46.
13. *NCAA Guide 1942*, inside front flap.
14. Wilson Sports Equipment advertisement in *NCAA Guide 1944*, no page number.
15. Little in *NCAA Guide* 1944, 21–22.
16. D.O. "Tuss" McLaughry in *NCAA Guide 1944*, 31.
17. Thomas J. Hamilton in *NCAA Guide 1943*, 31.
18. *Football: The Naval Aviation Physical Training Manuals*, Office of the Chief of Naval Operations (Annapolis, Md.: United States Naval Institute, 1943), 7.
19. Hamilton, op. cit., 35.
20. Thomas J. Hamilton quoted in Rominger, op. cit.; Arch Ward in *Chicago Tribune*, Mar. 29, 1942, quoted in Rominger.
21. Powers in game program, op. cit.
22. John A. Gunn, *The Old Core* (Costa Mesa, Calif.: J&J Publishing, 1992), 160.
23. Philip "Moon" Calabrese quoted by John "Ox" DaGrosa and Edward H. Nichterlein in *NCAA Guide 1945*, 30.
24. John L. Griffith in *NCAA Guide 1944*, 29.
25. Bernard F. "Bunny" Oakes in the *Denver Post*, noted in *The Football 1943 Review: Yearbook of the Football News, 1944*, 18.
26. John R. Lovell and Clinton B. Conger quoted from *Michigan Alumni Review* (Oct. 27, 1945) in Douglas A. Noverr and Lawrence E. Ziewacz, *The Games They Played: Sports in American History, 1865–1980* (Chicago: Nelson-Hall, 1983), 162.
27. George T. Davis in the *Los Angeles Evening Herald and Express* quoted in game program, Fourth Air Force vs. Randolph Field, Los Angeles, Calif., Dec. 10, 1944.
28. Byron F. Boyd in *The Football News: The American Collegiate Sports Weekly*, Oct. 9, 1943.
29. Furman Bisher, "You're in the Army, Mr. Trippi," in *Southern Living*, Sep. 1984.
30. R.R.M. Emmit quoted in *Football Pictorial Yearbook, 1943*, 6; James G. Schneider, *The Navy V-12 Program: Leadership for a Lifetime* (Champaign, Ill.: Marlow Books, 1987), 270.
31. "Great Lakes, America, and the Two-Ocean War: 1941–1943," www.nsgreatlakes.navy.mil.
32. Game program, Camp Lejeune at Jacksonville Naval Air Technical Training Center, Nov. 27, 1943.
33. Game program, Fleet City Naval Receiving Station vs. El Toro Marine Corps Air Station, San Francisco, Calif., Sep. 29, 1945.
34. Bob MacLeod and Pat Lahey quoted in John A. Gunn, *(Quite) A Few Good Men* (Costa Mesa, Calif.: J&J Publishing, 1992), 15.
35. Game program, Fleet City Naval Receiving Station vs. Pacific Fleet All-Stars, San Francisco, Calif., Dec. 2, 1945.
36. Wilfred Smith in *Football Rule and Record Book, 1945*, 53.
37. Game program, Brooklyn Bond Bowl Game, First Air Force vs. Army Air Forces Training Command, Brooklyn, N.Y., Nov. 11, 1945.
38. *Ibid.*
39. Thomas Harbrecht and C. Robert Barnett, "College Football During World War II," *The Physical Educator*, March 1979.
40. DaGrosa and Nichterlein in *NCAA Guide 1945*, op. cit., 28.
41. General Douglas MacArthur, from the Philippines, quoted in "Army—1944 National Champions," "Two Cousins College Football Emporium," www.2cuz.com (site discontinued).
42. United Press article in unknown newspaper, dateline New York, N.Y., Dec. 16, 1944.
43. Fourth Air Force (March Field, Riverside, Calif.) Information Booklet, 1943.
44. Game program, Fourth Air Force vs. Randolph Field, Los Angeles, Dec. 10, 1944.
45. Fourth Air Force Booklet, op. cit.

46. *NCAA Guide 1945*, 100.
47. *Great Lakes Bulletin*, Dec. 3, 1943.
48. *The Football News: The American Collegiate Sports Weekly*, Oct. 9, 1943.
49. Game program, Fleet City vs. Pacific Fleet All-Stars, op. cit.
50. Griffith in *NCAA Guide 1944*, 30.
51. John DaGrosa and Bob Hall in *NCAA Guide 1946*, 20.
52. Game program, Fleet City vs. Pacific Fleet All-Stars, op. cit.
53. Oakes, op. cit.
54. Grantland Rice in *Illustrated Football Annual 1945*, 3.
55. Rice in game program, North Carolina at Duke, Nov. 24, 1945.

## Chapter 3

1. Weldon Hart in *NCAA Guide 1944*, 120.
2. *Ibid.*
3. *Ibid.*, 121.
4. Curtis Bishop in *Illustrated Football Annual, 1944*, 42.
5. "Southwest Louisiana Institute and Arkansas A&M, 1943–44," www.raginpagin.com.
6. John A. Gunn, *The Old Core* (Costa Mesa, Calif.: J&J Publishing, 1992), 141.
7. James G. Schneider, *The Navy V-12 Program: Leadership for a Lifetime* (Champaign, Ill.: Marlow Books, 1987), 264.
8. *Ibid.*, 57.
9. *Carolina Magazine* quoted in *Carolina Alumni Review*, Fall 1987.
10. John "Ox" DaGrosa and Edward H. Nichterlein in *NCAA Guide 1944*, 22.
11. Schneider, op. cit., 8–9.
12. "The Navy V-12 Program," Navy Memorial Foundation, www.lonesailor.org.
13. Schneider, op. cit., xi.
14. *Ibid.*, 10.
15. *Ibid.*, 12–14.
16. *Ibid.*, 152, 153, 159.
17. *Ibid.*, 144.
18. *Ibid.*, 134.
19. John A. Gunn, *(Quite) A Few Good Men* (Costa Mesa, Calif.: J&J Publishing, 1992), 140, 160, 270.
20. *Chicago Tribune* quoted in Ray Schmidt, "The Purdue Marines," *College Football Historical Society Newsletter*, August 1988, 12, 13.
21. *Ibid.*, 41–42, 149.
22. *Football Prevues 1944*, 3.
23. Schneider, op. cit., 301.
24. Donald W. Rominger, Jr., "From Playing Field to Battleground: The United States Navy V-5 Preflight Program in World War II," *Journal of Sport History*, Winter 1985.
25. *Ibid.*
26. Schneider, op. cit., 262.
27. *Ibid.*
28. *The State: A Weekly Survey of North Carolina*, Feb. 27, 1943.
29. Bernie Bierman in *NCAA Guide 1943*, 37.
30. Game program, Camp Lejeune at North Carolina Pre-Flight, Nov. 13, 1943.
31. United States Navy Pre-Flight School, Chapel Hill, N.C. Second edition of informational monograph, ca. 1943.
32. *Football: The Naval Aviation Physical Training Manuals*, Office of the Chief of Naval Operations (Annapolis, Md.: United States Naval Institute, 1943), Preface.
33. Byron F. Boyd in *The Football News: The American Collegiate Sports Weekly*, Oct. 23, 1943, 4.
34. Frank H. Wickhorst in *NCAA Guide 1944*, 33–34.
35. Jerald Kirsten in correspondence to author from Moraga (Calif.) Historical Society, Jul. 2005.
36. Game program, St. Mary's Pre-Flight at Washington, Nov. 14, 1942.
37. Iowa Navy Pre-Flight School football press guide, 1942.
38. Harry Borba in game program, Camp Lejeune at North Carolina Pre-Flight, op cit.; Mark Stillwell in *Naval Aviation News*, Sep.–Oct. 1989.
39. Borba, op. cit.
40. Everett B. Morris in unknown magazine article, 1942, "Navy Pre-Flight Schools."
41. For the following three paragraphs: North Carolina Pre-Flight, North Carolina Collection, P27: University of North Carolina Library; *Carolina Alumni Review*, Fall 1987; Game program, Camp Lejeune at North Carolina Pre-Flight, op. cit.; LCDR Gerald Ford, USNR, www.history.navy.mil; *Football Record and Rule Book 1944*.
42. Jane Stancil, "It Was Wartime!," in *Carolina Alumni Review*, Fall 1987.
43. Unknown 1942 magazine article.
44. Stancil, op. cit.
45. Rominger, op. cit.

## Chapter 4

1. Lou Little in *NCAA Guide 1942*, 25.
2. *Ibid.*

3. *Ibid.*
4. John "Ox" DaGrosa and Joseph T. Gardner in *NCAA Guide 1943*, 17.
5. Bob Hall and John DaGrosa in *NCAA Guide 1942*, 40.
6. Harry Wismer in *Football Pictorial Yearbook 1944*, 8.
7. *Ibid.*, 13.
8. *Ibid.*, 14.
9. DaGrosa and Gardner, op cit., 15–17.
10. Ed Pollock in *NCAA Guide 1943*, 73.
11. Jake Wade in *ibid.*, 83.
12. Homer F. Cooke, Jr., in *ibid.*, 50.
13. Joe Hoppel, Mike Nahrstedt, and Steve Zesch, eds., *College Football's Twenty-Five Greatest Teams* (St. Louis, Mo.: The Sporting News, 1988), 371.
14. Walter R. Okeson in *NCAA Guide 1943*, 9.
15. DaGrosa and Gardner, op. cit., 18.
16. Jack Troy in *Football Pictorial Yearbook 1943*, 49.
17. O.B. Keeler in *NCAA Guide 1943*, 81.
18. Troy, op. cit., 43.
19. Weldon Hart in *Football Pictorial Yearbook 1943*, 52.
20. George T. Davis in *NCAA Guide 1944*, 126.
21. C.E. McBride in *Football Pictorial Yearbook 1943*, 68.
22. Ed Pollock in *NCAA Guide 1944*, 98.
23. Chet Nelson in *NCAA Guide 1944*, 124.
24. Les Goates in *Football Pictorial Yearbook 1943*, 72.
25. John "Ox" DaGrosa and Edward H. Nichterlein in *NCAA Guide 1944*, 27–28.
26. Wismer, op. cit.
27. John L. Griffith in *NCAA Guide 1944*, 30.
28. Jerry Nason in *NCAA Guide 1945*, 93–94.
29. John "Ox" DaGrosa and Edward H. Nichterlein in *NCAA Guide 1945*, 30.
30. Weldon Hart in *Football Pictorial Yearbook 1944*, 70.
31. Les Goates in *Football Pictorial Yearbook 1944*, 82.
32. Weldon Hart in *NCAA Guide 1945*, 118.
33. Jack Troy in *Football Pictorial Yearbook 1945*, 46.
34. Cooke, op. cit., 54.
35. DaGrosa and Nichterlein in *NCAA Guide 1945*, 29; Jack Byrne in *Illustrated Football Annual 1943*, 25; George Trevor in *Illustrated Football Annual 1944*, 15.
36. Sid Luckman in game program, First Air Force vs. Army Air Forces Training Command, Brooklyn, N.Y., Nov. 11, 1945.
37. *Illustrated Football Annual 1945*, 4.
38. *Football: The Naval Aviation Physical Training Manuals*, Office of the Chief of Naval Operations (Anapolis, Md.: United States Naval Institute, 1943), 184.
39. DeGrosa and Nichterlein in *NCAA Guide 1944*, 25.
40. *Illustrated Football Annual 1945*, 4.
41. *Illustrated Football Annual 1944*, 4.
42. *NCAA Guide 1945*, 4 (supplement).
43. Hall and DaGrosa in *NCAA Guide 1942*, 35.
44. *Football: Naval Aviation Manuals*, op cit., 184.
45. *Illustrated Football Annual 1944*, 4.
46. Walter R. Okeson in *NCAA Guide 1942*, iv.
47. D.O. McLaughry in *NCAA Guide 1944*, 31.
48. Grantland Rice in *The Football 1942 Review: Yearbook of the Football News*, 1943, 5.
49. Bernard F. "Bunny" Oakes in *Denver Post* quoted in *The Football 1943 Review: Yearbook of the Football News*, 1944, 18.
50. F.T. Ward in *Football: Naval Aviation Manuals*, op. cit., 8.
51. Okeson in NCAA *Guide 1943*, 9.
52. Furman Bisher, "You're in the Army, Mr. Trippi," in *Southern Living*, Sep. 1984.
53. L.H. Baker, *Football: Facts and Figures* (New York: Rinehart, 1945), 605.

## Chapter 5

1. Shirley Povich quoted in Bob Quincy and Julian Scheer, *Choo Choo: The Charlie Justice Story* (Chapel Hill, N.C.: Bentley Publishing, 1958), 44.
2. *Mainsheet*, Nov. 13, 1943.
3. *Ibid.*
4. *The Daily Tar Heel*, Nov. 29, 1999.
5. Charlie Justice in *All the Way Choo Choo*, TV documentary by David Solomon Productions, DVD excerpt, July 1984; Hereafter cited as Justice DVD interview.
6. Furman Bisher, "You're in the Army, Mr. Trippi," *Southern Living*, Sep. 1984.
7. Ken Rappoport, *Tar Heel: North Carolina Football* (Huntsville, Ala.: The Strode Publishers, 1976), 22.
8. Bisher, op. cit.
9. Joe Maniaci quoted in Justice DVD interview.

10. Justice quoted in Rappoport, op. cit., 22–23.
11. Justice quoted in *The Daily Tar Heel*, op. cit.
12. Bob Terrell, *All Aboard: Charlie "Choo Choo" Justice* (Alexander, N.C.: Alexander Books, 1996), 68.
13. Quincy and Scheer, op. cit., 40; Joe Maniaci quoted in *ibid.*
14. Rappoport, op. cit., 23.
15. Justice quoted in the *New York Times*, Oct. 20, 2003.
16. *Mainsheet*, Sep. 4, 1943, and Oct. 9, 1943.
17. *Baltimore* (Md.) *Sun*, Oct. 25, 1943; hereafter cited as *Sun*.
18. *Sun*, Nov. 7, 1943.
19. Paul Scalera in *Sun*, Nov. 14, 1943.
20. Quincy and Scheer, op. cit., 43.
21. *Mainsheet*, Nov. 27, 1943.
22. *Mainsheet*, Nov. 13, 1943.
23. John "Ox" DaGrosa and Edward H. Nichterlein, *The National Collegiate Athletic Association Football Guide 1945*, 28–29.
24. *Mainsheet*, Sep. 23, 1944.
25. *Sun*, Oct. 1, 1944.
26. *Sun*, Oct. 9, 1944.
27. *Sun*, Oct. 11, 1944.
28. *Mainsheet*, Oct. 14, 1944.
29. Game program, Camp Lejeune at Bainbridge, Oct. 8, 1944.
30. *Sun*, Oct. 16, 1944.
31. *Mainsheet*, Oct. 21, 1944.
32. *Sun*, Oct. 18, 1944.
33. *Ibid.*
34. *Ibid.*
35. Telephone interview with William Friday, Oct. 5, 2005.
36. *Mainsheet*, Oct. 28, 1944.
37. *Sun*, Oct. 30, 1944.
38. *Mainsheet*, Nov. 4, 1944.
39. Smith Barrier in the *Greensboro Daily News*, Nov. 6, 1944.
40. Bisher, op. cit.
41. Terrell, op. cit., 70–71.
42. Justice quoted in Terrell, op. cit., 70.
43. *Camp Lejeune Globe*, Nov. 22, 1944.
44. Justice quoted in *The Daily Tar Heel*, op. cit.
45. Quincy and Scheer, op. cit., 44.
46. Game program, Army Air Forces vs. Navy, Pearl Harbor, Nov. 4, 1945.
47. Interview with Robert H. Koontz, Sep. 17, 2003.
48. Telephone interview with Joe Augustine, Oct. 17, 2003.
49. Justice quoted in Rappoport, op. cit., 23.
50. Quincy and Scheer, op. cit., 46.
51. Rappoport, op. cit., 23–24.
52. Dick Baddour quoted in www.Inside Carolina.com, Oct. 17, 2003.

## Chapter 6

1. John "Ox" DaGrosa and Edward H. Nichterlein in *NCAA Guide 1944*, 26.
2. John DaGrosa and Bob Hall in *NCAA Guide 1946*, 20.
3. Jack Byrne in *Illustrated Football Annual 1943*, 18.
4. Mark Stillwell in *Naval Aviation News*, Sep.–Oct. 1989.
5. Ray Bray quoted in Mark Stillwell in *ibid.*
6. Game program, Del Monte Pre-Flight at California, Nov. 27, 1943.
7. Game program, Fleet City vs. El Toro Marine Corps Air Station, San Francisco, Calif., Sep. 29, 1945.
8. DaGrosa and Hall in *NCAA Guide 1946*, op. cit., 23.
9. Game program, Pearl Harbor All-Stars vs. Fleet City, San Francisco, Calif., Dec. 2, 1945.
10. John B. Scott in *College Football Historical Society Newsletter*, Nov. 1998, 10.
11. Game program, Camp Lejeune at Jacksonville NATTC, Nov. 27, 1943.
12. W.A. Alexander in *NCAA Guide 1944*, 86.
13. George Trevor in *Illustrated Football Annual 1944*, 14; Wilton Hazzard in *Illustrated Football Annual 1944*, 9.
14. *Football Pictorial Yearbook 1945*, 10.
15. John "Ox" DaGrosa and Edward H. Nichterlein in *NCAA Guide 1945*, 24.
16. George Trevor in *Illustrated Football Annual 1945*, 6; Leonard Lewin in *Football Prevues 1945*, 18.
17. Jack Byrne in *Illustrated Football Annual 1943*, 20.
18. Game program, Sampson Naval Training Station at Cornell, Oct. 21, 1944.

## Chapter 7

1. *NCAA Guide 1943*, 10.
2. Theodore P. Bank in *NCAA Guide 1942*, 17.
3. Furman Bisher in "You're in the Army, Mr. Trippi," in *Southern Living*, Sep. 1984.

4. *Football Prevues 1945*, 4.
5. College Football Recap, www.infoplease.com.
6. Two Cousins College Football Emporium website: 2cuz.com/features/army1944 (site discontinued); George Trevor in *Illustrated Football Annual 1944*, 15.
7. Harold "Spike" Claassen in *NCAA Guide 1946*, 27; George Trevor in *Illustrated Football Annual 1945*, 6.
8. Ernie Palladino in Joe Hoppel, Mike Nahrstedt, and Steve Zesch, eds., *The Sporting News — College Football's Twenty-Five Greatest Teams* (St. Louis, Mo.: The Sporting News, 1988), 21.
9. Two Cousins College Football Emporium Website, op. cit.
10. Game program, Camp Davis vs. Catawba, Wilmington, N.C., Oct. 10, 1942.
11. Game program Camp Davis at Camp Lejeune, Oct. 30, 1943.
12. Theodore P. Bank in *NCAA Guide 1943*, 27.
13. Game program, Camp Grant at Wisconsin, Madison, Sep. 19, 1942.
14. Game Program, Fort Warren at Colorado, Sep. 25, 1943; Game Program, Fort Warren at Utah, Oct. 2, 1943; *The Football News: The American Collegiate Sports Weekly*, Oct. 23, 1943, 2.
15. Unknown Denver, Colo., newspaper, Oct. 22, 1943.
16. Game Program, Fleet City vs. Fourth Air Force, San Francisco, Calif., Nov. 25, 1945.
17. Game Program, Fourth Air Force at Washington, Oct. 23, 1943.
18. Game program, St. Mary's Pre-Flight vs. Fourth Air Force, San Francisco, Calif., Oct. 29, 1944.
19. *Keesler Field News*, Nov. 11, 1943.
20. *Football Prevues 1944*, 3–4.
21. *The Sporting News*, Nov. 9, 1944.
22. *Football Prevues 1945*, 4.
23. Bank in *NCAA Guide 1943*, 27.
24. Game program, Second Air Force vs. Fourth Air Force, Los Angeles, Calif., Sep. 14, 1945.
25. Charles Ben Kopp in *NCAA Guide 1945*, 38.

## Chapter 8

1. Quotation in John A. Gunn, *(Quite) A Few Good Men* (Costa Mesa, Calif.: J&J Publishing, 1992), 14.
2. Jack Byrne in *Illustrated Football Annual 1943*, 23.
3. John A. Gunn, *The Old Core* (Costa Mesa, Calif.: J&J Publishing, 1992), 76.
4. Gunn, *(Quite) A Few Good Men*, 8–9; Archie Rackley in Gunn, 9.
5. James G. Schneider, *The Navy V-12 Program: Leadership for a Lifetime* (Champaign, Ill.: Marlow Books, 1987), 270.
6. Joe Verducci in *Football Prevues 1944*, 34.
7. Gunn, *(Quite) A Few Good Men*, op. cit., 32.
8. *Camp Lejeune Globe*, Nov. 22, 1944.
9. Gunn, *(Quite) A Few Good Men*, op. cit., 280.
10. Game program, Cherry Point Marine Corps Air Station at Bainbridge Naval Training Center, Nov. 11, 1944.
11. Gunn, *(Quite) A Few Good Men*, op. cit., 58.
12. *Ibid.*, 18.
13. Bill Leiser in *Illustrated Football Annual 1945*, 24.
14. Gunn, *(Quite) A Few Good Men*, op. cit., 11.
15. *Ibid.*, 29–30.
16. Jerry Nason in *The National Collegiate Athletic Association Football Guide 1945*, 93.

## Chapter 9

1. George Trevor in *Illustrated Football Annual 1943*, 24.
2. *Great Lakes Bulletin*, Dec. 3, 1943, www.nsgreatlakes.navy.mil.
3. John "Ox" DaGrosa and Joseph T. Gardner in *NCAA Guide 1943*, 13.
4. *The Football 1942 Review: Yearbook of the Football News 1943*, 13.
5. Sec Taylor in *NCAA Guide 1943*, 97.
6. *Illustrated Football Annual 1943*, 29.
7. Homer Cooke in *NCAA Guide 1943*, 51.
8. Jack Byrne in *Illustrated Football Annual 1943*, 16.
9. Oliver Kuechle in *National 1944 Review and Preview 1945*, 71.
10. Bill Leiser in *Illustrated Football Annual 1943*, 37.
11. Weldon Hart in *NCAA Guide 1944*, 122, 123.
12. Chet Nelson in *Ibid.*, 124.
13. Dewey Luster quoted by Floyd Olds in *Illustrated Football Annual 1943*, 58.

14. George T. Davis in *NCAA Guide 1944*, op. cit., 126.
15. www.raginpagin.com.
16. *Camp Davis AA Barrage*, Nov. 1943.
17. James G. Schneider, *The Navy V-12 Program: Leadership for a Lifetime* (Champaign, Ill.: Marlow Books, 1987), 266.
18. L.W. St. John quoted by Francis Powers in *Illustrated Football Annual 1943*, op. cit., 46.
19. Jack Byrne in *ibid.*, 49.
20. www.ntcgl.navy.mil/history/1943football (site discontinued).
21. Homer F. Cooke, Jr., in *NCAA Guide 1944*, 69.
22. Oliver Kuechle in *National 1944 Review*, op. cit., 71.
23. Jack O'Sullivan in *Illustrated Football Annual 1944*, 44.
24. *Football Prevues 1945*, 4.
25. www.2cuz.com/features/army1944 (site discontinued).
26. John "Ox" DaGrosa and Edward H. Nichterlein in *NCAA Guide 1945*, 24.
27. O'Sullivan, op. cit., 46.
28. Ed Danforth in *Football Prevues 1944*, 8; Jake Wade in *NCAA Guide 1945*, 105; *Illustrated Football Annual 1945*, 62.
29. *Illustrated Football Annual 1945*, 63.
30. Weldon Hart in *NCAA Guide 1945*, 118.
31. Fred Russell and Smith Barrier in *Illustrated Football Annual 1945*, op. cit., 33.
32. Francis J. Powers in *ibid.*, 25.
33. Furman Bisher, "You're in the Army, Mr. Trippi," *Southern Living*, Sep. 1984.
34. Bernie McCarty, "The Man from Smackover," *College Football Historical Society Newsletter* 4 no. 3 (May 1995), 3–6, www.la84foundation.org/SportsLibrary/CFHSN/CFHSNv04/CFHSNv04n3b.pdf.
35. Ed Pollock in *NCAA Guide 1946*, 109.
36. John DaGrosa and Bob Hall in *NCAA Guide 1946*, 21.
37. Telephone interview with Clyde Luther "Smackover" Scott, Oct. 26, 2006.
38. *The Football 1945 Review: Yearbook of the Football News*, 7.
39. John A. Gunn, *(Quite) A Few Good Men* (Costa Mesa, Calif.: J&J Publishing, 1992), 15.
40. *Los Angeles Times* and *Los Angeles Herald Examiner* quoted in *ibid.*, 15–16; *College Football Historical Society Newsletter*, Aug. 1992, 2–3.
41. *Los Angeles Herald Examiner* quoted in Gunn, *(Quite) A Few Good Men*, 16.

42. *The New York Times*, Dec. 2, 1945, quoted in Thomas Harbrecht and C. Robert Barnett, "College Football During World War II: 1941–1945," *The Physical Educator*, March 1979.
43. Game program, Second Air Force vs. Fourth Air Force, Los Angeles, Calif., Sep. 14, 1945.
44. DaGrosa and Hall, op. cit., 24–25.
45. Emmons Byrnes in *Football Prevues 1945*, op. cit., 8–9.

## Chapter 10

1. Telephone interview with Julian Pressly, Oct. 3, 2006.
2. Alexander Durley in *National 1944 Review and Preview 1945*, 116.
3. Pressly interview.
4. *Great Lakes Bulletin*, Oct. 6, 1944.
5. Paul W.L. Jones in *The National Collegiate Athletic Association Football Guide 1943*, 114.
6. E.P. Hurt in *The National Collegiate Athletic Association Football Guide 1945*, 130.
7. Alexander Durley in *National 1944 Review*, op. cit., 114.
8. *Ibid.*
9. *Ibid.*, 115.
10. Robert W. Peterson, *The Early Years of Pro Football* (New York: Oxford University Press, 1997), 127, 136.
11. Elmer Layden quoted in *ibid.*, 138.
12. Professional Football Researchers Association, www.profootballresearchers.org.
13. Bob Dove quoted in Peterson, op. cit., 142–43.
14. Pro Football Hall of Fame, www.profootballhof.com/history.
15. George Strickler in *Illustrated Football Annual 1944*, 64.
16. *Ibid.*, 65.

## Chapter 11

1. George L. Shiebler in *The National Collegiate Athletic Association Football Guide 1945*, 65.
2. John A. Gunn, *The Old Core* (Costa Mesa, Calif.: J&J Publishing, 1992), 130.
3. John "Ox" DaGrosa and Edward H. Nichterlein in *NCAA Guide 1945*, 30.
4. John A. Gunn, *(Quite) A Few Good Men* (Costa Mesa, Calif.: J&J Publishing, 1992), 1.

5. Game program, Navy vs. Marines, Pearl Harbor, T.H., Oct. 27, 1945.
6. *Honolulu Advertiser*, Nov. 28, 1943.
7. Undated (1943) unknown Honolulu newspaper.
8. *Honolulu Advertiser*, Dec. 17, 1943.
9. Undated Hawaii newspaper, 1943.
10. *Illustrated Football Annual 1944*, 52.
11. Game program, Navy All-Stars vs. Army Air Forces Pacific Ocean Areas, Pearl Harbor, Jan. 7, 1945.
12. Red McQueen in *Honolulu Advertiser*, Jan. 1945.
13. *National 1944 Review and Preview 1945*, 155.
14. Gunn, *The Old Core*, op. cit., 136.
15. *Ibid*., 110, and supplemental material.
16. *Ibid*.
17. Bill Lazetich quoted in miscellaneous John A. Gunn material.
18. Gunn, *The Old Core*, op. cit., 110 and supplemental material.
19. Douglas A. Noverr and Lawrence E. Ziewacz, *The Games They Played: Sports in American History, 1965–1980* (Chicago: Nelson-Hall, 1983), 138.
20. Pat Harmon quoted in Blair Kerkhoff, *Kansas City Star*, June 26, 1999, www.kcstar.com.
21. Don Fambrough quoted in Blair Kerkhoff, *ibid*.
22. Lawrence Robinson in *Football Pictorial Yearbook 1946*, 4.

## Chapter 12

1. Professional Football Researchers Association, www.profootballresearchers.org.
2. Bernie McCarty (1980) in *ibid*.
3. John "Ox" DaGrosa and Edward H. Nichterlein in *NCAA Guide 1945*, 30.
4. Game program, U.S. Navy Training and Distribution Center, Camp Peary, vs. Bainbridge (Md.) Naval Training Center, at Williamsburg, Va., Oct. 22, 1944.
5. *The Football News: The American Collegiate Sports Weekly*, Nov. 27, 1943.
6. Telephone interview with Dave Rankin, Oct. 25, 2006.
7. Game program, Fort Knox at Ohio State, Sept. 26, 1942.
8. *Great Lakes Bulletin*, Sep. 15, 1944.
9. James G. Schneider, *The Navy V-12 Program: Leadership for a Lifetime* (Champaign, Ill.: Marlow Books, 1987), 288.
10. Telephone interview with Julian Pressly, Oct. 3, 2006.
11. William R. "Killer" Kane in *NCAA Guide 1945*, 42–43.
12. Undated (1943), unknown newspaper article.
13. *Milwaukee Journal*, Sep. 26, 1943.
14. Sid Gray in undated (Sep. 1943) *Camp Davis AA Barrage*.
15. Telephone interview with George "Sonny" Franck, Sep. 2, 2005.
16. Furman Bisher, "You're in the Army, Mr. Trippi," *Southern Living*, Sep. 1984.
17. Frank Murray quoted by Dick Williamson and Fred Russell in *Illustrated Football Annual 1943*, 63.
18. *The Football News: The American Collegiate Sports Weekly*, Nov. 13, 1943, 4.
19. Dick Williamson and Fred Russell in *Illustrated Football Annual 1943*, 64.
20. *Mainsheet*, Nov. 20, 1943.
21. *Mainsheet*, Nov. 27, 1943.
22. McCarty in *College Football Historical Society Newsletter*, op cit.
23. Telephone interview with Clyde Luther "Smackover" Scott, Oct. 26, 2006.
24. Harold Classes and Whitney Martin quoted in McCarty in *College Football Historical Society Bulletin*, op. cit.
25. McCarty in *College Football Historical Society Bulletin*, op. cit.
26. Scott interview.
27. *Ibid*.
28. Telephone interviews with Scott and Leslie Hampton Scott, Oct. 26, 2006.
29. John A. Gunn, draft unpublished magazine article notes, 1983.
30. Grantland Rice in game program, Camp Lejeune at North Carolina Pre-Flight, Nov. 13, 1943.
31. Jonas H. Ingram quoted in *Football: The Naval Aviation Physical Training Manuals*, Office of the Chief of Naval Operations (Annapolis, Md.: United States Naval Institute, 1943), 7.

# *Selected Bibliography*

## Periodicals

*Bainbridge Mainsheet*, Bainbridge (Md.) Naval Training Station/Center, numerous 1943–45.
*Baltimore* (Md.) *Sun*, numerous 1943–44.
*Baltimore & Ohio* [Railroad] *Magazine*, August 1946.
*Camp Davis* (N.C.) *AA Barrage*, several 1943.
*Camp Lejeune* (N.C.) *Globe*, numerous 1943–44.
*Carolina Alumni Review*, University of North Carolina Alumni Association, Jan.–Feb. 2004; Fall 1987; May–June 1998.
*College Football Historical Society Newsletter*: Aug. 1988; Aug. 1992; May 1995; May 1999, Nov. 1999.
*Daily Tar Heel*, University of North Carolina, Nov. 29, 1999.
*Great Lakes Bulletin*, Great Lakes (Ill.) Naval Training Center, numerous 1943–45.
*Greensboro* (N.C.) *Daily News*, Nov. 6, 1944.
*Honolulu Advertiser*, various 1943, 1944.
*Naval Aviation News*, Sep.–Oct. 1989.
*New York Times*, Oct. 20, 2003.
*Our Navy Magazine*, Mid-Nov. 1943.
*Screaming Eagle*, 101st Airborne Division Newsmagazine 1, no. 1 (Sept. 17, 1945).
*The State: A Weekly Survey of North Carolina*, Feb. 27, 1943.
*Wilmington* (N.C.) *Sunday Star-News*, Sep. 26, 1943

## Articles

Barnett, Robert, and Harbrecht, Thomas. "College Football During World War II: 1941–1945." *The Physical Educator*, March 1979.
Bisher, Furman. "You're in the Army, Mr. Trippi." *Southern Living*, Sept. 1984.
Parker, Don. "The World of Sports." In *While You Were Gone*, Jack Goodman, ed. New York: Simon and Schuster, 1946.
Rominger, Donald W., Jr. "From Playing Field to Battleground: The United States Navy V-5 Preflight Program in World War II." *Journal of Sport History* 12, no. 3 (Winter 1985).

## Interviews

Joe Augustine, Oct. 17, 2003
Albert F. Bagley, Jr., July 21, 2004
Clifton Brubaker, July 21, 2004
Robert "Bob" Cox, July 28, 2005
George "Sonny" Franck. Sep. 22, 2005
John A. Gunn, Several 2005–06
William Friday, Oct. 4, 2005

Sarah Justice, Oct. 17, 2003
Robert H. Koontz, Oct. 17, 2003
Mike Miklas, July 21, 2004
Julian Pressly, Oct. 3, 2006
Dave Rankin, Oct. 25, 2006
Clyde Luther Scott, Oct. 26, 2006
Leslie Hampton Scott, Oct. 26, 2006

## Internet sources

AAFLA.org/la84foundation. org
abooks.com
army.mil
cae.wisc.edu
collegefootball.org
cornell-magazine.cornell.edu
databasefootball.com
dcmilitary.com
ericthrall.com
espn.go.com
footballfoundation.org
footballresearch.com
fortsheridan.com
HawkTalkOnLine.com
hickoksports.com
history.navy.mil
infoplease.com
insidecarolina.com
iowa.theinsiders.com
jhowell.net
kcstar.com
lib.unc.edu
lonesailor.org
marchfield.org
military.com
montereyherald.com
ntcgl.navy.mil (site discontinued)
nsgreatlakes.navy.mil
ObituariesOnTheNet.com
phys.utk.edu
profootballhof.com
RaginPagin.com
sccotton.org
shrine-bowl.com
shrpsports.com
sportsecyclopedia.com
strategic-air-command.com
time.com
2cuz.com (site discontinued)
usntcbainbridge.org

## Football Guides and Periodicals

Bingham, W.J., ed. *The Official National Collegiate Athletic Association Football Guide* (New York: A.S. Barnes and Co.), 1944–47. Cited as *NCAA Guide.*
Boyd, Byron D., ed. *The Football 1942 Review: Yearbook of the Football News, 1943.*
_____. *The Football 1943 Review: Yearbook of the Football News, 1944.*
_____. *The Football 1944 Review: Yearbook of the Football News, 1945.*
Byrne, Jack, and Reiss, Malcolm, eds. *Illustrated Football Annual*, Fiction House, Inc., 1943–45.
*CFRA (College Football Researchers Association) Bulletin* No. 99, Oct.–Nov. 1992.
*The Football News: The American Collegiate Sports Weekly,* numerous 1943–45.
*Football Pictorial Yearbook.* Street & Smith Publications, 1942–46.
*Football Prevues 1945.* Athletic Publications, Inc.
Hirschfield, Leo, ed. *Football Prevues 1944,* Gorham Press.
Iowa Pre-Flight Press Guide, 1942.
Okeson, Walter R., ed. *The Official National Collegiate Athletic Association Football Guide* (New York: A.S. Barnes and Co.), 1942–43.
Spink, J.G. Taylor, ed. *Football Rule and Record Book 1945,* St. Louis, Mo.

# Books

*Bainbridge Naval Training Center—1968 Unofficial Directory & Guide.* Lubbock, Tex.: Boone Publications, 1968.
Baker, L.H. *Football: Facts and Figures.* New York: Rinehart, 1945.
Danzig, Allison. *The History of American Football: Its Teams, Players, and Coaches.* Englewood Cliffs, N.J.: Prentice-Hall, 1956.
Davies, Richard O. *Sports in American Life: A History.* Malden, Mass.: Blackwell Publishing, 2007.
Gunn, John A. *The Old Core.* Costa Mesa, Calif.: J&J Publishing, 1992.
\_\_\_\_\_. *(Quite) A Few Good Men.* Costa Mesa, Calif.: J&J Publishing, 1992.
Hoppel, Joe, Mike Narhstedt, and Steve Zesch, eds. *College Football's Twenty-Five Greatest Teams.* St. Louis: The Sporting News, 1988.
Kroger, Jim. *Upon Other Fields on Other Days: College Football's Wartime Casualties.* Atlanta: Longstreet Press, 1991.
MacCambridge, Michael, ed. *America's Game: The Epic Story of How Pro Football Captured a Nation.* New York: Random House, 2004.
\_\_\_\_\_. *ESPN Sports Century.* New York: Hyperion, 1999.
McCarty, Bernie. *All-America: The Complete Roster of Football's Heroes, Vol. 1, 1889–1945.* University Park, Ill., self-published, 1991.
Mendell, Ronald L., and Timothy B. Phares. *Who's Who in Football.* New Rochelle, N.Y.: Arlington House, 1974.
Noverr, Douglas A., and Lawrence E. Ziewacz. *The Games They Played: Sports in America History, 1965–1980.* Chicago: Nelson-Hall, 1983.
Office of the Chief of Naval Operations. *Football: The Naval Aviation Physical Training Manuals.* Annapolis, Md.: United States Naval Institute, 1943.
Osborne, Richard E. *World War II Sites in the United States: A Tour Guide & Directory.* Indianapolis: Riebel-Roque Publishing, 1996.
Peterson, Robert W. *The Early Years of Pro Football.* New York: Oxford University Press, 1997.
Quesenbery, Erika L., and Bainbridge Historical Association. *Images of America: United States Naval Training Center, Bainbridge.* Charleston, S.C.: Arcadia Publishing, 2007.
Quincy, Bob, and Julian Scheer. *Choo Choo: The Charlie Justice Story.* Chapel Hill, N.C.: Bentley Publishing, 1958.
Rader, Benjamin G. *American Sports: From the Age of Folk Games to the Age of Spectators.* Englewood Cliffs, N.J.: Prentice-Hall, 1983.
Rappoport, Ken. *Tar Heel: North Carolina Football.* Huntsville, Ala.: Strode Publishers, 1976.
Schneider, James G. *The Navy V-12 Program: Leadership for a Lifetime.* Champaign, Ill.: Marlow Books, 1987.
Smith, Elaine J., ed. *History of Sport and Physical Activity in the United States,* 2nd ed. Dubuque, Ia.: Wm. C. Brown, 1978.
Terrell, Bob. *All Aboard: Charlie "Choo Choo" Justice.* Alexander, N.C.: Alexander Books, 1996.
United States Navy Pre-Flight School, Chapel Hill, N.C., second edition of monograph, ca. 1943, Merin-Baliban Studios, Philadelphia, Pa.
Vaccaro, Mike. *1941: The Greatest Year in Sports.* New York: Doubleday, 2007.

## Football Game Programs

Alameda Coast Guard vs. California, Berkeley, Nov. 4, 1944.
Bainbridge Naval Training Station vs. Camp Peary U.S. Navy Training and Distribution Center, Camp Peary, Va., Oct. 22, 1944.
Camp Lejeune vs. Bainbridge Naval Training Center, Bainbridge, Md., Oct. 8, 1944.
Camp Lejeune Marine Corps Base vs. Jacksonville Naval Air Station/Air Technical Training Center, Jacksonville, Fla., Nov. 27, 1943.
Camp Lejeune Marine Corps Base vs. North Carolina Pre-Flight, Chapel Hill, Nov. 13, 1943.
Cherry Point Marine Corps Air Station vs. Bainbridge Naval Training Center, Bainbridge, Md., Nov. 11, 1944.
Curtis Bay Coast Guard vs. Bainbridge Naval Training Station, Bainbridge, Md., Oct. 16, 1943.
Del Monte Pre-Flight vs. California, Berkeley, Nov. 27, 1943.
El Toro Marine Corps Air Station vs. Army Air Force Training Command, Los Angeles, Calif, Oct. 28, 1945.
El Toro Marine Corps Base vs. Fleet City Naval Receiving Station, Los Angeles, Calif., Dec. 9, 1945.
First Air Force vs. Army Air Force Training Command, Brooklyn, N. Y., Nov. 11, 1945.
Fleet City Naval Receiving Station vs. Second Air Force, San Francisco, Calif., Sep. 23, 1945.
Fleet City Naval Receiving Station vs. El Toro Marine Corps Air Station, San Francisco, Calif., Sep. 29, 1945.
Fleet City Naval Receiving Station vs. Fourth Air Force, San Francisco, Calif., Nov. 25, 1945.
Fleet City Naval Receiving Station vs. Pacific Fleet All-Stars, San Francisco, Calif., Dec. 2, 1945.
Fort Francis E. Warren vs. Colorado, Boulder, Sep. 25, 1943.
Fort Knox vs. Ohio State, Columbus, Sep. 26, 1942.
Fourth Air Force vs. Randolph Field, Los Angeles, Calif., Dec. 10, 1944.
Fourth Air Force vs. Washington, Seattle, Oct. 23, 1943.
Great Lakes Naval Training Center vs. Northwestern, Evanston, Ill., Oct. 16, 1943.
Great Lakes Naval Training Center vs. Notre Dame, Notre Dame, Ind., Dec. 2, 1944.
Jacksonville Naval Air Station/Air Technical Training Center vs. North Carolina, Chapel Hill, 1943.
Maxwell Field vs. Bainbridge Naval Training Station, Bainbridge, Md., Dec. 3, 1944.
Navy All-Stars vs. Army All-Stars, Pearl Harbor, Jan. 7, 1945.
Navy All-Stars vs. Marine All-Stars, Pearl Harbor, Oct. 27, 1945.
University of Nevada-Reno Air Base vs. Utah, Salt Lake City, Oct. 16, 1943.
St. Mary's Pre-Flight vs. UCLA, Los Angeles, Calif., Oct. 2, 1942.
St. Mary's Pre-Flight vs. Santa Ana Army Air Base, Los Angeles, Calif., Nov. 8, 1942.
St. Mary's Pre-Flight vs. Washington, Seattle, Nov. 14, 1942.
St. Mary's Pre-Flight vs. Fourth Air Force, San Francisco, Calif., Oct. 29, 1944.
St. Mary's Pre-Flight vs. Fleet City, San Francisco, Calif., Nov. 4, 1945.
St. Mary's Pre-Flight vs. El Toro Marine Corps Air Station, San Francisco, Calif., Nov. 18, 1945.
Santa Ana Army Air Base vs. Loyola, Los Angeles, Calif., Nov. 15, 1942.
Second Air Force vs. Fourth Air Force, Los Angeles, Calif., Sep. 14, 1945.
Texas Tech vs. Lubbock Army Air Field, Lubbock, Tex., Sep. 18, 1943.

## Miscellaneous sources

*All the Way Choo Choo*, July 1984 TV documentary by David Solomon Productions, DVD excerpt.
*Army Town: Greensboro, 1943–1946*, Greensboro (N.C.) Historical Museum, 1994.
"Bainbridge Naval Training Center: The Orphan Sister," brochure, USNTC Bainbridge Historical Association, Inc.
Fourth Air Force information booklet, 1943.
John A. Gunn, draft magazine unpublished manuscript notes, 1983.
*True Sport Picture Stories* (New York: Street & Smith Publications) 2, no. 4, Dec. 1943 (comic book).
VARIOUS RESEARCH MATERIAL PROVIDED BY:
  The Historical Society of Cecil County, Md.
  Jack Hilliard, Greensboro, N.C.
  John A. Gunn, Gulf Breeze, Fla.
  John R. Witt, Elkmont, Ala.
  John Thorpe, DeBary, Fla.
  J.Y. Joyner Library, East Carolina University
  Larry Clark, Wilmington, N.C.
  Moraga (Calif.) Historical Society
  Jerry Sanders e-mail, Sep. 1, 2008
  Randall Library, University of North Carolina Wilmington

# *Index*

Numbers in **bold italics** indicate pages with photographs.

Aberdeen (Md.) Ordnance School 89; team 212
Aberdeen (Md.) Proving Ground 42, 89
Aberdeen (Md.) Proving Ground (Black) 93, 195
Abilene (Tex.) Army Air Base Flyers 89, 145
Adams, Hobbs 120
Afrika Korps 43
Agase, Alex 174, ***212***, 213
Aiken, Md. 27
Air Medal 71, 144
Air Service Command team 205
Air Transport Command (Tenn.) Rockets 41, 42, 89, 131, 141, 145, 147, 156, 187
Akin, Leonard "Len" 31, 33–35, ***36***, 40, 41, 104
Alabama State University 190
Alameda, Calif. 151
Alameda (Calif.) Coast Guard Station Sea Lions 18, ***88***, 89, 109, 112, 127, 151, 152, 169, 176, 181, 218
Alaska Air Transport Command Clippers 89, 200
USS *Albacore* (SS-218) 221
Albert, Frank (Frankie) 18, 66, 126, 165, 174, ***175***
Albuquerque (N.M.) Air Base Colin Kellys 89, 166
Aldrich, Ki 206
Alexander, Bill 173, 180
Alexandria, Egypt 43
Algeria 4
Algiers (La.) Navy 89, 142, 195
All-America Conference (postwar) 215
All-America: players v, 16–18, 21, 31, 34, 57, 68, 75, 79, 82, 94, 96, 98, 99, 103, 106, 109, 115, 118, 120, 124, 126, 133, 135, 137, 140, 142, 143, 145–47, 154, 156, 157, 159, 164, 168–70, 175, 177, 179, 184, 185, 190, 191, 201, 202, 206, 208, 210–13, 217, 218, 220; teams 174, 181, 187; *see also* "All-Purple Heart Collegiate All-America"; 1943 Consensus All-America; 1944 Consensus All-America; 1945 Consensus All-America; Rice, Grantland
All-Pacific Recreation Fund 53
"All-Purple Heart Collegiate All-America" 4, 185, 186
All-South team 95
All-Southern team 95
"All the Way Choo Choo" 106
Allen Academy (Tex.) 144
Allen University (S.C.) Yellow Jackets 191
Allies 17
Amador Valley, Calif. 111
Amarillo (Tex.) Army Air Field Sky Giants 89, 124, 145, 146, 181
American Association 196
*The American Collegiate Sports Weekly* 48
American Council on Education 58
American Football Coaches Association 46
American Football League 196
American International 156
American League all-stars 34
Amherst 208
Amling, Warren 187
"Anchors Aweigh" 25
Anderson, Paul 115, 116, 172, 173
Angsman, Elmer 184
Annapolis, Md. 31, 54, 121, 222; *see also* Navy (U.S. Naval Academy, Annapolis, Md.)
Ann Arbor, Mich. 115
Appalachian State University (Mountaineers) 136
Appomattox (Courthouse, Va.) 1
Arab Bowl, Oran, Algeria (Oran Refrigeration Termites vs. Casablanca Ordnance Rabchasers) 204, ***205***

# Index

Arkansas A&M (Boll Weevils) 57, 58, 142; Arkansas-Monticello (present) 58
Armed forces (military) 1–3, 8, 9, 11, 14–16, 18–23, 43, 44, 47–50, 53, 77, 94, 109, 117, 123, 162, 168, 171, 175, 179, 187, 189, 191, 192, 194, 195, 198, 199, 201, 202, 204, 209
Army (U.S. Military Academy, West Point, N.Y.) 3, 9, 17, 41, 52, *53*, 54, 80, 81, 99, 102, 106, 122, 123, 130, 132–35, 160, 168, 172–74, 176, 177, 179, 180–83, 186, 187; Army-Navy games 3, 15, 39, 52, *53*, 54, 79, 82, 122, 128, 131, 177, 183, 220–22
Army, U.S. *see* U.S. Army (army)
Army Air Forces Aid Society 52, 175
Army Air Forces Championship (U.S.) 52
Army Air Forces Training Command (Tex.) Skymasters 43–45, 50, 51, 89, 113, 131, 141, 143–45, 147, 187, 206, 213
Army (Pacific) All-Stars team *201*
Army Pacific Olympics, Tokyo, Japan (11th Airborne Angeles vs. Honolulu All-Stars) 207
Army Personnel Distribution Command (Ky.) Comets 89, 109, 113, 131, 135, 141, 145, 147, 187
Army Relief 52
Army teams vs Navy teams (various bowl or postseason games) 204–206
"Army Town: Greensboro (N.C.), 1943–1946" 83
Aschenbrenner, Frank 124
Asheville, N.C. 10, 25, 40, 41, 94, 95, 98, 99, 102, 104
Associated Press (AP) 33, 53, 54, 98, 99, 164, 168, 174, 221; All-Service team 104, 119, 135, 147, 174, 181, 187; Mid-Atlantic (All) Service team 25, 33, 98, 104; polls 2, 5, 20, 62, 88, 106, 109, 111, 112, 115, 118, 133, 162, 163, 165, 168, 172, 173, 179, 186
ASTP (Army Specialized Training Program) *see* U.S. Army (officers, soldiers)
Athens, Ga. 64, 113
*Athletic Journal* 44
Atlanta Ga. 13, 14
Atlanta (Ga.) All-Stars 193
Atlantic City, N.J. 42, 222
Atlantic City (N.J.) Naval Air Station Flyers 42, 179, 218
Atom Bowl, Nagasaki, Japan (Isahaya Tigers vs. Nagasaki Bears) 4, 207
Auburn Tigers 31, 40, 78, 98, 114, 119, 175, 181, 182, 201
Augustine, Joe 104
Aulds, Tex 172
Axis (Powers) 47, 88

B-29 *Superfortress* bomber 146
Bachiak, Aurel 154
Badaczewski, John 40
Baddour, Dick 106

Bagley, Albert 28
Bainbridge, William 11, 28
Bainbridge (Md.) Naval Training Station/Center Commodores vii, 4, 10, 11, 12, 25, *26*, 27–29, 32–42, 48, 73, 88, 89, 94, 95, *96*, 97–100, *101*, 102–05, 107–09, 111, 115, 126, 153–56, 163, 172–74, 176, 180, 181, 190, 201, 211, 218, 220, 223; (The) "Bainbridge Eleven" 11, 12, 25–42; establishment/history 25–29; Jacob Tome Institute/Tome Field 27, 28, 36, *37,* 96; *Mainsheet* newspaper 27, 29, 31, 33–37, 98, 101, 102, 220; Naval Academy Preparatory School 28; 1943 team 29–34; 1944 team 34, 35, *36, 37,* 38–41; 1945 team 41, 42; PI (physical instructors) School 27, 28, 41; players as Marylanders 37, 102; Recruit Training Command 27
Bainbridge Naval Training Center Historical Association viii
Baker, John 141
Baker, L.H. 39, 119, 165, *165*; football service (Baker Football Information Service) 39, 119, 165, 180
Baker, Sam 190
Balasz, Frank 159
Baltimore, Md. 27, 52, 177
Baltimore & Ohio Railroad 27
*Baltimore (Md.) Sun/Evening Sun* 31, 32, 97, 98, 100
Bambino Bowl, Bari, Italy (Technical School vs. Playboys) 205
Bamboo Bowl, Manila, Philippines (Clark Field Acpacs vs. Leyte Base) 207
Banonis, Vince 118, 119, 174
Barber, Jim *108*
Barber, Red 195
Bari, Italy 205
Barksdale Army Air Base (La.) 89
Barnhill, John H. 180, 223
Barron, Bill 122
Barwegan, Dick 206
Bates Bobcats team 160
Baugh, Sammy 198
Bauman, Bob v, 208
Baylor University 31, 34, 40, 56, 69, 82, 124, 144
Beaumont Hospital (Tex.) 89
Beaumont team 159
Bechtol, Hubert 187
Bednarczyk, Leo vii
Beebe, Hank 106
Behan, Chuck v, 154, 208
Behrens, William F. 28
Belfast, Ireland 200, 204
Belichick, Bill 4
Belichick, Steve 4, 114
Bell, Marvin 153
Bell, Matty 63
Bell, William N. 194

Benedict Tigers team 193
Bergstrom Air Field (Tex.) 89
Berkeley, Calif. 151, 218
Berlin, Germany 144
Berry Field (Tenn.) 89
Berstein, Howard 80
Bertelli, Angelo "the Springfield Rifle" 18, 75, 149, 154, 168, 174, 207, 213
Berwanger, Jay 214
Bible, Dana X. 56, 173
Bierman, Bernie 3, 18, 64, 118, 162, 218
Big Six (Conference) 80, 123, 169, 182, 210
Big Ten (Midwestern Conference) 15, 20, 54, 62, 68, 75, 80, 108, 118, 137, 162, 168, 171, 179, 182, 212, 216
Biloxi, Miss. 142
Bisher, Furman xi, 13, 16, 96
Blackland Field (Tex.) Eagles 56, 89, 144, 174
Blaik, Earl "Red" 18, 52, 82, 132–34, 173, 177, 179
Blanchard, Felix "Doc," "Mr. Inside" 3, 17, 132, *133,* 134, 181, 187, 218, 221; as a "Touchdown Twin" 132
Blozis, Al 198
Blue Network 7
*Bluejackets Manual* 28
Bogue Field (N.C.) Marines 89, 150, 155, 156
Bombers (team) 141
Border Intercollegiate Athletic Conference 76
Boston, Mass. 14, 28
Boston College (Eagles) 79, 80, 111, 124, 164, 171, 175, 190
Boston Red Sox 71
Boston Yanks 105, 196, 197
Bottari, Vic 126
Bougainville 47, 154
Boulevard AC (Hi.) 203
Bowen, Dinky 178
Bowman Field (Ky.) 89
Bradford, Brick 31
Bradley Tech Braves 137
Brandt, Bill 185
Bray, Raymond 109, 174
Brazinski, Sam *158*
Breckinridge, Ky. 210
Breeding, George *136*
Brennan, Terry 184
Britain (Great) 17; British 43, 200, 217
Brominski, Ed 35
Bronze Star 2, 62, 151, 208, 212
Brooklyn, N.Y. 50, 151, 206
Brooklyn Bond Bowl Game, Brooklyn, N.Y. (First Air Force vs. Army Air Force Training Command) *51,* 206; *see also* Treasury Bowl, New York, N.Y
Brooklyn Dodgers (NFL) 29, 30, 50, 118, 126, 196, 197
*Brooklyn (N.Y.) Eagle* 50
Brooklyn Tigers 196
Brown, Bo cartoons 44, 75, 213, 219

Brown, Earl 173
Brown, Joe E. 53
Brown, Paul E. xi, 2, 18, 63, *116,* 117, 171, 180, 181
Brown University Bears 82, 128, 134, 135, 160
Bryan Air Field (Tex.) Raiders 89, 144, 191
Bryan Air Field (Tex.) (Black) 195
Bryant, Paul "Bear" 2, 18, 63, 71, 113, 124, 163
Buckingham, Morris 177
Bucknell Bison 80
Bulge (Battle of the, tour) vii
Bunker Hill (Ind.) Naval Training Station Blockbusters 89, *119,* 120; *see also* Peru (Ind.) Navy
Burma 186
Burnham, Elmer 172
Bush, George H.W. 71
Bushnell General Hospital (Ut.) 89
Buster Sports viii
Butkovich, Tony v, 18, 154, 168, *169,* 208, 213
Butler 126
Butts, Wallace 218

C-54 cargo aircraft *150*
Cain, Bob 185, 186
Cairo, Egypt 43
Calabrese, Philip "Moon" 47
Calahan, Ross 169
Caldwell, Chan 185
California 20, 78, 196
California Collegiate Athletic Conference 76
California Ramblers 151
Calvelli, Tony 145
Camden (N.J.) Blue Devils 99
Cameron, Eddie 76, 100, 172, 180, 218
Camp Ashby (Calif.) 89
Camp Barkeley (Tex.) 89
Camp Beale (Calif.) 89, 112
Camp Butner (N.C.) 89, 156, 191
Camp Campbell 220th Armored (Ky.) 89
Camp Cooke (Calif.) 187
Camp Davis (N.C.) Fighting AA's/Blue Brigade 33, 36, 89, 124, 135, 136, 153, 155, 165, 166, 170–72, 174, 217
Camp Detrick (Md.) 42, 89, 155
Camp Gordon (Ga.) 3rd Armored Division Tankers 89, 142
Camp Gordon Johnson (Fla.) 121
Camp Grant (Ill.) Warriors 89, 117, 119, 137, 139, 165, 166, *216,* 217
Camp Holabird (Md.) 191
Camp Hood-North, Fourth Army (Tex.) 89
Camp Hood-South (Tex.) 90
Camp Kilmer (N.J.) 90
Camp Lee (Va.) Travelers 33, 34, 39, 42, 90, 98, 99, 109, 156
Camp Lejeune (N.C.) Marine Corps Base Marines v, 17, 18, 29, 30, 33, 34, 39, 40, 48, 49, 67, *77,* 90, 95, 99, 102, 103, 121, 124, 125, 136, 149, 152–54, *155,* 159, 174,

208; as New River Marine Corps Barracks 152
Camp Lejeune (N.C.) Marine Corps Base (Montford Point) (Black) Panthers 92, 193, 195
Camp MacKall (N.C.) Chutists 90, 155, 156
Camp MacKall (N.C.) (Black) Paratroopers 93, 194
Camp McCoy (Wisc.) 90
Camp Peary (Va.) Pirates 37, 39, 40, 90, 100, 101, 104, 108, 109, 126, 156, 180, 181, 211, 223
Camp Plauche (La.) (Black) 195
Camp Polk (La.) 90, 145
Camp Pickett (Va.) 166, 191
Camp Swift (Tex.) 191
Campbell, Orville 106
Canada 205
Canadeo, Tony 214
Canale, Rocco 187
Cantor, Leo 141
Cape Gloucester 152
Capitol Classic (game) 191
Card-Pitt Combine "Carpets" 196, 197
Carlisle Barracks-Medical Field Service (Pa.) Medicos 90, 166
Carlson'S 3-Deep 174
Carnegie Tech 35, 82, 109
Carolinas (championship) 135, 136
Carver, Gordon 177
Case, Ernie 185, 186
Catawba Indians 124, 136
Cecil County, Md. 25
Cecil County (Md.) Historical Society viii
Central Collegiate Athletic Conference 76
Central Intercollegiate Conference 76
Central Pacific Armed Forces League (Hawaii teams) 200
Chapel Hill, N.C. 3, 10, 14, 64, 69, 97, 102, 109, 124–26
Charleston (S.C.) Coast Guard 90, 136, 147, 151
Charlestown, Md. viii
Charlotte, N.C. 147, 148
Charlotte (N.C.) Bees 193
Chase, Benjamin S. 181
Chatham Army Air Base (Field) (Ga.) Blockbusters 90, 113, 147, 156
Cheatham, Hilliard Lloyd "Upan" 31, 33, 35, 37, 39, 40, 98, 104, 201
Cherry Point (N.C.) Marine Corps Air Station Marines 40, 81, 90, 109, 114, 121, 124, 126, 136, 142, 147, 150, 155, 156, 193
Cherryville, N.C. 10, 106
Chesapeake Bay 11, 25
Chevigny, Jack v, 2, 18, *153*
Cheyenne, Wyo. 137
Chicago, Ill. 14, 54, 114, 168, 171, 173, 194
Chicago Bears 29–31, 33, 34, 52, 83, 84, 105, 111, 120, 126, 135, 146, 154, 175, 185, 195, 197, 198, 202, 210–13

Chicago Cardinals 68, 115, 118, 126, 153, 172, 196, 197, 202
*Chicago (Ill.) Daily News* 45, 159
Chicago (Ill.) Rockets (postwar) 215
Chicago (Ill.) Service Men's Center 52, 175
*Chicago (Ill.) Tribune* 47, 159
Chigger Bowl, Dutch Guiana — Army Air Forces teams 205
China 4, 185
China Bowl, Shanghai 207
Christmas, Paul 68, 109
Cifers, Ed 68
Citadel Bulldogs 136
Clark, George 177
Clark, Larry viii
Clark, Potsy 126
Clark (Ga.) Panthers 194
Classes, Harold 221
Clay, Walter *158*, 189
Clements, Johnny 102
Clemson Tigers 69, 78, 114, 121, 206, 218
Cleveland, Oh. 50, 54
Cleveland Browns (postwar) 116
Cleveland Rams 30, 31, 33, 34, 68, 109, 176, 177, 196, 197
Coast Guard Academy (U.S) Bears 80, 151, 153, 160
Coast Guard Pilots (Calif.) 112
Coast Guard Receiving Station (Calif.) 90
Coast (Pacific) *see* Pacific Coast
Coconut Bowl, New Guinea 206
Coffee Bowl, London (USA vs. Canada) 205
Colby Mules team 160
Colella, Phil 183
Colgate Raiders 82, 134, 213
College All-Stars (game/team) 52, 106, 117, 168, 175, 183, 210, 212, 218
College Football Historical Society 184
*College Football's Twenty-Five Greatest Teams* 11, 20, 134
College of Idaho Coyotes team 146
College of Pacific 62, 78, 154, 202, 213; Tigers team 109, 112, 127, 129, 141, 151, 152, 169, 173
*Colliers* 162, 164; *see also* Rice, Grantland, for *Colliers/Grantland Rice* All-America/Service/Navy teams
Collier's/Grantland Rice teams *see* Rice, Grantland
Collins, Spot *57*
Colorado A&M 82; present Colorado State 82, 138
Colorado College Tigers 62, 138, 146, 169, 173
Colorado Springs, Colo. 145
Colorado Springs (Colo.) Air Base 90, 166
Colored Intercollegiate Athletic Association 191, 192
Columbia, S.C. 191
Columbia Lions 35, 44, 73, 83, 123, 134, 149, 157, 164, 171, 184, 214

Columbus, Oh. 117, 186
Columbus Army Air Field (Ga.) (Black) team 195
Comiskey Park, Chicago, Ill. 171, 173
Compton College 129
Congress (U.S.) 60
Connecticut Huskies 160
USS *Constitution* 28
Cook, Beano vii, viii, 1, 5
Cornell Big Red v, 123, 128, 134, 168, 208, 212
Coronado (Calif.) Amphibious Training Base Amphibs 89, 129
Corpus Christi (Tex.) Naval Air Station Comets 89, 121, 144, 164–66, 174, 187, 212, 217, 218
Cotton Bowl, Dallas, Tex. (Randolph Field vs. Texas) *49*, 56, 106, 143, 204
Coulter, DeWitt "Tex" 133, 134, 187
Cowhig, Gerry 209
Cravath, Jeff 179, 180
Creighton Blue Jays team 139
Crisler, Fritz 117, 172, 180
Crosby, Bing 202
Crowley, James H. "Jim" "Sleepy" 18, 63, *64*, 71, 124, 128
Cuba 1
Curtis Bay (Md.) Coast Guard Cutters 31, 33, 34, 90, 98, 151
Czarboski, Zygmont "Ziggy" 41, 209

Daley, William "Bill" 79, 104, 112, 168, 174
Dallas, Tex. 34, 144, 192, 204
Dancewicz, Frank 183
Daniel Field Air Base (Ga.) Fliers 90, 114, 121, 136, 166, 181
Daniel Field Air Base (Ga.) (Black) 195
Daniell, Jim *108*
Dark, Alvin 57, 154, 170, 202
Dartmouth Indians 21, 50, 61, 82, 173, 186, 202
David, Bob *155*
Davidson Wildcats 136
Davies, Richard O. 14
Davis, Bill 164, 174
Davis, Fred 146, 185
Davis, Glenn "Mr. Outside," "California Comet" 3, 17, 99, 102, 106, *132*, 133, 181, 183, 187; as a "Touchdown Twin" 132
Davis, Jasper "Jap" *74*
Davis, Joe *36*, 37, 40
Davis, Ken 154
Davis, Tom 177, 213
Day, Ollie 177
DeBary, Fla. viii
December 7, 1941 attack on Pearl Harbor *see* Pearl Harbor, Hi
deCorrevont, Bill 25, 30, 32, 33, 41, 98, 115
Defruiter, Bob *140*
DeGreve, Red v, 208

DeKalb Teachers (Ill.) v, 137, 208
Del Monte (Calif.) Pre-Flight School Navyators 68, *88*, 90, 109, 112, 122, 123, 152, 169, 172–74, 176, 223; U.S. Naval Postgraduate School (present) 68
Del Monte Hotel, Monterey, Calif. 64, 68
Deming Army Air Field (N.M.) 90
Denver, Colo. 214
*Denver (Colo.) Post* 185
Department of the Navy 7, 8, 19, 58; Secretary of the Navy 9, 154; Under Secretary 63; *see also* U.S. Navy (navy)
Depauw Tigers 172, 210, 211
Depression (Great) 14, 45, 135
Detroit Lions 68, 109, 114, 126, 145, 146, 154, 179, 185, 197, 223
Detroit University 118
Disney, Walt 157
Distinguished Flying Cross 71, 144, 216
Dixie League 196
Dixon, Mike viii
Dobbs, Glenn 18, 104, *143*, 146, 164, 174, 206, 210
Dobler, Fred 33
"Don't Sit Under the Apple Tree 71
Dorsey, Tommy 160
Doss, Noble 69
Dove, Bob 18, 145, *157, 158*, 159, 196, 214
Drew Army Air Field (Fla.) 90, 147
Duden, H. Richard "Dick" 122, 187, 221
Dudley, William "Bullet Bill" 18, 143, 144, 164, 181
Dugger, John 181
Duke v, 3, 29, 31, 33, 34, 39, 52, 61, 62, 71, 74, 76–78, 80, 100, 104, 114, 115, 120, 121, 123, 124, 126, 135, 155, 156, 168, 154, 172, 173, 177, 180, 182, 186, 201, 208, 213, 218, 219, 222, 223; Junior varsity team 155; 1942; "Transplanted Rose Bowl Game" 2, 73, 74
Dunagan, Al *167*
Duquesne Dukes 40, 75, 101
Durdan, Donald "Don" 25, 31, 33, 34, *36*, 37, 39, 40, 73, 98, 100, 220
Durham, N.C. 2, 29, 34, 73, 74, 177, 222, 223
Dutch Guinea 205
Dutton, Bill 30, 31, 98
Dyer, Roy *60*

Eagle Mt. Lake (Tex.) Rangers 90
East Coast 104, 196
Eastern Flying Training Command (Ala.) 90
Eastern Kentucky University 154
Eastern Washington Eagles 146
Ebbets Field, Brooklyn, N.Y. 50, 51
Edgewood Arsenal (Md.) 90
Edmiston, Art 69
EFTC team 187
Eighth Air Force (8th AF, England) 205

El Alamein, Egypt 43
11th Airborne Division (Pacific) team 207
11th Marines vs. 5th Marines 200
Eliot, Ray 180, 216
Elkmont, Ala. viii
Ellington Field (Tex.) Flyers 90, 144
Elliott, Chalmers "Bump" 202, 213
Ellis, Thad 80
El Paso, Tex. 146, 204
El Toro (Calif.) Marine Corps Air Station Flying Marines 4, 17, 18, 50, 82, 90, 103, 111, 112, 127, 129, 138, 141, 145–47, 149, *150*, 151, *157, 158*, 159, 179, 180, 181, 184, 185, 187, 189, 190, 196, 214, 215, 218, 223; "Flying Bull" patch 157; 1945 games vs. Fleet City 50, 111, 112, 159, 184, 185, 190, 214
Emporia Teachers 139
Enright, Rex 68, 77, 113
USS *Enterprise* (CV-6) 2, 63, 216
Erb, Charles, Jr. 202, 203
Erdelatz, Eddie 66
Eshmont, Leonard "Len" 18, 68, 109, *123*, 124, 126, 172, 174, 181
ESPN vii, 5
*Esquire* 212
Eureka, Calif. 34
Europe (European) 17, 130, 146, 168, 199; European Theater of Operations 204
Evans, Frederick "Dippy" 144
Evans, Ray 146, 164
Evanston, Ill. 171
Evashevski, Forest 68, 118
*Evening Herald and Express* (Los Angeles, Calif.) 48

F4F *Wildcat* fighter 212–213
F4U *Corsair* fighter 212, 218
Fabulous Forties 219
Fairfield team 159
Fairfield-Suisun (Calif.) Army Air Base 90
Fambrough, Don 209, 214
Far West 145
Far Western Conference 76
Farkas, Andy 31
Farragut (Ida.) Naval Training Station 27, 90, 138
Faurot, Don 18, 63, 68, 118, 172
Fayetteville State Broncos 193
Fears, Tom 146
Feathers, Beattie 177
Feeney, John 40
Fenimore, Bob 187
Ferraro, John 181
Fessenden, Doug 144
Field, Jack (Jackie) 40, 99, 100, *201*
56th Engineers Training Battalion (Wash.) (Black) 93, 195
Filchock, Frank 69, 113
Filipowicz, Steve 113, 210

Filley, Pat 174
Finch, Robert 174
First Air Force (1st AF, Mitchell Field, N.Y.) Aces 18, 50, 51, 90, 113, 131, 141, 145, 147, 187, 206, 213
Fisher, Dick 118, 165, 174
Fitch, Bob 153
Flanagan, Dick *186*
Flanigan, Hugh 31
Fleet City Naval Training Center/Naval Receiving Station/Naval Personnel Training and Distribution Center/Shoemaker Field (Calif.) Bluejackets 4, 18, 49, 50, 54, 55, 70, 90, 105, 107, *110*, 111, 127, 138, 141, 152, 159, 176, 181, 187 223; 1945 games vs. El Toro 50, 111, 112, 159, 184, 185, 190, 214; *see also* Pleasanton (Calif.) Naval Personnel Distribution Center
Florence, Italy 206
Florida A&M Rattlers 191, 192
Foldberg, Ed 134
Fonvielle, Chris viii
Football: adjustments, development, operations vii, 2, 5, 7, 11, 16, 18–22, 45, 74–76, 78, 79, 80, 82, 162, 166, 168, 183, 216; as a combat conditioner 7–9, 13, 15, 19, 23, 43–47, 63–72, 73, 87, 88, 171, 215, 216 (*see also* V-Programs, V-1, V-5, V-7, V-12); history 11, 14, 15; rules, formations, strategies/tactics 4, 5, 16, 20, 22, 82–88, 133, 140, 168; season highlights (1942) 162–66, (1943) 161, 166–74, (1944) 174–82, (1945) 183–88; segregation and racial conditions 189–93; and war effort 2, 8, 14, 22, 23, 48, 54, 72, 188, 191, 192, 195, 199, 200, 215, 216; as war game 1–3, 5, 43–45, 72, 86, 224
*Football Facts and Figures* 165
*Football: The Naval Aviation Physical Training Manuals* 87
"Football! Navy! War!" 7, 46
*The Football News* 31, 41, 48, 52, 65, 115, 174
*Football Pictorial Yearbook* 13, 16, 48, 49, 57, 60, 64, 75, 78, 81, 88, 96, 103, 119, 120, 132, 133, 140, 145, 162, 170, 175, 176, 184, 211, 212, 216, 220
*Football Prevues* 48
*Football Review: Yearbook of the Football News* 48
*Football Rule and Record Book* 48, 50
Football Writers Association 8
Ford, Gerald 63, 71
Fordham Rams 29, 68, 109, 113, 122, 123, 124, 126, 159, 164
Forrestal, James 63
Fort Benning (Ga.) Doughboys 4, 90, 113, 117, 121, 142, 145, 166, 179, 187
Fort Benning (Ga.) (Black) 93, 195
Fort Benning (Ga.) 1st Student Training Regiment 90
Fort Benning (Ga.) 4th Infantry (Black) 195

Fort Benning (Ga.) 4th Infantry Raiders 90, 121, 142
Fort Benning (Ga.) 176th Infantry 90
Fort Benning (Ga.) 124th Infantry 90
Fort Benning (Ga.) 3rd Infantry 121, 142, 147
Fort Benning (Ga.) 300th Infantry 90
Fort Bliss (Tex.) 90, 159, 214
Fort Bragg (N.C.) 42, 91, 109, 136, 193
Fort Bragg (N.C.) 3rd Field Artillery Replacement Training Center 90, 91
Fort Crook (Neb.) 93, *167*
Fort Dix (N.J.) 80
Fort Douglas (Ut.) 91, 146, 165
Fort Hamilton (N.Y.) 166
Fort Knox (Ky.) 91; Armoraiders team 119, 137, 165, 166, 190, 194, 210, 213
Fort Leonard Wood (Mo.) (Black) 195
Fort MacArthur (Calif.) 91, 129, 179
Fort McClellan (Ala.) (Black) 195
Fort Monmouth (N.J.) 91, 165
Fort Monroe (Va.) Gunners 33, 34, 91, 109, 136, 155, 170
Fort Ord. (Calif.) 91, 129
Fort Pierce (Fla.) Naval Amphibious Base Amphibs 18, 91, 104, 112, 113, 121, 142, 145, 147, 180, 181, 187, 223
Fort Riley (Kans.) Replacement Training Center Centaurs 91, 117, 119, 124, 137, 138, *139,* 146, 165
Fort Riley (Kans.) (Black) 93, 195
Fort Sheridan (Ill.) Comets 91, 117, 214
Fort Totten (N.Y.) 165, 166
Fort (Francis E.) Warren (Wyo.) Broncos 112, 117, 120, 137–39, 141, 146, 147, 181, 190, 191
Fort Worth, Tex. 143
Forte, Al *110*
41st (Infantry) Division 207
49th Army 124
Foston, John 190
"Four Horsemen" backfield *see* Notre Dame
Fourth Air Force (4th AF, March Field, Calif.) Flyers 4, 18, 48, 53, *66,* 78, 88, 91, 104, 111, 112, 127–29, 131, 138, 140, 141, 145–48, 152, 157, 159, 165, 169, *170,* 173, 177, 179–81, 187, 189, 206, 223; as "Buck Rogers Outfit" and "GI Juggernaut" 14
Foxx, Bobby 69
France 132; St. Lo 186
Franck, George "Sonny" viii, 212, 217, 218
Franklin & Marshall 62, 213
Franklin Field, Philadelphia, Pa. 54
Freeman, Jack 187
Friday, William 100
*Friday Night Lights* 215
Fries, Sherry 36
Frink, Fred F. 120
Frnka, Henry 173
Frost, Merrill 186
Fruitig, Ed 164, 174
Fuqua, Bill 31

Furlong Field, Pearl Harbor, Hi. 201
Furman 40, 115, 201
Fuson, Herschel "Ug" 134

Gagne, Vern *158,* 159
Gaines, Clarence 191
Galveston (Tex.) Army Air Field 91
Galveston (Tex.) Naval Station (Black) 195
Gardner, Jack 87
Garfield, N.J. 40
Gatewood, James "Jim" 31, 35, *36,* 37, 39–41, 98, 100
Gatewood, Lester 40
Geiger, Roy 185
Gentry, Howie 33
Georgetown 40, 75; Hoyas team 124
Georgetown, Tex. 56
Georgia Pre-Flight School Skycrackers 68, 91, 113, 114, 121, 124, 126, 147, 154, 156, 164, 165, 166, 174, 181, 223
Georgia Tech Ramblin' Wreck 54, 62, 78, 80, 114, 122, 123, 173, 174, 177–82
Gerber, Elwood *35, 36,* 41
Germany 43, 47, 69, 87, 186, 210
Gerometta, Art 134
Gher, Buzzy 80, 175
GI Bill 59, 72, 81
G.I. Bowl, London, England 205
GI Jane 52
GI Joe 22, 52
Gianelli, Bart 213
Gilbert Islands 202
Gipp, George 96
Glenview, Ill. 109
Godman Army Air Field (Ky.) 91
Godman Army Air Field (Ky.) (Black) 193, 195
Golden Age of American sports 14; "Mini-Golden Age" 18
Goleta (Calif.) Marine Corps Air Station 91
Gonzaga Bulldogs 33, 214
Governali, Paul "Pitchin' Paul" 18, 149, 157, 164, *184,* 185, 187, 214
Graham, Otto 18, 39, 71, 124, *163,* 164, 174, 177, 181, 210
Grape Bowl 62
Graves, George "Potsy" 154
Gray, Bill 202
Gray, Gordon 179
Great Falls (Mont.) Army Air Base 91
Great Lakes, Ill. 114, 171, 173
Great Lakes (Ill.) Naval Training Station/Center xi, 4, 12, 18, 34, 43, 49, 54, 61, 66, 91, 107, *108,* 114–17, 123, 126, 138, *139,* 147, 159, 161–66, 171, 168, 171, 172, *173,* 174, 176, 180–82, 185, *186,* 187, 190, 192, 214, 223; establishment/history 27, 114; *Great Lakes Bulletin* 139, 161, 190, 192; 1943 game vs. Notre Dame 18, *52,* 115, 116, 161, 168, 171, 172, *173,* 178; Ross Field 171, *173*

*Great Lakes Bulletin see* Great Lakes (Ill.) Naval Training Station/Center
Green, Jack (John/Johnny) F. 133, 134, 187
Green Bay Packers 33, 35, 119, 126, 128, 197, 198
Greensboro, N.C. vii, 83
Greensboro (N.C.) Army Air Base 223
Greensboro (N.C.) Army Air Forces Overseas Replacement Depot Tech-Hawks *83*, 156
Greensboro (N.C.) Historical Museum 83
Greenville (N.C.) Army Air Base 91
Gregg, John 123, 180
Griffith, Andy 106
Griffith, John L. 54
Grosse Isle (Mich.) Naval Air Station 166
Guadalcanal v, 47, 62, 152–54, 206, 207
Guam 126
Guepe, Art *119*
Gulf Breeze, Fla. vii
Gulf Coast 142
Gulfport (Miss.) Army Air Field 91, 142; in "the Gulfport Classic" 142
Gulfport (Miss.) Naval Air Station 91
Gulfport (Miss.) Naval Station Seabees 91, 142
Gunn, John A. vii, 11, 20, 47, 62, *74, 77, 116, 123, 136, 150, 151, 153,* 153, 154, *155, 157, 158, 169, 191, 194,* 200, 207, 208; Gunn children vii; World War II teams 223

Hackett, William C. 181
Hagberg, Oscar 122, 179, 221
Halas, George 63, 83, 84
Hale vs. Yarvard 200
Halifax, (Ambassador) Lord 217
Hall, Linus Parker 68, 109, 126, *176*
Hall of Fame (Basketball) 191
Hall of Fame (College Football) 18, 66, 68, 75, 80, 81, 106, 120, 156, 159, 210, 218
Hall of Fame (Professional Football) 57, 71, 83, 116, 117, 159
Halsey, ("Bull") 94
Hamberg, Hal 121, 122
Hamilton, Bermuda 204–06
Hamilton, Thomas J. 3, 8, 46, *47*, 63–65, 71, 107, 223; as 1942 football "Man of the Year" 8, 63
Hampton (Scott), Leslie 222
Hampton (Va.) Pirates team 191
Hanley, Richard E. "Dick" 18, *157,* 180, 185, 189, 214, 215
Harder, Pat 113, 210
Hardin-Simmons Cowboys 145, 146, 162, 164, 185, 204
Hare, Cecil 33
Hart, Weldon 56
Harvard Crimson 15, 19, 79, 124, 134, 160, 163
Havelock, N.C. 155
Hawaii (Hawaiian) (T.H, Territory of) 20, 54, 104, 105, 150, 157, 196, 200, 203
Hawaii Air Force viii

Hawaii (navy) all-stars 115
Hawaiian Pine (Hi.) (team) 203
Hawaii Senior Football League 202
Hayes, Woody 63
Hearn, Bill 185, 186
Healani (Hi.) (team) 203
Hebner, Arnie 196
Hebrank, John v, 208
Heisman Trophy 2, 3, 21, 75, 106, 115, 126, 132–34, 145, 146, 149, 164, 168
Helms Foundation Award 132
Hendrickson, Brian viii
Heywood, Ralph 174, 213
Hickey, Howard "Red" 33, 35, 36, 115, 220
Higgins, Luke 209
High Point College Panthers team 136
Hightower, Don 69
Hill Field (Ut.) 91; Flyers team 166
Hilliard, Jack vii
Hinde, Hubbard v, 208
Hines, Mike *155*
Hinkle, Tony 18, 114, 115, 116, 171, 172
Hirsch, Elroy "Crazy Legs" 3, 17, 102, *103*, 149, 154, *158,* 159, 168, 184, 185, 215
*The History of American Football: Its Teams, Players, and Coaches* 11
Hitler, Adolf 45, 218
Hoernschemeyer, Bobby 122
Hoffman, N.C. 193
Holloway, Edwin 135
Holly Ridge, N.C. 135
Hollywood, Calif. 202
Hollywood (Calif.) Bears 141
Hollywood (Calif.) Rangers 112, 159
Holmes, Bill 145
Holovak, Mike 164
Holy Cross 39, 124, 154; Crusaders team 160, 179, 186
Hondo (Tex.) Army Air Field 91; Comets team 138
Honolulu, Hi. 73, 104, 202, 205
*Honolulu (Hi.) Advertiser* 206
Honolulu (Hi.) Bears 202, 203
Hopp, Bill 156
Hopp, Harry "Hippety" 39–41, 100, 103, 104, 111
USS *Hornet* (CV-12) 218
Horvath, Les 18, 132, 181
Houma (La.) Air Base 91; team 142
Howard, Frank 78
Howard Bison team 192
Hrabatin, Frank *36,* 41, 201
Hudacek, Steve 164, 174
Huertz, Joe 164
Huffman, George B. 142
Hughes, Tom 213
Humble, Weldon 57, 170
Humboldt State 137, 190, 191
Hume, Hillis 53
Huneke, Chuck *158*

Hutchinson (Kans.) Naval Air Station 91, 139, 187
Hutson, Don 198

Idaho Vandals 137, 146
"I'll Be Seeing You" 71
Illinois 218
Illinois Wesleyan 104
*Illustrated Football Annual* 30, 41, 48, 86, 108, 118, 161, 164
Indiana University (Hoosiers) 20, 69, 113, 117, 119, 122, 180, 181, 186, 187
Indiantown (Pa.) Military Reservation 166
Ingram, Jonas H. 224
International News Service 174
Interstate Conference 76
Iowa City, Ia. 64, 118
Iowa Field House 68
Iowa Intercollegiate Athletic Conference 76
Iowa Pre-Flight School Seahawks 3, 4, 18, 31, 64, 68, 82, 87, 88, 91, 108, 118, *119*, 120, 138, 139, 146, 162, 164–66, 168, 171, 173, 174, 176, 179–81, 223; B team 166
Iowa Stadium, Iowa City 118
Iowa State Cyclones 119
Iranian Bowl, Tehran (Camp Amirabad vs. Camp Khorramshahr) 205
Ireland 4
Irvine, Calif. 157
Italy 69, 186, 206
Italian Campaign 130
Ivy League 160, 182
Iwo Jima v, 2, 18, 62, 151, 153, 156, 157, 186, 200, 202

Jackson (Miss.) Air Base Bombers 91, 181
Jacksonville, Fla. 109, 120, 192
Jacksonville (Fla.) Naval Air Station Air Raiders 91, 108, 113, 114, 120, 121, 126, 155, 156, 165, 166, 174, 187
Jacksonville (Fla.) Naval Air Station (Black) 195
Jacksonville (Fla.) Naval Air Technical Training Center Raiders 18, 36, 49, 91, 120, 121
Jacksonville, N.C. 151, 193
Jacobs, "Indian" Jack 104, 140, 141, *170*, 176, 177, 206
Japan 4, 44, 47, 73, 80, 87, 104, 105, 116, 154, 179, 185, 200, 201, 208, 215
*Java* (British frigate) 28
Jenkins, Robert "Bobby Tom," "Bob," "Talladega Thunderbolt" *120*, 122, 178, 181
Johnson, Don 159
Johnson, Harvey "Stud" 31, 33, 35, *36*, 37, 39–41, 98, 102–04, 172
Johnson, Henry A. 135
Johnson C. Smith Golden Bulls 193
Johnston, Wayne "Rusty" v, 208
Jones, Andrew viii
Jones, Buck 213
Jones, Carroll viii
Jones, David viii
Jones, Dub 122
Jones, Edgar "Special Delivery" 111, 202, 203
Jones, Ray 115
Jones, Wilbur 2–5; as "Grantland Rice Jones" 10
Jordan, Michael 10, 101
*The Journal of Sport History* 63
Jungle Bowl (All-Stars vs. Marines) 206
Jungmichel, Buddy 164, 174
Justice, Charlie (Charley) "Choo Choo" vii, 3, 10; at Bainbridge 10, 11, 25, 30–33, *35*, 39–41, *95*, *96*, 97, 154, 218, 220; "Choo Choo" nickname 96–98, 220; playing in Hawaii 81, 95, 104, *105*, 115, 201; postwar at North Carolina and death 10, 81, 95, 97, 103, 105, 106; pre-navy life 30, 94, 95, 97; starring role/honors 1943–44 at Bainbridge 98–100, *101*, 102–104, 154
Justice, Sarah 10, 95, 104, 105
Juzwik, Steve *110*, 111, 115

Kaalas (Hi.) (team) 203
Kane, Joe 40, 100
Kane, William R. "Killer" 215, 216
Kansas City, Mo. 162
Kansas College Athletic Conference 76
Kansas State Wildcats 87, 120, 139
Kansas Wesleyan Coyotes 139, 146
Karangelen, Pete 33
Karmazin, John *148*
Kasprzak, Don 202
Kearney (Neb.) Army Air Field Raiders 91, 138, 139
Kearns Army Air Base (Ut.) 91
Keesler (Miss.) Air Field Commandos viii, 4, 18, 91, 113, 142, 145, 147, 156, 203; in "the Gulfport Classic" 142
Kellagher, Bill 159
Kelleher, Dick 31
Kelly, Bob 122
Kenan Stadium, Chapel Hill, N.C. 102, 219
Kenna, Doug 133; "Kenna Team" 133
Kennedy, Bill *158*
Kennedy, Bob *148*, 210
Kentucky 190
Kern, Bill 109, 172
Kerns, "Black Mike" 154
Key, William S. 204
Keyes, Geoffrey 130
Kezar Stadium, San Francisco, Calif. 50, 70, 109, 111
Killinger, Glenn 71, 124
Kimbrough, Frank 124
Kimbrough, John 206
Kinard, Frank "Bruiser" *110*, 187
Kinston (N.C.) Marines 91, 150, 155, 193
Kirkland Field (N.M.) 91
Klamath Falls (Ore.) Marines 91, 150, 151

Klink, Quentin 36, *110*
Kmetovic, Pete *108*
KMPC, Los Angeles, Calif. 159
Knox, Frank (Secretary of the Navy) 9, 60, 63
Knox, Frank X. (Frank's nephew) 154
Knoxville (Tenn.) Engineers 92
Koontz, Robert H. 104
Korte, Bob 185, 186
Koslowski, Stan 39, 124
Krall, Stan *148*
Kuczynski, Bernard 40
Kutner, Mal 118
Kuzman, John 126

Lach, Steve 104, *115,* 116, 172, 173, 201, 206
Lafayette, La. 57
Lafayette Leopards 134
LaGarde Hospital (La.) 92
Lake Charles (La.) Army Air Field 92
Lake Michigan 114
Lake Village, Ark. 222
Lakehurst (N.J.) Naval Air Station Blimps 92, 166
Lambert Trophy 122, 132, 177
Lanakilas (Hi.) (team) 203
Langhurst, Jim 118
LaRue, Jim 177
Layden, Elmer 195
Layden, Pete 144
Leahy, Frank 172
Lee H. Edwards High School (Asheville High), Asheville, N.C. 94, 95, 103
Legion Bowl, Memphis, Tenn. (Fourth Air Force vs. AAFTC) 206
Legion Stadium, Wilmington, N.C. 136
Lehigh v, 208; Engineers team 80
Leiser, Bill 168
"Lend-Lease": definition 17; players/schools 3, 17, 56, 57, 107, 166, 168, 176
Letlow, Russell 181
Lewis, Cliff 177
Lewis, Ernie *158*
Lily Bowl, Hamilton, Bermuda 204, 205, 206
Lincoln (Neb.) Army Air Field Wings 92, 138, 181
Lincoln University (Pa.) Lions 192, 212
Lipka, Chester *148*
Little, Lou 44, 46, 73, 83
Little Creek (Va.) Naval Amphibious Base 42, 92, 109, 113, 187
Little Rock, Ark. viii, 223
Locke, Bruce 154
Logan (Ut.) Naval Training Station 92
Lombardo, Tom 33; "Lombardo Team" 133
London, England 204, 205; Crimson Tide Artillerymen vs. Fighting Irish Engineers *204*
Lone Star Conference 76
Long Beach, Calif. 214
*Look Magazine* (Bill Stern) 174

Lopp, Frank *148*
Los Alamitos (Calif.) Navy team 141
Los Angeles, Calif. viii, 14, 21, 48, 146, 159, 197
Los Angeles (Calif.) Broncos 112
Los Angeles (Calif.) Bulldogs 159
*Los Angeles (Calif.) Herald Examiner* 185
*Los Angeles (Calif.) Times* 184
Los Angeles Coliseum, Los Angeles, Calif. 18, 20, 74, 140, 184
Los Angeles Rams (postwar) 189
Louis, Joe 106
Louisiana-Lafayette (postwar) *see* Southwestern Louisiana Institute
Louisiana State 57, 154, 170, 202; Tigers team 87, 114, 170, 186
Lowry Field (Colo.) Bombers 92, 138, 139
Loyola (Calif.) 152; Freshmen/junior varsity team 129
Loyola (La.) 41
Lubbock (Tex.) Army Air Base (Field) 44, 75, 124, 172, 181, 219
Luckman, Sid 83, 84, 198
Lujack, Johnny 75, 112, 172, 209
Lukacs, John vii
Luster, Dewey "Snorter" 78, 169

MacArthur, Douglas 52
MacDill (and Daniel Fields) (Ala.) (Black) 93, 195
Macleod, Bob 50
Magar, F.E. *194*
Magnani, Dante *37,* 40
*Mainsheet see* Bainbridge (Md.) Naval Training Station/Center
Major, Mark 179
Makin Island 126, 154
Malevich, Jack 111
Man 'O War 34
Mancha, Vaughn 187
Manhattan Beach (N.Y.) Coast Guard 92, 151, 165
Manhattan University (Jaspers) 124, 202
Maniaci, Joe 18, *29,* 30, 34, 35, 96, 97, 100, 102, 173, 180
Manila, Philippines 206, 207
Manila Bowl, Manila, Philippines 206
Manske, Ed 126
Mariana Islands 202
Marquette Warriors v, 98, 117, *119,* 120, 124, 137, 208
Marseille, France 206
Marshall Islands 202
Marshall University 159
Martin, Jack 122
Martin, Whitney 221
Maryland 10, 27, 33, 194
Mather Field (Calif.) 141, 152, 165
Matusa, Al 201, 202
Maui, Hi. 200

"Maui (Hi.) Marines" (4th Marine Division) 200
Maxwell Award (Trophy) 2, 132–34, 149, 157, 164, 171, 184
Maxwell (Ala.) Field Marauders 38–40, 101, 102, 142, 145, 147, 181
Mayport (Fla.) Naval Air Station 92, 113
McAfee, George 18, 104, 120, 165, 174, 201
McCardle, Mickey **157, 158**, 213, 214
McCarty, Bernie 210, 221
McClellan Field (Calif.) Rangers 92, 165
McCollum, Harley 159
McCook Army Air Base (Neb.) 92
McDonald, Jim 68, 109, 126
McFadden, Darren 106
McKeever, Ed 180
McMurdo, James T. 156
McTamney, John 40
McWilliams, Tom 134
Meagher, Jack 119, 180
Mediterranean 200, 204
Mehelich, Charles 40, 101
Melbourne Cricket Ground 200
Mello, Jim 117
Mellus, John 18, 135, 170, 174
Melville (R.I.) Naval Patrol Torpedo Boat Base Night Raiders 80, 92, 135, 178, 179, 181, 183
Memphis, Tenn. 145, 206
Memphis (Tenn.) Naval Air Technical Training Command 58, 92
Meneweather, Earl 137, 138, 190, **191**
Menton, Paul 97, 98
Merriman, J.S. 160
Merritt, Frank **148**, 187
Meter, Bernie **155**
Mexico City team 144
Meyer, Leo "Dutch" 81, 179
Miami (Fla.) Army Air Field 92
Miami (Fla.) Naval Air Station team 147
Miami (Fla.) Naval Training Center Navaltars 92, 113, 121
Michaels, Joe **36,** 39
Michie, Dennis 1
Michigan State Spartans 36, 41, 80, 117, 135, 175, 182
Micka, Mike 213
Mid-Atlantic 76, 79, 80, 98
Middlebury Panthers 160
Midway 202
Midwest(ern)(ers) 68, 78, 87, 116, 118, 157, 190, 191
Miklas, Mike viii
military *see* armed forces
Military Academy, West Point, N.Y. *see* Army (Military Academy, West Point, N.Y.)
Miller, Creighton 174
Miller, Jack 185, 186
Milwaukee (Wisc.) Chiefs 34
Milwaukee (Wisc.) Falks 137

Minisi, Anthony "Tony," "Skippy" 122, 183, 184
Minor, Alex 179
Minor, Max 133
Minter Field (Calif.) Flyers 92, 165
Miss America pageant 222
Mississippi Ordnance 142
Mississippi Southern 142, 203
Mississippi State Bullfogs 19, 78, 80, 175
Missouri 79
Missouri College Athletic Union 76
Missouri Valley Conference 76, 182
Mobley, Rudy "Little Doc" 164
Modesto Junior College team 112 , 127
Molenda, John J. "Bo" 128
Monica, Russ 33
USS *Monterey* (CVL-26) 63
Monterey, Calif. 64, 109
Montgomery, Bernard 43
Montgomery, Ala. 101
Montgomery Teachers (Ala.) team 195
Moore, Iris Jean 32
Moore General Hospital (N.C.) 92
Moraga, Calif. 64, 126
Moran, Charles 17
Morgan, Robert 217
Morgan State Bears 191, 193, 195
Morris, Max 187
Morris Brown Fighting Wolverines 194
Morrison, Ray 63
Morrow, Bob 104, 202
Mosher, Clure 41
Mosquito Bowl (4th Marines vs. 29th Marines) v, 206–08
"Mosquito Network" 207
Motley, Marion 18, 117, 190, **192**
Moton Field *see* Tuskegee (Ala.) Army Air Field (Black)
Mountain States (Big Seven) Athletic Conference 76
Mucha, Rudy **108**
Mugg, Garvin 41
Muhlenberg Mules 36, 40, 79, 128
Mulleneaux, Carl 33, 41, **108**
Munger, George 163, 173
Municipal Stadium, Cleveland, Oh. 54
Murphy, George Edward v, 154, 208
Murray, Frank 177, 218
Myslinski, Casimir 174

Nagasaki, Japan 4, 207
Nagurski, Bronco 196
National Basketball Association 14
National Collegiate Athletic Association (NCAA) 7, 8, 15, 22, 23, 44, 46, 47, 58, 74, 77, 79, 82, 87, 107, 111, 144, 164, 166, 172, 182, 184, 211; annual football guides viii, 16, 46, 47, 48, 53, 66, 77, 79, 127, 167, 173, 186, 190, 204; Division II (present) 58; Division III (present) 56; organization,

policies, and procedures 15, 16, 45, 54, 85, 86, 122; staff 77, 87
National Football League (NFL) 4, 8, 13, 19, 20, 21, 33, 50, 52, 84, 103, 116, 171, 175, 183, 192, 195–98, 208, 210, 213
Naval Reserve Officer Training Corps *see* U.S. Navy (navy)
Navy (U.S. Naval Academy, Annapolis, Md.) Midshipmen (Middies) 3, 8, 9, 31, 33, 34, 39, **53**, 54, 63, 66, 71, 79, 82, 99, 104, 107, 108, 120–24, 126, 132, 134, 135, 168, 172–74, 176–80, 181–83, 186, 187, 216, 220–24; Army-Navy games 3, 15, 39, 52, **53**, 54, 79, 82, 122, 128, 131, 177, 183, 220–22
Navy Cross v, 2, 62, 151, 208, 216
Navy "V Programs" for officer training *see* U.S. Navy (navy); V-Programs; V-1; V-5; V-7; V-12
*The Navy V-12 Program: Leadership for a Lifetime* 11
Nazi Germany 17; Nazi-held Europe 144
NCAA *see* National Collegiate Athletic Association
N.C. College (for Negroes) Eagles 195
N.C. State University (Wolfpack) 78, 124, 136, 177
Nebraska Intercollegiate Athletic Conference 76
Nelson, Bob **108**
Nelson, Jimmy 141, 206
Nemeth, Eddie 216
Nemetz, Al 134
Nevada vs. Alaska Clippers 200
Nevers, Ernie 189
New England 80, 160, 178
New Guinea 200, 206
New Hanover County, N.C. 45
New Hanover High School, Wilmington, N.C. 74
New Jersey 28
New London, Conn. 160
New London (Conn.) Submarine Base Diesels 92, 194, 195
New Mexico Intercollegiate Conference 76
New Mexico Lobos team 146
New River (N.C.) Marine Corps Air Station 92
New York (City), N.Y. 33, 52, 61, 145, 146, 165, 194, 205
New York Giants 68, 109, 122, 123, 128, 135, 170, 195, 197, 218
*New York (N.Y.) Sun* 174
New York University (Violets) 175
New York Yankees 128
New Zealand 200
Newberry College 36, 114
Newman, Harold 206
Newton, Doc 78, 177
Neyland, Bob 52
Nimitz, (Chester) 94

1943 Consensus All-America 174
1944 Consensus All-America 181
1945 Consensus All-America 187
Ninth Air Force (9th AF, Europe) 205
Noble, Charlie 36, 98
Noble, Tom "Knobby" 31
Nomellini, Leo 156
Norberg, Hank 174
Norfolk, Va. 100
Norfolk (Va.) Fleet Marines 92, 151, 155
Norfolk (Va.) Naval Training Station (Black) 93, 195
Norman, Okla. 123
Norman (Okla.) Naval Air Station Zoomers 4, 92, 122–24, 139, 146, 176, 180, 181
North Africa 43, 200
North Carolina Pre-Flight School Cloudbusters 33, 37, 40, 64, 67, **69,** 70, 71, 75, 92, 102, 109, 114, 121–24, **125,** 126, 136, 155, 156, 163–66, 174, 177, 179, 181, 223; B team 136
North Central Intercollegiate Conference 76
North Texas Agricultural College (Aggies) 56, 144–46, 169
North Texas State 41, 149
Northern Illinois State Teachers 218
Northwestern University (Wildcats) 20, 25, 39, 43, 54, 62, 71, 79, 98, 115–17, 119, 124, 126, 145, 157, 159, **163,** 164, 168, 171, 173, 174, 177, 187, 211
Norwich Cadets 160
Notre Dame (Fighting Irish) v, 2, 12, 18, 20, 21, 31, 33, 36, 41, 50, 54, 62, 68, 74, 75, 79, 87, 102, 111–13, 115–19, 122, 123, 126, 132, 134, 135, 141, 143, 144, 149, 153–55, 157, 159, 161, 164, 168, 173, 174, 177, 178–80, 183, 184–86, 202, 208, 209, 211, 213, 221; "Four Horsemen" backfield 64, 124, 195; 1943 game vs. Great Lakes 18, **52,** 115, 116, 161, 168, 171, 172, **173,** 178; T formation (Box) 82, 114, 141
Noverr, Douglas A. 15
NROTC (Naval Reserve Officer Training Corps) *see* U.S. Navy (navy)

Oahu, Hi. 201
Oak Grove (N.C.) Marines 150, 156, 193
Oak Leaf Clusters 144
Oceana (Va.) Naval Air Station 42, 92
Odell, Bob 149, 171, 174
Odessa, Tex. 215
O'Donnell, J. Hugh 171
Officer candidate training *see* U.S. Army (officers, soldiers), ASTP; U.S. Navy and U.S. Marine Corps, V-Programs, V-1, V-5, V-7, V-12
Ohio State University (Buckeyes) 17, 20, 50, 68, 78, 82, 109, 116–19, 132, 162, 171, 179–82, **186,** 187, 194, 211, 213
Oil Bowl 57

# Index

Okeson, Walter 16, 87
Okinawa v, 2, 18, 62, 151–54, 168, 169, 208;
  Kiyuma Gusuku castle 208; Naha 208;
  Sugar Loaf Hill 208
Oklahoma A&M Cowboys 123, 124, 182, 186, 187
Oklahoma City (Okla.) 34
Oklahoma Collegiate Conference 76
Olathe (Kans.) Naval Air Station 92, 120;
  Zippers team 139
Oliver, Tex 63, 66, 126, 206
Olympics (1948) 223
1005th Army Engineers 129
Operation Iraqi Freedom 10
Oran, Algeria 4, 204, **205**
Oregon State Beavers 25, 34, 40, 73, 98, 140;
  1942 "Transplanted Rose Bowl Game" 2, 73, 74
O'Rourke, Charles (Charlie) 111, 190
Orr, Maurice 30
Osmanski, Bill 154, 207
Ottumwa (Ia.) Naval Air Station Skyers 92, **167**

Pacific (Ocean, islands, Theater, War) 7, 9, 47, 62, 71, 84, 105, 122, 144, 146, 149, 152, 183, 199, 200, 201, 207, 212, 214–16, 218;
  Central Pacific 200; South Pacific xi, 18, 154, 186, 207; Southwest Pacific 116, 200
Pacific Coast 111, 140, 151, 168
Pacific Coast Conference 34, 60, 78, 80, 179, 182; present PAC-10 60
Pacific Coast Professional Football League 196
Pacific Fleet All-Stars 50, 92, 105, 141, 190, **201**
"Pacific Fleet at Play" 201
Pacific Northwest Intercollegiate Conference 76
Palaus 126
Palermo, Sicily 130
Palmer, D.F. 206
Palo Alto, Calif. 14
Panelli, John 184
Parc des Princes Bowl, Paris, France (Ninth Air Force vs. First General Hospital) 205
Paris, France 205
Parnell, Jerry viii
Parris Island, S.C. 152, 154, 169
Parris Island (S.C.) Marine Corps Recruit Depot 92, 213
Pasadena, Calif. 2, 73
Paschal, Bill 187
Patterson, Billy 69
Patterson, Paul 190
Patterson Field (Oh.) Stars 92, 166
Patton, George S. 130, 132
Pearcy, Jim 159
Pearl Harbor, Hi. 2, 73, 104, 114, 185, 190;
  December 7, 1941 attack (Pearl Harbor Day) 2, 14, 15, 73, 117, 196, 202

Pearl Harbor (Hi.) Navy All-Stars 92, 112
Peleliu 152
Penn, William 179
Penn State Nittany Lions 40, 123, 124, 154
Pennsylvania State Teachers College Conference 76
Pensacola, Fla. 125
Pensacola (Fla.) Naval Air Station Goshawks 65, 69, 92, 121, 165, 166
Perkins, Bob 202
Perkins, Ed 190, **194**
Perpich, George 139
Perry, Johnny v, 208
Peru (Ind.) Navy 146; *see also* Bunker Hill (Ind.) Naval Training Station
Peterson, Robert W. 195
Petro, Joe 36, 40
Phil-Pitt Combine "Steagles" 4, 196, 197
USS *Philadelphia* 2
Philadelphia, Pa. 28, 31, 54, 68, 69, 135, 183, 221
Philadelphia Eagles 4, 30, 33–35, 105, 106, 154, 156, 183, 196, 197, 202, 223
*Philadelphia (Pa.) Inquirer* 221
Philadelphia (Pa.) Yellow Jackets 128
Philippine Sea 215
Philippines 52
Pierce, Paul 41
Pirkey, Cecil 172
Pittsburgh Steelers 4, 33, 126, 143, 179, 196, 197
Pleasanton (Calif.) Naval Personnel Distribution Center Bluejackets 92, 109; *see also* Fleet City Naval Training Center/Naval Receiving Station/Naval Personnel Training and Distribution Center/Shoemaker Field (Calif.)
Pocatello (Ida.) Naval Ordnance Marine Barracks Marines 92, 150, 150, 151
Podesta, John (Johnny) 154, 202, 213
Poi Bowl, Honolulu, Hawaii (Navy vs. Army Air Forces) 205
Pollard, Arthur 40
Polo Grounds, New York, N.Y. 52, 194
Pomona (Calif.) Army Ordnance Base Gunners 92, 129
Pond, Raymond W. "Ducky" 113
Pool, Hampton 18, 112, 180, 187
Poole, George Barney 18, 80, **81,** 133, 134
Poole, Jim 69, 164, 174
Pooles of Ole Miss 80
Port Deposit, Md. 11
Port St. Lucie, Fla. 112
Porter, William 192
Portland (Ore.) Trail Blazers viii
Portland (Ore.) University Pilots 146
Portsmouth Fleet 92
Potato Bowl, Belfast, Ireland 204
Povich, Shirley 94
Prairie View Panthers 192

Presbyterian Blue Hose 136, 193
Presidential Unit Citation 71, 216
Pressly, Julian viii, 189, 190, 214, 215
Preston, Fred **108**
Preston, Pat 154, 213
Primavera, Ralph 135, 217
Princeton Tigers 1, 19, 79, 80, 123, 134, 146, 175, 179, 218
Pro All-Stars 141
Proctor, Dewey 40, 115, 172, 201
Providence (R.I.) 202
PT (patrol torpedo) boats 122, 179
Pulley, Andy 40
Purdue Boilermakers v, 20, 31, 33, 35, 62, 117, 120, 123, 137, 154, 166, 168, 173, 202, 206, 208, 212, 213
Purple Heart 208, 212

Quillen, Frank 159
Quincy, Bob 97, 98, 104
Quinn, Jim v, 208

Rader, Benjamin G. 14
Radford, Arthur 63
Radovich, Bill **108**
Rafalko, Ed 133
Ragazzo, Phil **30**, 33, 34, 36, 218
Raisin Bowl 62
Ramsey, Garrard S. "Gerry," "Buster" 18, 31, 33, 35, **36**, 41, 104, 174, 201, 206
Randolph Field (Tex.) Army Air Base Ramblers 4, 18, 39, 48, **49**, 56, 88, 92, 102, 131, 143–47, 164, 170, 172–74, 176, 179–82, 204, 205, 218, 223; as "the Notre Dame of service football" 143; as "the West Point of the Air" 143, 176
Randolph Field (Tex.) (Black) 93, 195
Rankin, Dave viii, 212, 213, 218
Raphael, Roland 35
Rappaport, Ken 96, 97
Ravensberg, Bob 187
Ravera, Bob 185, 186
Red and Green Sport Star 165
Red Cross 53, 198
Redlands University (Bulldogs) 129, 141, 171
Reese, William "Bill," "Red" 146, 180
Reinhart, William J. 111
Reno (Nev.) Army Air Base 92
Rensselaer Polytechnic Institute Red Hawks 128, 160
Rentz, Joe 126
Rice 57, 80, 202; Owls team 56, 144, 145, 149, 170, 175
Rice, Grantland 22, 33, 52, 55, 87, 115, 178; Grantland Rice (*Collier's*) All-America team 115, 174, 175; Grantland Rice (*Collier's*) All-Service team 164; *Collier's*/Grantland Rice All-Navy All-America team 174, 175; Rice poems 55, 224
Rice Bowl, Tsingtao, China (3rd Battalion/29th Marines vs. 3rd Battalion/22nd Marines) 206
Richmond, Va. 40
Richmond (Va.) Army Air Base Thunderbirds 36, 92, 156
Riddick, Ray 126
Rinehart & Company 165
Riverside, Calif. 53, 140
Riverside (Calif.) Chamber of Commerce 53
Riviera Bowl, Marseille, France (R.R. Shop Battalion vs. Army All-Stars) 206
Roanoke College 31
Robesky, Ken **108**
Robins Army Air Field (Ga.) (Black) 195
Rochester Shipbuilding Oldenbacks 128
Rockenboch, Lyle "Rocky" 36, 41
Rockford, Ill. 137
Rockne, Knute 2, 96, 171
Rocky Mountain Athletic Conference 76
Rocky Mountains (Rockies) 79, 80, 164, 169, 179
Rodgers, Hosea 202
Rodgers, Rajah 202
Rogers, Marion 174
Rohrig, Herman "Hurryin' Herman" 142
Rollins Tars team 121
Rome (N.Y.) Army Air Field 92, 128
Rominger, Donald J. 63, 72
Rommel, Erwin 43
Roosevelt, Franklin D. 14, 28, 53, 63
Rose, Glen 137
Rose Bowl 2, 25, 60, 73, 74, 77, 80, 126, 128, 140, 162; 1942 "Transplanted Rose Bowl" 2, 34, 73, 74
Rosecrans (Mo.) Army Air Base 92
Roskie, Ken 139
Ross Field, Great Lakes (Ill.) Naval Training Station/Center *see* Great Lakes (Ill.) Naval Training Station/Center
Ruby, Martin 144
Ruby, Paul 40
Ruertz, Joe 174
Ruggerio, Frank 184
Rushing, Randall 179
Russell, C.F. 28
Russell, Jack 18, 144, 174, 181
Russell, Rosalind 205
Rutgers 1, 80
Rykovich, Julie **155**
Rymkus, Lou 36, 37, 41, 104

Saia, Joe 80, 175
Sailers, John 179
St. Augustine's Falcons 191
St. Louis, Mo. 54
St. Louis Billikens 139
St. Martin's (Wash.) Saints 146
St. Mary's College (Calif.) Gaels 40, 64, 66, 108, 109, 112, 126, 152, 157, 159, 185–87
St. Mary's Pre-Flight School Air Devils **66**,

68, 70, 71, 93, 112, 122, 123, 126, *127*, 141, 152, 159, 164–66, 169, 174–77, 180, 181, 187, 223
St. Norbert's Green Knights 137
St. Onge, Bob 133
St. Paul's (Va.) Tigers 191
Saipan 126, 151
Salem, Ore. 73
Salt Lake (Ut.) Army Air Base Wings 92, 138
Sampson, N.Y. 128
Sampson (N.Y.) Naval Training Station Bluejackets 27, 33, 34, 64, 93, 128, 134, 141, 212
San Antonio, Tex. 143
Sanders, Orban 69
San Diego, Calif. 128
San Diego (Calif.) Amphibious Training Base 159
San Diego (Calif.) Bombers 129, 141, 196
San Diego (Calif.) Marine Corps Air Station 157
San Diego (Calif.) Naval Training Center Bluejackets 27, 93, 108, 128, 129, 159, 164, 169, 174, 179, 181, 187, 223
San Diego State Aztecs 141; Freshmen/junior varsity team 129
Sandig, Curtis *110*
USS *San Francisco* (CA-38) 122
San Francisco, Calif. 50, 73, 105, 111
San Francisco (Calif.) Clippers 138
San Francisco (Calif.) Packers 137, 152
San Francisco Bay (Calif.) Coast Guard Receiving Station Pilots 93, 112, 151, 159
San Francisco 49ers (postwar) 66
San Joaquin (Calif.) Cowboys 112
San Jose State Spartans 73, 112, 126, 152, 177
San Pedro (Calif.) All-Stars 129
San Phillipe Stadium, Oran, Algeria 204, 205
San Salvador 28
Santa Ana (Calif.) Army Air Base Flyers 93, 141, 166
Santa Barbara (Calif.) Junior College (postwar) 214
Santa Barbara (Calif.) Marine Corps Air Station Marines 93, 129
Santa Cruz 216
Santora, Frank 40
Saunders, (Laverne G.) "Blondie" 186
Savitsky, George 80, 175, 187
Scheer, Julian 97, 98, 104
Schissler, Paul 18, *140*, 173, 180
Schneider, James G. 58, 59, 60, 61
Schreiner, David Nathan v, 208
Schuler, Bill 185, 186
Schultz, C.W. 206
Schwarting, Joseph 40
Schwartz, Perry 118
Scott, Clyde Luther "Smackover" viii, 3, 81, 82, 122, 183, 184, 210, *220*, 221, *222*, 223; "Smackover" nickname 220, 221
Scott, Richard 187

Scott, Vince 184
Scranton University Royals 40, 128, 160
Second Air Force (2nd AF, Washington (State), Colo.) Superbombers 18, 52, 80, 93, 104, 112, 120, 124, 131, 138, 139, 141, 142, 145–47, 162, 165, 175, 176, 179, 180, 181, 185, 187, 204, 205, 214, 223
Selman (La.) Army Air Base (Black) 93, 195
Selman (La.) Army Air Base Cyclones 93, 142
Seneca Lake, N.Y. 128
Senior League All-Stars (Hi.) 203
Seven Seas 224
Seventh Air Force (7th AF, Hawaii) Hawaiian Flyers 202, 203
Sewell, Billy 145, 146
Shanghai, China 207
Shaughnessy, Clark 2, 43, 83, 175
Shaw Bears team 191
Shepherd, Lemuel, Jr. 207
Sherman tank 134
Shoemaker, Calif. 111
Shrine Bowl 95
Sicily 130, 164, 206
Siegfried, Win 31
Signaigo, Joe *155*
Sikes, Jules 126, 180
Silver Star 2, 62, 151, 208
Sinkwich, Frank (Frankie), "Flat-Foot Frankie," "the Georgia Fireball" 82, *145,* 146, 149, 164, 185, 214, 215
Sitko, Emil 115, 123, 126, 172, *173,* 209
Skladany, Joe 35
Skyline Conference 182
Smackover, Ark. 220, 221; *see also* Scott, Clyde Luther "Smackover"
Smith, Bruce 18, *66,* *108,* 114, 126, 164, 165, 174, 177
Smith, Lieutenant Robert B. Trophy *see* Washington (D.C.) Touchdown Club
Smith, Willis 137
Solomon, Dan 135
Solomons Islands 206, 213
Sossamon, Lou 33, *36,* 40, 201
South Atlantic 224
South Bend, Ind. 14
South Carolina 33, 95
South Carolina State 117, 190, 192, 193
South Dakota Intercollegiate Conference 76
South Plains (Tex.) Army Air Field Winged Commandos 93, 174
Southern Conference 76–78, 80, 168, 177, 182
Southern Cross 224
Southern Idaho University (Golden Eagles) 138, 139, 146
Southern Illinois University (Salukis) 80, 175
*Southern Living* xi
Southern Methodist University (Mustangs) v, 56, 102, 144, 145, 208
Southwest Teachers 144
Southwestern Association 191

Southwest(ern) Conference 56, 78, 81, 144, 169, 179, 182
Southwestern Louisiana Institute (SLI) Ragin' Cajuns 56, 57, 142–45, 170, 213; Louisiana-Lafayette (postwar) 57
Southwestern University Pirates 56, 57, 58, 145, 168
Soviet Union 17
Spadaccinni, Vic 145
Spaghetti Bowl, Florence, Italy (Fifth Army vs. 12th Air Force) 206
Spanish-American War 1, 128
Spence Field (Ga.) team 121, 165
Spokane, Wash. 145
Spokane (Wash.) Air Service 93
*The Sporting News* viii, 174
Stagg, Amos Alonzo 78, 81, 169, 173
Stahley, Skip 128
Standlee, Norm 33, 135, **136**, 172
Stanford, Fred **88**
Stanford University (Indians) 2, 19, 33, 79, 83, 112, 126, 127, 129, 135, 136, 145, 146, 175, 177
Stanowicz, Joe 133
*Stars and Stripes* 174, 200
Stautner, Ernie 156
Stealy, Dick 139
Steffy, Joe 134
Stern, Bill 174
Steuber, Bob 3, 18, 162–64, 172, 210, **211**
Stevens, Inc. 223
Stickney, William 153
Stinson Field (Tex.) team 144
Stockton (Calif.) Army Air Base 93
Strader, Norman P. "Red" 108
Stratton, Harold 202
Street & Smith's viii, 19, 81, 88, 96, 103, 119, 120, 132, 133, 140, 145, 162, 170, 175, 176, 184, 211, 212, 216, 220
Strode, Woodrow Wilson Woodwine "Woody" 189, 190, 214
Strohmeyer, George 119, 181
Strong, Ken 196
Stryzkalski, John 187
Stydahar, Joe 18, 111, 181
Suffridge, Bob 69, 111, 206
Sugar Bowl 106, 123, 177
Sullivan, Jim **155**
Sullivan Award 134
Sumpter, Tony **158**
Sun Bowl 62, 145, 146, 162, 204; Second Air Force vs. Hardin-Simmons 204
Surdyk, Florian 36, 40
Suseoff, Nick 18, 146, 181, 187
Susquehanna River 27, 37
Svendsen, George 119, 126, 165, 174
Swarthmore Garnet 179
Sweiger, Bob 104, **108**, 115, 202
Swenson, Harold 80
Syracuse Orangemen 80, 124, 128, 175

Tampa, Fla. 147, 148
Tarawa 47, 126, 153
Tatum, Jim 18, 63, 68, 77, 121
Tavener, John 181
Tea Bowl, London (Air Service Command vs. Eighth Air Force) 205
Tea Bowl, London (Canada vs. USA) 205
Tehran, Iran 205
Temple Owls 79, 124, 134, 171
Tennessee 58
Terrell, Bob 94, 97
Texas 214, 217
Texas A&I 69
Texas A&M Aggies 40, 56, 118, 119, 126, 144, 206, 215, 217
Texas Christian University (Horned Frogs) 56, 78, 81, 179, 182, 183, 185, 206
Texas Collegiate Athletic Conference 76
Texas State Teachers 41
Texas Tech Red Raiders 44, 75, 164, 169, 219
Tharp, Jim 41
Third Air Force (3rd AF, Morris Field, N.C.; Drew Field, Fla.) Gremlins 18, 93, 113, 114, 117, 131, 141, 142, 145–47, **148**, 156, 176, 179, 187
Thompson, David 101
Thorpe, Jim 1
Thorpe, John viii
*Time* 21
Timmons, Charles 206
Tinian 126, 153, 186
Tinsley, Philip 181
Titchenal, Bob 126
Todd, Richard "Dick" 18, **118**, 164, 174
Toepfer, Meryl **167**
Tokyo, Japan 207, 215
Tokyo Bowl, Tokyo, Japan (11th Airborne Division vs. 41st Division) 207
Tomasello, Carl 40
Tonapah (Nev.) Fourth Air Force 93
*Touchdown Illustrated* 97
Townsend, Bob 145
Treasury Bowl, New York (Randolph Field vs. Second Air Force) 52, 205; *see also* Brooklyn Bond Bowl Game, Brooklyn, N.Y
Trevor, George 161
Triangle, N.C. viii
Trinity (College, Conn.) Bantams 160
Tripoli (Tunisia) 28
Trippi, Charley xi, 18, **83**, 147, 176, 210
Tritico, Frank M. 143, 179, 180
Truk 126
Tsingtao, China 206
Tucker, Arnold 18, 134
Tufts Jumbos 160
Tulagi 153
Tulane Green Wave 40, 78, 114, 122, 159, 182
Tulis, Bob 159
Tulsa (Okla.) Air Base Bombers 93
Tunney, Gene 63

Turner, Bon 80, 175
Turner, Clyde "Bulldog" 146, 185, 187, 214
Tuscaloosa, Ala. 14
Tuskegee, Ala. 194
Tuskegee (Ala.) Army Air Field (Black) 4, 93, 193–95; Moton Field 194
Tuskegee Airmen 194
Tuskegee Institute (Golden Tigers) 192, 194

United Press 174; United Press All-Service team 115
United Service Organizations (USO) 198
U.S. Air Force (present) 1
U.S. Army (army) 2, 9, 16, 17, 19, 52, 53, 131, 133, 138, 145
U.S. Army (officers, soldiers) 19, 47, 199, 212; ASTP (Army Specialized Training Program) 16, 58, 59; as football players/teams 2, 7, 46, 130, 131, 135, 137, 143, 154; as officer candidates 16, 17, 19, 133
U.S. Army (units): Army Service Forces/Special Services Division 200; Second (2nd) Armored Division 130; 3rd Army Ground Forces 217; 3rd Infantry Division 130, 199; Fifth Army 206; Quartermaster Corps 137; Seventh Army (U.S.) 130; Womens Army Corps (WACs) 204, 205, 217; see also War Department
U.S. Army Air Forces (air forces, officers, airmen) 8, 17, 19, 50, 143, 164, 176; as football players 46, 104, 206; as officer candidates see U.S. Army soldiers; 12th Air Force 206
U.S. Coast Guard 2, 8, 15, 17, 58, 151, 163; as officer candidates (integrated with navy) 58–72, 78, 87, 107, 108; see also V-Programs, V-1, V-5, V-7, V-12
U.S. Coast Guard Academy see Coast Guard Academy (U.S.)
U.S. forces/troops 200, 206
U.S Marine Corps (units): First (1st) Marine Division 152; Second (2nd) Marine Division 153, 207; 3rd Battalion/22nd Marines 206; 3rd Battalion/29th Marines 206; Fourth (4th) Marine Division 200; 4th Marines 206–208; 5th Marine Raiders 200; Sixth (6th) Marine Division 207; 11th Marines 200; 29th Marines 206–208; Marine (Corps) Reserve 149; Marine Fleet Air Wing West Coast 157; Marine Raiders 154; VMF-221 212; Women Marines *48*, 154
U.S. Marine(s) (officers, Marines, officer candidates) v, vii, 2, 3, 7–9, 15–17, 23, 46, 47, 50, 56, 59, 75, 118, 120, 131, 149, 150, 157, 168, 177, 190, 199, 200, 207, 217–218; as football players 2, 17, 21, 46, 47, 49, 57, 78, 104, 105, 149, 151, 153, 154, 162, 196, 200, 202, 207, 208, 213; as officer candidates 15–17, 58–72, 107, 108, 159, 169, 171, 212, 213, 217, 219; see also Department of the Navy; V-Programs, V-1, V-5, V-7, V-12

U.S. Military Academy see Army (U.S. Military Academy, West Point, N.Y.)
U.S. Naval Academy see Navy (U.S. Naval Academy, Annapolis, Md.)
U.S. Navy (navy, naval) 2, 7, 9, 15–17, 20, 23, 25, 28, 58–72, 78, 79, 131, 150, 168, 177, 190, 199, 201, 210, 217; as football players 2, 7, 17, 21, 46, 49, 78, 98, 104, 115–17, 128, 143, 162, 166, 171, 175, 202, 206; as officer candidates 15–17, 58–72, 78, 87, 107, 108, 113, 121, 122, 169, 171, 217, 219; see also Department of the Navy; V-Programs, V-1, V-5, V-7, V-12
U.S. Navy (units): Bureau of Aeronautics 47, 63; Bureau of Personnel 63; Chief of Naval Operations 65, 87; Naval Reserve 78, 219; NROTC (Naval Reserve Officer Training Corps) 2, 15, 58, 61, 62, 75, 217; Seabees 111; VF-10 "Grim Reapers" 216; WAVES 28, 32, 116
"U.S. Navy Pre-Flight School, Chapel Hill, N.C., 1942–1943" 69
U.S. Office of War Information (OWI) 199
University of Alabama (Crimson Tide) 33, 35, 41, 113, 120, 122, 126, 141, 142, 146, 175, 177, 185–87, 206
University of Arizona (Wildcats) 146
University of Arkansas (Razorbacks) 33, 56, 58, 82, 115, 124, 137, 212, 220, 223; postwar 106
University of California (Golden Bears) 68, 79, 109, 112, 118; 126, 127, 152, 179, 218; Freshmen team 129
University of California at Los Angeles (UCLA) (Bruins) 68, 109, 127, 129, 141, 152, 162, 164, 179, 185, 189
University of Chicago 15, 114, 171
University of Colorado (Buffaloes) 138, 146, 179
University of Delaware 128
University of Denver (Pioneers) 126, 139, 179
University of Florida (Gators) 19, 121, 175
University of Georgia (Bulldogs) 31, 40, 82, 83, 87, 98, 113, 121, 126, 145, 146, 149, 162, 164, 182, 185, 186, 218
University of Hawaii (Rainbow Warriors) 73, 203
University of Illinois (Fighting Illini) v, 20, 40, 50, 54, 111, 117, 120, 126, 137, 144, 154, 168, 169, 180, 182, 190, 208, 212, 213, 216
University of Iowa (Hawkeyes) 20, 31, 54, 68, 117–20, 137, 159
University of Kansas (Jayhawks) 119, 126, 139, 146, 164, 209; B team 139
University of Kentucky (Wildcats) 78, 175
University of Louisville 40
University of Maryland (Terrapins) 31–34, 68, 71, 98
University of Miami (Fla.) Hurricanes 113, 121
University of Miami (Oh.) 116

University of Michigan (Wolverines) v, 3, 17, 20, 54, 62, 68, 78, 82, 103, 112, 115, 117–20, 123, 128, 135, 137, 149, 154, 159, 164, 168, 173, 174, 179, 180, 186, 190, 208, 213, 215
University of Minnesota (Golden Gophers) 3, 20, 66, 78, 79, 104, 112, 115, 118–20, 137, 138, 126, 145, 159, 162, 166, 177, 206, 211, 217, 218
University of Mississippi [Ole Miss] (Rebels) 68, 69, 78, 80, 81, 109, 146, 164, 176
University of Missouri (Tigers) 68, 109, 117–20, 139, 142, 162, 164, 202, 210, 211, 213; B team 139
University of Nebraska (Cornhuskers) 40, 68, 100, 111, 140, 142, 185
University of Nevada (Wolf Pack) 112, 117, 152, 185, 190, 192, 200
University of North Carolina Wilmington (UNCW, postwar) vii, viii; Cameron School of Business viii; Randall Library viii
University of North Carolina (Tar Heels) 3, 10, 11, 33, 36, 58, 62, 68, 69, 71, 75, 77, 80, 81, 98, 100, 102, 106, 113, 121, 124, 133, 135, 149, 150, 156, 177, 202, 213, 217, 219; B team 155; Navy Field *69*; postwar 10, 105, 106
University of Ohio 206
University of Oklahoma (Sooners) 56, 68, 78, 80, 123, 124, 140, 169, 170, 177, 182, 206, 209; Junior varsity 124
University of Oregon (Ducks) 19, 60, 111, 126, 127, 206, 220
University of Pennsylvania (Quakers) 3, 40, 54, 69, 80, 114, 122, 123, 134, 135, 149, 154, 159, 163, 171, 173–75, 183, 186, 187, 221
University of Pittsburgh (Panthers) 3, 31, 33, 35, 54, 82, 98, 109, 111, 117, 135
University of Rochester 62
University of San Francisco (Dons) 109, 112, 152
University of Santa Clara (Broncos) 127, 146
University of South Carolina (Gamecocks) 33, 40, 68, 77, 113, 114, 177 201, 218
University of Southern California 3, 36, 40, 60, 79, 141, 157, 174, 177, 181, 202, 214; Trojans team 80, 127–29, 140, 141, 169, *170*, 175, 179, 180, 186; USC Song Girls (postwar) 3
University of Tampa (Spartans) 121
University of Tennessee (Volunteers) 52, 68, 69, 80, 179, 180, 185, 186, 206
University of Texas (Longhorns) 2, 30, 40, *49*, 56, 69, 99, 115, 118, 143–45, 149, 164, 168, 169, 173, 186, 187, 201, 204, 217, 218; Freshmen team 144
University of Tulsa (Golden Hurricanes) 70, 78, 120, 143, 144, 159, 164, 173, 180, 182, 186, 206, 211, 212
University of Utah (Utes) 82, 138, 179
University of Virginia (Cavaliers) 123, 126, 143, 160, 177, 182, 185, 218

University of Washington (Huskies) 127, 141, 146, 173, 179
University of West Virginia 109, 111
University of Wisconsin (Badgers) v, 3, 17 20, 78, 79, 103, 113, 117, 123, 137, 154, 159, 162, 208, 215, *216*, 217
Uram, Andy 206
Urban, Gaspar *155*
Utah State (Aggies) 33, 80

V-Programs 2, 16, 58–72
V-1 Program 58, 61
V-5 Program 2, 3, 15, 46, 47, 58, 63–72, 127, 190
V-7 Program 2, 15, 58, 61
V-12 Program 2, 15, 16, 33, 56–63, 87, 127, 151, 154, 162, 168–71, 190, 211–14, 217
Vaccaro, Mike 14
Valor Tours vii
Vanderbilt Commodores 31, 78, 79, 82, 113, 178
Vanderweghe, Alfred "Al" *36*, 40, 98, 103, 104
Van Every, Hal 145
Van Order, Ed v, 208
Vargo, Tom 40
Verducci, Joe J. *151*, 152
Vero Beach, Fla. 112
Veteri, Tony 179, 218
Victory Bond Drive 55
Vietnam (War) 1; Operation Linebacker 1
Villanova Wildcats 33, 40, 123, 128, 134, 135, 170
Virginia 33, 194
Virginia Polytechnic Institute (VPI) Gobblers 134
V-J Day 3, 50, 144
Vosges Mountains, France 198
Vranka, Ray 156

Wade, Wallace 52, 76
Wahpeton (N.D.) Naval Training Station 166
Wake Forest University (Demon Deacons) v, 124, 135, 136, 156, 170, 177, 182, 186, 208, 211, 217, 218
Wake Island 126, 202
Waldorf, Pappy 172
Walker, Ed 146
Walker, Paul 181
Walker, Peahead 177
Walter Camp Trophy 132, 143
Walterhouse, Dick 134
War Department 9, 52
War Football Fund, Inc. 52
War of 1812 11, 28
War Wounded Fund 111
Ward, Arch 47
Ward Island (Tex.) 144
Warrington, Caleb 181
Washburn (College) Ichabods 139
Washington, D.C. 17, 33, 104, 157, 191, 194, 214

*Washington (D.C.) Post* 94
Washington (D.C.) Touchdown Club 108, 111, 118, 133, 134, 164; Lieutenant Robert B. Smith Trophy 115, 118, 143, 164
Washington Intercollegiate Conference 76
Washington Redskins 31, 33, 34, 74, 84, 96, 105, 106, 113, 115, 118, 126, 146, 156, 159, 177, 185, 195, 197, 198, 210
Washington State Cougars 145, 146
Waterfield, Bob 164
Watkins Ed 214
Webb Institute of Naval Architecture 61
Weber, John W. 174
Wedemeyer, Herman 185, 187
Welch, Ralph 173
Wemple, Don 50
West Coast 54, 157, 162, 169, 170, 184, 187, 196, 201
Western Plains 78
Wesleyan Cardinals 160
West Point, N.Y. 54, 132, 222; *see also* Army (U.S. Military Academy, West Point, N.Y.)
Western Michigan Broncos 109, 115, 117, 214
Western Reserve 30, 34, 40, 114
West Virginia Athletic Conference 76
West Virginia State Yellow Jackets team 191
"What It Was Was Football" 106
Whatley, Ben 192
Whelchel, Johnny 121, 172
White, Byron "Whizzer" 179
White, Hal 173
White, Jack 202
White, James J. 174
White City Stadium, London, England **204**
Whitman (College) Missionaries 146
Whitmire, Don 18, 174, 181
Wichita (Kans.) Aero Commandos 144
Wichita (Kans.) Pros 139
Wichita team 139
Wicker, Tom 217
Wickham, John 159
Widoes, Carroll 179
Wiley (Tex.) Wildcats 192
Wilkin, Wilbur "Wee Willie" 18, **157, 158**, 159, 214
Wilkinson, Bud 2, 18, 63, 68
Will Rogers Army Air Base (Okla.) 93, 124, 166
Willamette University 73
William & Mary Indians 31, 36, 40, 98, 100, 123, 124, 201, 206
William Jewell College Cardinals 79
Williams, Don 145
Williams, Hoyer 31
Williams, Jack 30

Williams, Joe 206
Williams, Ted 71
Williams Trophy 132, 177
Williamsburg, Va. 100, 108
Williamson, Paul B. 165
Williamson National Football Rating and Prediction System 31, 108, 111, 112, 129, 165, 181, 187, 193
Wilmington (Calif.) Army Engineers 93
Wilmington, Del. 27
Wilmington Engineers (Tex.) 93
Wilmington, N.C. 10, 74, 135, 136
Wilmington (N.C.) Coast Guard 93, 151, 156
*Wilmington (N.C.) Star-News* 10
Wink, Jack 162
Winston-Salem State Rams 191
Wismer, Harry 7, 8, 75, 79
Witt, John viii, 203
Witt, Robert E. "Bob" 142, **203**
Wolf, Al 184
Wolf, Raymond "Bear" 63, 68, 113
Wong, Mun Charn 202
Worcester Tech Engineers 160
World Series 217
World War I 1, 12, 47, 137, 172
World War II v, 1, 7, 8, 13–15, 45, 59, 94, 105, 130, 189; assigning and training personnel 11, 15–17, 27–29, 44–47, 56–72, 104, 107, 108; Operations Goalpost and Varsity 1; veterans/football players vii, viii, 75, 81, 122, 199; World War II history 10, 11
Woudenberg, John 126, 181
Wyatt, Bowden 68
Wyoming 137

Yablonski, Ventan **148**
Yale Bulldogs 15, 21, 80, 82, 113, 123, 134, 160, 175, 179, 181, 185
Yamamoto, Admiral (Isoroku) 3
Yank, Lou 144
*Yank: The Army Weekly* 48
Yankee Stadium, New York, N.Y. 54, 135
Yanks (NFL) 196, 197
Yap 126
Yokohama, Japan 213
Yonakor, John 18, 102, 154, **155,** 174, 202
York Vikings 128
Young, Bill 201
Young, Claude "Buddy" 18, **110**, 111, 184, 185, 187, 190
Young, Tom 177
Young, Waddy 50
Yuma (Ariz.) Army Air Base 93; Gremlins team 169

Ziewacz, Lawrence E. 15

www.ingramcontent.com/pod-product-compliance
Ingram Content Group UK Ltd.
Pitfield, Milton Keynes, MK11 3LW, UK
UKHW041931140426
5217IPUK00014B/415